DATE DUE

APR 30 '91			
NOV 14 '91			
DEC 17 '92			
OCT 04 '95			
APR ? '96			
AP 23 '96			
12/10/12			

#47-0108 Peel Off Pressure Sensitive

■ Nietzsche's New Seas

Nietzsche's New Seas

Explorations in
Philosophy,
Aesthetics,
and Politics

*Edited by
Michael Allen Gillespie
and Tracy B. Strong*

THE UNIVERSITY OF CHICAGO PRESS
Chicago and London

MICHAEL ALLEN GILLESPIE, assistant professor of political science at Duke University, is the author of *Hegel, Heidegger, and the Ground of History* (1984).
TRACY B. STRONG, professor of political science at the University of California, San Diego, is the author of *Friedrich Nietzsche and the Politics of Transfiguration* (1976) and coauthor (with Helen Keyssar) of *Right in Her Soul: The Life of Anna Louise Strong* (1984).

The University of Chicago Press, Chicago 60637
The University of Chicago Press, Ltd., London
© 1988 by The University of Chicago
All rights reserved. Published 1988
Printed in the United States of America

97 96 95 94 93 92 91 90 89 88   5 4 3 2 1

Library of Congress Cataloging-in-Publication Data

Nietzsche's new seas : explorations in philosophy, aesthetics, and
    politics / edited by Michael Allen Gillespie and Tracy B. Strong.
        p. cm.
    Includes index.
    ISBN 0-226-29378-5. ISBN 0-226-29379-3 (pbk.)
    1. Nietzsche, Friedrich Wilhelm, 1844–1900. I. Gillespie,
Michael Allen. II. Strong, Tracy B.
B3317.N498 1988
193—dc19   88-6413
                                                            CIP

Contents

■ *Nach neuen Meeren*

Dorthin—*will* ich; und ich traue
Mir fortan und meinem Griff.
Offen liegt das Meer, ins Blaue
Treibt mein Genueser Schiff.

Alles glänzt mir neu und neuer
Mittag schläft auf Raum und Zeit—:
Nur *dein* Auge—ungeheuer
Blickt mich's an, Unendlichkeit!

(V 2, 333)

Toward New Seas

That way is my *will;* I trust
In myself and in my grip.
The sea is open, into the blue
Drives my Genoan ship.

Everything shines for me new and newer,
Noon sleeps upon space and time—:
Only *your* eye—monstrously
stares at me, infinity!

▪ Introduction

Nietzsche once remarked that some men are born posthumously, and of no one has this perhaps been truer than of Nietzsche himself. Indeed, one might say that he has been reborn again and again as different generations of commentators repeatedly thought they had uncovered his true meaning. In the past decade, we have witnessed yet another rebirth of this apparently most protean of protean thinkers. Yet this new birth is different from the previous ones. In this new incarnation, Nietzsche no longer appears primarily as the prophet and purveyor of nihilism but as the thinker who marks a kind of ending to, or at least a rift in, the continuity of the West. He plumbs the depths of nihilism and in that exploration opens a way out of the abyss to a new and different way of thinking and being.

We suggest that this new birth may be somewhat different from the others because the labor that brings it into our world does not start with the assumption that we should look first at the "content" of what Nietzsche says, as if his texts were simply the containers for his "meaning." The new approach to Nietzsche begins rather with the claim that we can best understand the meaning of what Nietzsche says by coming to terms with how he says it, that the meaning of Nietzsche's enigmatic utterances can best be understood by examining the style or structure of his thought. As a result, the traditional questions about the philosophical, theological, and political significance of Nietzsche's thought are seen as integral parts of the way Nietzsche thinks.

This approach must therefore be concerned with how Nietzsche's texts work, with what their activities are as texts. The goal of this volume is to bring together a representative sample of the best recent

1

scholarship that works with and in this approach to Nietzsche. The volume includes work from American, French, and German scholars here made available to the larger English-speaking public for the first time. The contributors to this volume come from diverse backgrounds and disciplines. Some are philosophers, some political theorists; still others historians, biographers, and literary critics. They represent a wide variety of schools of thought that differ not only methodologically but also ideologically. Thus, while the essays that follow are united in their basic approach to Nietzsche, they come to divergent and often contradictory conclusions about the philosophical and political significance of his work. Nonetheless, they are all concerned to explore the relation between the text and the reader, and in doing so they inevitably transcend the view of Nietzsche as simply an iconoclast.

Nietzsche's readers have long been perplexed about how to read his works. The form of the texts he left when he lapsed into insanity in 1889 are among the most strange in philosophical literature; they fit none of the received forms of writing "philosophy." Nietzsche's writings are not dialogues, treatises, essays, or critiques. In fact, they contain examples and elements of all these, and in addition present aphorisms, riddles, lyric poems, invective, confession, and exhortation, as well as what often appears to be little more than bombast. If this were all there was to Nietzsche's texts, however, we would be tempted to dismiss him as a minor experimental writer whose thought did not measure up to that of the great thinkers of the Western tradition. However, it is hard to avoid the sense that this is not all; it is even harder, though, to be explicit about what else there might be. The experience of reading Nietzsche is not one which lends itself easily to dismissal of the author, yet a next step seems unclear.

The early reception of Nietzsche's thought was colored by his madness, and many critics still read his insanity back into his works, although they often disagree about whether his was a "divine madness" and prescience that pointed the way to a new future or only a lamentable megalomania that distorted the world and man's task. The tendency to read Nietzsche's works in this way was exacerbated by his sister's mishandling of his manuscripts and especially her insistence that *The Will to Power,* the chaotic work she had assembled and published from his discarded notes, was his magnum opus. A new interpretation of Nietzsche thus only began to emerge when his manuscripts became available to scholars in the 1930s, but this was cut short by his adoption and perversion by the Nazis and by the war that followed. Nietzsche consequently was seen as the apostle of German nationalism and as the spiritual father of Nazism.

In the Anglo-American world, modern readings of Nietzsche date from Walter Kaufmann's *Nietzsche: Philosopher, Psychologist, Antichrist* (Princeton: Princeton University Press, 1950), which helped to free Nietzsche from the association with Nazism. This book had many merits, but it was not sensitive to the decisive question of style. Kaufmann recognized that Nietzsche was a great stylist but did not really investigate the relationship between how Nietzsche wrote and what he said. Kaufmann's seminal work set the tone for much of the Nietzsche scholarship of the 1950s and 1960s. The directions taken by this scholarship have mirrored the split that Kaufmann unconsciously established between the "philosophical" and the "stylistic" Nietzsche.

Some scholars during this period were principally concerned with translating his work into contemporary philosophical discussions. These men, including F. A. Lea, Arthur Danto, Richard Schacht, and J. P. Stern, whether sympathetic or not to Nietzsche's enterprise, attempted to discern and describe a consistent philosophic system in his work. In trying to do so, however, they ran into the enormous difficulties posed by the many apparent contradictions in his thought. How, for instance, was it possible to reconcile the agent-oriented, bright vigor of what Nietzsche said about the will to power with the dark, cosmic circularity of the doctrine of the eternal recurrence of the same?

These philosophically oriented scholars found two types of solutions to this problem. Some sought to ignore the doctrines that they found unbelievable. Thus, Kaufmann dismissed the eternal recurrence as "a dubious doctrine which was to have no influence to speak of." The problem with this approach is that it allows a commentator to pick and choose which parts of Nietzsche he or she finds acceptable. Such an approach fails to accept Nietzsche's thoughts as they present themselves and attempts instead to remold them into what the interpreter has preconceived as a legitimate form.

Other scholars saw a second solution, which was in many ways the mirror image of the first. They agreed that Nietzsche's thought was contradictory, but, instead of denying one side of the contradiction, they simply asserted that Nietzsche's thought is necessarily and intentionally contradictory because he describes a fundamentally contradictory and chaotic world. Jaspers, for instance, argued that, since the world for Nietzsche is not structured by nature and is ultimately chaos, there can be no object for knowledge and hence no epistemology. This approach captures an important claim Nietzsche is making about the world but also seems to show the impossibility of Nietzsche's making such a claim. Nietzsche, in his view, is merely a negative thinker.

Parallel to this attempt to construe Nietzsche philosophically was the attempt to analyze him poetically or stylistically. Two broad views also dominate this approach. The more traditional sees Nietzsche as a German "stylist." This view was already in evidence during his lifetime. An early reviewer, for example, suggested that "Herr N should pay attention to content as well as style." Most often those who take this approach see Nietzsche as an "aphoristic" writer and place him in the same category as Lichtenberg and La Rochefoucauld. While Nietzsche was certainly the master of the aphorism, he did not write only aphoristically but in a variety of modes. Even more important, this view never raises the question of why Nietzsche might have written in so many modes, let alone the question of the means by which he reconciles and unites them.

All these writers tend to view the content of Nietzsche's writings as secondary or even as unimportant and indeed embarrassing. A second group, strongly influenced by or participating in contemporary developments in literary criticism in France, argues that Nietzsche's style is such that his writing stands without any referent other than itself. Jacques Derrida, for instance, has suggested that Nietzsche's texts have a relativity of reference so great that it destroys the notion of reference altogether. For these critics, Nietzsche's writing is thus not about anything in particular. It is simply what it does to the reader. Important here is thus an emphasis on the fragmentary character of Nietzsche's thought, such that a coherent reading of his texts becomes impossible.

It is the premise of this volume that these ways of approaching Nietzsche do not take seriously enough his claim that he developed a new way of thinking that transcends the traditional distinction between philosophy and poetry. The distinction itself implies a division of the world into that which can be made objectively available to others, thus tested and validated, and that which can be known only subjectively and represented, but not measured or validated, by any external standard. Nietzsche thinks that his writings achieve a relation to the world they interpret which is not tacitly exempt from the way they understand the world. More specifically, if one were to claim that all the world was to be understood as perspectival, as Nietzsche appears to assert, the claim would be self-contradictory unless the claim itself were somehow compatible with its own conclusions. The evolution and demonstration of this mode of thinking must await the essays that follow; it is clear, however, that for Nietzsche the necessity for thinking and understanding the world in this radically non-self-privileging fashion was a consequence of his experience of nihilism.

The central importance and meaning of nihilism for Nietzsche's thought was first made apparent by Martin Heidegger in his Nietzsche lectures in the 1930s. These remained relatively unknown, however, until their publication in German in 1961 and in English in 1979–87. Increasingly, they have been seen as the most profound interpretation of Nietzsche available and have consequently come to play a decisive role in shaping the contemporary understanding of his thought. Indeed, while many of the authors in this volume disagree with Heidegger's fundamental proposition that Nietzsche is a metaphysical thinker, the new approach to Nietzsche represented by the essays here would have been impossible without Heidegger's interpretation of Nietzsche. Heidegger's insight was that Nietzsche's thought was above all the thought of nihilism and his concern with such matters as the revaluation of all values, the will to power, the eternal recurrence, and the overman could only be understood within the horizon established by the question of nihilism. While the approach in this volume goes beyond Heidegger to try to show how Nietzsche's own practice might serve as a model for overcoming nihilism, it still accepts and indeed is predicated upon Heidegger's insight about the centrality of nihilism.

For Nietzsche, the meaning of nihilism is summed up in the dictum "God is dead." In one sense, this insight is not new, since Hegel had announced it some seventy-five years earlier. However, in contradistinction to Hegel, who saw the death of God as inextricably bound up with the resurrection of the divine in and as spirit, Nietzsche asserts "God is dead. God remains dead" (V 2, 159).* The consequences of this death are cosmic and catastrophic. In general, one might say that it means an end to life as we know it, for God and all eternal standards that have served as guideposts for understanding, morality, ethics, and politics are obliterated. Furthermore, this end is the result of human action. In a terrifying manner, Nietzsche asks, "Who gave us the sponge to wipe away the whole horizon? What did we do when we unchained the earth from this sun? Where does it move now? Where

*All Nietzsche references in this volume, unless otherwise specified, are to Friedrich Nietzsche, *Werke: Kritische Gesamtausgabe,* ed. G. Colli and M. Montinari (Berlin: de Gruyter, 1972–), by division, volume and page.

do we move? Away from all suns? . . . Does not the night and only the night come constantly on?" (V 2, 159). Although "rhetorical," these images should not be dismissed as mere rhetoric. According to Nietzsche, the death of God and the subsequent loss of standards and meaning ensure the slow and progressive collapse of the social and political structures that have characterized the West. No one can fathom, he writes,

> how much must collapse now that this faith has been un-
> dermined because it was built on this faith, propped up by
> it, grown into it; for example the whole of our European
> morality. This plenitude and sequence of breakdown, de-
> struction, ruin, cataclysm that is now impending—who
> could guess enough of it today to be compelled to play the
> teacher and advance proclaimer of this monstrous logic of
> terror, the prophet of a gloom and eclipse of the sun whose
> like has probably never yet occurred on earth. (V 2, 255)

Our century has become only too well acquainted with the process that Nietzsche announced. Not all the consequences of the death of God, however, are negative. It is important to realize that the death of God has opened up a radically new space for thought and life. In the continuation of the passage quoted above, Nietzsche reveals that

> we philosophers and "free spirits" feel, when we hear the
> news that "the old God is dead," as if a new dawn shone
> upon us; our heart overflows with gratitude, amazement,
> premonitions, expectation. At long last, the horizon appears
> free to us again, even if it should not be bright; at long last,
> our ships may venture out again, venture out to face any
> danger; all the daring of the lover of knowledge is permitted
> again; the sea, *our* sea, lies open again; perhaps there has
> never yet been such an "open sea." (V 2, 256)

If God is dead, then in Nietzsche's view nothing is true and every-
thing is permitted. On the one hand, this means the liberation of the most subterranean passions from the bounds of ethics and morality and a consequent disaster whose proportions cannot even be imagined, let alone predicted or controlled. On the other hand, this im-
pending twilight and world midnight harbors the possibility of a new dawn, for, if nothing is true, then not merely every horrible thing but also every magnificent thing is permitted. If every limit on the human imagination is abolished, man is no longer restrained by nature or logic and indeed can create nature and logic. Whether or not humans

can become overmen, at least the space for that which is not "human, all-too-human" is now available.

It is important to note that Nietzsche did not think that a new dawn would necessarily and automatically follow the twilight of nihilism. One cannot simply decide to cast off morality, even if one thinks it is not grounded. Human will was so structured by the genealogy of the West that, in the end, as he remarks in the closing lines of *On the Genealogy of Morals,* man would rather "will the void, than be void of will" (VI 2, 430). Nietzsche does, however, hold open the possibility of a new dawn, of a new way of thinking and being that would not be subject to nihilism. To begin to understand what this might be requires an investigation of what Nietzsche means by the end of philosophy. To understand the end of philosophy, however, requires that we understand its beginning.

Philosophy for Nietzsche begins with the Greeks and at first is not dissociated from poetry, nor indeed from politics. The pre-Socratic achievement, he claims, is extraordinary, for previously the Greeks had thought that "man was the truth and core of all things. . . . For this reason [the Greeks] found it unbelievably difficult to comprehend concepts as such" (III 2, 309). The pre-Socratics tried to preserve the agonistic basis of public life that had been the legacy of the Homeric world and at the same time to solve the question of the origins of human and divine arrangements. They attempted to bring together knowledge of the world without destroying a way of life and were thus in Nietzsche's view "genuine statesmen" (IV 1, 178–79). Their greatness lies precisely in what is unique to each of them. He writes, "Philosophical systems are wholly true for their founders only. For all subsequent philosophers, they usually represent one great mistake. . . . On the other hand, whoever rejoices in great human beings will also rejoice in philosophical systems, even if they be completely erroneous. They always have one incontrovertible point: personal mood, color" (III 2, 295).

In Nietzsche's view, the pre-Socratics and indeed all philosophers are thus indistinguishable from poets. They seek to put their stamp on the world, to reshape it in their own image. "The philosopher seeks to hear within himself the echoes of the world symphony and to reproject them into the form of concepts. What verse is for the poet, dialectical thinking is for the philosopher" (III 2, 311). It is in this sense that they establish laws and customs for humanity.

The pre-Socratics failed, however, because they were unable to deal with the contradiction between what one is and knows as an individual and what one is and knows as a being like other beings. This is the import of the dynamic between the Apollonian and Dionysian that Nietzsche finds central to Greek life and that achieves its most sublime expression in Greek tragedy. For the tragedians, this contradiction is made bearable by the metaphysical comfort provided to "the profound Hellene" by tragedy, in which "state and society and, quite generally, the gulfs between man and man give way to an overwhelming feeling of unity leading back to the very heart of nature. . . . Art saves him and through art life" (III 1, 52).

There was, however, another approach—that of discovering a logical argument which resolved the contradiction. This in Nietzsche's view was the path followed by Socrates. The tragedians' approach required that each member of the audience overlook what he knew of the everyday world in order to gain a new and transfigured world for himself. Socrates and his philosophic followers, on the contrary, sought to subordinate the contradictions of the world to reason, to a dialectical and ultimately syllogistic understanding that confined contradictions to the realm of mere appearances and posited in place of this actual world a noncontradictory world of eternal placidity. To produce such a logical solution to tragic circumstances required, however, that poetry and music be separated from philosophy. It further required that poetry be subordinated to philosophy, as, in Nietzsche's view, Plato had made clear in the *Republic.*

For Nietzsche, then, the history of the West is characterized by this separation of philosophy and poetry. Philosophy aims at relieving suffering by constructing a "real" world in opposition to the actual world, which henceforth is characterized as the "apparent" world. This "apparent" world of sensation and feeling is subordinated as a result to the rules of reason that govern the imagined "real" world. This subordination has as its consequence the diminution of human life, for it relieves suffering not by resolving the fundamental contradictions of the passions but by denying the validity of passion altogether, by crushing what Nietzsche takes to be man's actual life experience with the great hammer of reason. The triumph of philosophy and the "real" world over poetry and the "apparent" world thus leads to a life devoid of all depths and heights, to the world of what Nietzsche's Zarathustra calls the last man. For Nietzsche, this is as much the consequence of the triumph of "Socratic" philosophy as it is of Christianity, which he characterizes as Platonism for the people. Fortunately, the will to truth that Christianity fosters ultimately leads to an investigation of the "real" world that reveals its emptiness, reveals, in other words, that God is dead. With this recognition, the hegemony of philosophy comes to an end.

Nihilism is the sign of this end. Nihilism, however, is thus also the sign of the possibility of a new birth and a new tragic age, structurally akin to that of the pre-Socratics. The Greeks had found it impossible to continue living such a life and saw the necessity of choosing between the Dionysian and the Socratic paths, between poetry (or music) and philosophy. Nietzsche proposes an alternative for this new tragic age that transcends this distinction. What is necessary is not poetry or philosophy but both united in the manner of the pre-Socratics, in other words, a "musical Socrates" or a "Socrates who practices music" (III 1, 92, 98, 107). However, whereas the Greeks had achieved this to a great degree accidentally, contemporary human beings will have to do it consciously. In his early work, Nietzsche seems to have believed that Wagner might fill the role of the new philosophical leader-artist; he soon rejected Wagner and came increasingly to see himself in this light and his works as a vehicle to this end. Nietzsche in this sense not merely proclaims the advent of nihilism but presents us with a new way of thinking that he believes opens up a new, unexplored space for life beyond nihilism.

This is the basis for the new approach to Nietzsche presented in this volume. His thought is examined not just for what it tells us but for what it does and does to us, not only as "philosophy" but also as "music" or "poetry," not just as information but as an informing and transforming force. The essays that follow are attempts to come to terms with Nietzsche in this way. They do not assume that Nietzsche is correct or that he offers a feasible way out of nihilism, nor do they agree about the political intentions or consequences of this way of thinking. Indeed, we have chosen the essays as much for their diversity as for their similarity. They represent what we believe to be a fair sampling of the various contemporary approaches to Nietzsche that seek to describe the course that Nietzsche charts for humanity, this course toward new seas, toward new ways of seeing and thinking that transcend the traditional distinctions of philosophy, aesthetics, and politics.

The volume is divided into three sections. The first section, which includes essays by Karsten Harries and Robert Pippin, attempts to show how Nietzsche takes leave of the traditional distinction between philosophy and poetry and to illuminate the course he sails through these dark seas.

In his essay, "The Philosopher at Sea," Harries argues that the attempt of recent philosophy, and especially of analytic philosophy, to reconstruct Nietzsche's thought in current academic terms must go astray. It will founder for two kinds of reasons. First, the attempt to translate Nietzsche into current philosophical vocabulary rests on the false belief that this vocabulary has attained a higher standpoint than Nietzsche's and thus has a more comprehensive understanding of what philosophy should be. The second reason is that much of recent philosophical discussion is oblivious to the rootedness of philosophy in the question of man's place in the world. For Harries, then, Nietzsche's philosophy demands not the simple and settled but the horizon of the questionable.

Thus, in Harries's reading, a central element in Nietzsche's thought is a concern for his readers. He must write in such a way that his text remains open to what lies under its apparent surface, "open to the absence of a single unspoken reading that could gather this text into a whole." Nietzsche does not seek to master the world in the manner of Descartes, nor to map out the island of truth in Kantian fashion, but rather to follow Ariadne's thread *back into* the labyrinth, to come face to face with the terrible.

If this reading of Nietzsche is correct, Western philosophy has almost always been "an evasion of life born of the spirit of revenge." To go back into the labyrinth is then the journey whereby philosophy comes home to itself. The journey is not without its risks. As Harries points out, when Nietzsche says that we must *zu Grunde gehen,* he means both that we must shipwreck and that we must go the ground of human existence.

For Harries, this journey is important and attractive; at the end, however, he also suggests that a steadier and more sober hand than Nietzsche's may be needed to preserve the ship. The accusation leveled by Harries against Nietzsche is that he has preserved that which he claims to have abandoned, in this case the notion of a *Grundtext.* This in turn is frequently linked to the argument that, despite his protestations to the contrary, Nietzsche remains a moralist. Such a judgment is the implicit target of Robert Pippin's essay.

In "Irony and Affirmation in Nietzsche's *Thus Spoke Zarathustra,"* Pippin tries, like Harries, to illuminate Nietzsche's attempt to develop a non(academic)philosophical discourse. He approaches this through what is often considered Nietzsche's most nonphilosophical work, *Thus Spoke Zarathustra.* Pippin points out that the story of Zarathustra is that of a person unable to rest content in any one place, either alone or in community with others. The dilemma is thus an age-old "political" one—that of the relation of the philosopher and the city.

The plot of the book involves two failures. The first is Zarathustra's apparent failure to establish the kind of relation to his audience that he had initially wished for. The second is the realization that his failure is "not simply the result of the corruption and deformity that he had encountered in the modern bourgeois culture of the town of the Motley Cow." Pippin argues that Nietzsche shows us that Zarathustra comes to realize that the "substance" of his teaching could one day, too, "appear like the pontifications of the last men," and that this is true even for doctrines like that of the overman. There is thus a substantial ironic distance between Nietzsche and his main character. Indeed, Pippin continues, most of the so-called Nietzschean themes in *Zarathustra* are merely stages in the main character's development and not *conclusions* for Nietzsche.

Through a careful dissection, not to say deconstruction, of key passages in *Zarathustra,* Pippin shows that Zarathustra's fate consists of irreconcilable options, neither a final going over nor a resigned going under, that Zarathustra's self-knowledge cannot be completed either alone or publicly. In this analysis, the irony of Nietzsche's writing becomes an alternative affirmation which eliminates the problem of relativism. With this, the "political problem" has changed. If man cannot be "overcome," then what should be said? And to whom? How? When and why? Speaking in masks may be the only way to avoid being caught in an image of one's own making.

The second section of the volume, which includes essays by Jean-Michel Rey, Curt Paul Janz, and Michael Allen Gillespie, considers more fully the character of this new form of discourse that Nietzsche develops. Rey, a member of the French deconstructionist school of interpretation and a leading French Nietzsche scholar, accepts and radicalizes the conclusions of Harries and Pippin in his essay, "Commentary." Nietzsche's text in his view represents a fundamental departure from all previous metaphysical thinking which rests upon the usurped mastery of the signified over the signifier, of the "truth" over the "author." Nietzsche, in Rey's view, is a fundamentally aphoristic writer who presents us not with the "truth" but with a variety of perspectives on speech itself. As he sees it, Nietzsche thus passes beyond the realm of philosophy and into the realm of fiction, which recognizes that there is nothing beyond the text and that the text is not *about* anything at all but directs and gives shape to our thinking and seeing. Still more strongly, he claims that there is not a determinate text for Nietzsche but merely a collection of signs subject to a variety of interpretations.

Recalling and radicalizing some of the themes in Harries and Pippin, Rey indicates that Nietzsche's writing thus produces a world for us which is precisely the world that "philosophy"—and rationalist Western thought in general—wants to censure and control. What Nietzsche's writing thus does is both to give us a world and to make us aware of our attempts to control it, that is, aware of what we hitherto justified in the name of "philosophy." Nietzsche gives us a world before, or without, "commentary" and makes us aware that we *are* commenting or interpreting and that our interpretations are both necessary and multiple.

In contradistinction to Rey, Janz and Gillespie suggest that, while Nietzsche passes beyond the confines of traditional philosophy, he not only gives up Western logic but also develops and employs in his writing a musical logic that is intended to have a specific effect on the reader-listener. Janz, who has written the definitive Nietzsche biography and is the leading expert on Nietzsche's music, begins his essay, "The Form-Content Problem in Friedrich Nietzsche's Conception of Music," by showing the importance of music and musical logic for Nietzsche's literary work. He then details the development of this musical logic in his musical compositions. He sees in this development a continual, although intermittent, transition from a conception of music as an expression of emotion and passion, that is, from a music that is the vehicle for the presentation of a specific content, to music as a formal language that is not clarified by words but clarifies them. He thus shows how Nietzsche's early attraction to Romanticism and Wagner gives way to a more mature love and appreciation for classical musical form.

Janz argues that it is only when Nietzsche begins reflecting on musical aesthetics after 1865 (starting with the *Birth of Tragedy*) that he makes innovations that later are repeated in the great modernist "serial constructions of Joseph Matthias Hauer and Arnold Schoenberg." Janz shows conclusively that the image of Nietzsche as simply following or elaborating Wagner's theories is quite wrong: his concerns were all along quite different, and he never argued for a realm of the "logic of the lower levels of consciousness." Nietzsche is in fact, as Janz calls him, a "court of conscience for German composers."

Janz shows us then that Nietzsche was preoccupied in the musical sphere with the same kinds of problems that Harries, Pippin, and Rey point to in the sphere of the text. Gillespie tries to show how this musical logic lies at the core of Nietzsche's thinking, in his essay

"Nietzsche's Musical Politics." Through a detailed investigation of *Twilight of the Idols*, Gillespie argues that we must reject the view of Rey and others that Nietzsche was a merely aphoristic or unsystematic thinker. Nietzsche, he argues, structures his work according to a rigorous musical logic that is meant to replace the logic of traditional philosophy that sets itself up in contradistinction to poetry. Nietzsche, as Gillespie portrays him, is the musical Socrates called for in *The Birth of Tragedy*, the new Aeschylus who is to give birth with his music to a new tragic age and a new politics. In Gillespie's view, this turn to a musical logic is a return for Nietzsche to the mode of thinking of the pre-Socratics. In this light, he suggests that musical structure is Nietzsche's primary vehicle for presenting his fundamental teaching, the doctrine of the eternal return. It is this music, then, that is meant to provide the basis for a Nietzschean republic that will replace the Platonic republic that Western philosophy in a variety of ways has always sought to establish.

The third section of the volume, with essays by Tracy B. Strong, Sarah Kofman, Eugen Fink, and Hans-Georg Gadamer, examines the consequences of such a new way of reading Nietzsche for our understanding of his substantive teaching. In his essay, "Nietzsche's Political Aesthetics," Strong presents us with an alternative view of Nietzsche's politics. As he sees it, Nietzsche is usually read in the context of traditional philosophy as advocating a politics of domination. Beginning with Nietzsche's new aesthetics, however, Strong tries to show that Nietzsche's politics is really a politics of transfiguration. Strong argues that Nietzsche's political model is drawn from the Greeks but tries to show that the essence of Greek political life in Nietzsche's view cannot be recovered in our world through politics but only by means of art. Nietzsche thus rejects the power politics of Bismarck as ultimately unpolitical and indeed antipolitical because Bismarck used the political to secure nonpolitical ends. What is necessary instead is a political aesthetics.

Strong shows how Nietzsche's thinking in this regard was fundamentally shaped by his reception of Schopenhauer's musical criticism, Wagner's social but not his musical doctrines, Burckhardt's philosophy of history, and Emerson's ontology. For Nietzsche, the central question for both Greek politics and nineteenth-century art was the relation of individual to collective judgment. In this sense, Nietzsche's politics is not concerned with facilitating and regulating the encounters of independent selves but with the question of what sorts of selves we ought to have. His politics does not accept the world as given and thus does not aim at security or reconciliation but at transfiguration and redemption. Strong, however, suggests that this attempt breaks down at the end of Nietzsche's life, as Nietzsche comes to despair of the possibility of ever accomplishing such a transfiguration. This in turn precipitates the explicitly and almost crudely political reflections of Nietzsche's last months, when he poses as the political opponent of European regimes and proclaims himself "ready to rule the world."

Just as Strong tries to show us how this new way of reading Nietzsche can save him from charges of advocating a politics of domination, Kofman, a French philosopher at the Sorbonne, argues in her essay, "Baubô: Theological Perversion and Fetishism," that Nietzsche is not a misogynist and that he in fact presents us with a profound new understanding of woman. While the traditional reading of Nietzsche has portrayed him as teaching the inferiority of women to men, Kofman argues that this is a mistaken conclusion based on an understanding of Nietzsche's thought within the framework of traditional philosophy. Nietzsche, in her view, must be read more subtly, with greater attention to the artistic or, in Rey's terms, fictional character of his work. Understood in the light, it becomes clear that what is perverse or denaturing of the world for Nietzsche is the use of sacred names to fix a reality that is in fact fundamentally perspectival. Behind this perversion, for Nietzsche, lie ascetic ideals, particularly as employed by theology to subordinate the strong and well-formed human being to the weak and ugly. As Kofman points out, perversion succeeds because it employs the art of seduction, which for Nietzsche is the art of women. Perversion and degeneracy thus seem to be tied to the feminine in Nietzsche's thought.

This superficial reading of Nietzsche, in Kofman's view, must be augmented by a reading that recognizes that seduction is also the art of Dionysus and consequently the art which Nietzsche himself employs. Kofman locates the difference between the noble and perverse for Nietzsche not in the difference between men and women but in two different perspectives of life, the noble view that looks at the world from top to bottom and the perverse view that peers up from the bottom to the top. On this basis, she is also able to describe two different types of women in Nietzsche—the affirmative, well-formed and modest woman who is profound in her superficiality and the negative and degenerate "scientific" woman who seeks to peer beneath the surface but remains shallow in her profundity. The affirmative woman is a reflection of ascending life itself, to which Nietzsche gives the name Baubô, whom Kofman argues is the female equivalent of Dionysus.

Just as Strong and Kofman try to show how we must alter our traditional interpretation of Nietzsche's teaching about politics and sexuality when we view him from this new perspective, Fink, a leading phenomenologist, tries to delineate how such a way of understanding Nietzsche changes our conception of his cosmology and anthropology in his essay "Nietzsche's New Experience of World." Fink argues that the old question of whether Nietzsche is a poet or a philosopher has remained unanswered because we have failed to grasp his new experience of world. This failure is due in large part to our repeated attempts to comprehend it in traditional metaphysical formulas. According to Fink, any interpretation of Nietzsche is a hazardous enterprise because of the peculiar mixture of revelation and concealment in his thought. Nietzsche in his view is neither a philosopher who considers matters systematically nor a poet who is guided by the internal logic of his creation. Nietzsche thinks rather in images that reflect his peculiar experience of the world. Fink first delineates Nietzsche's anthropology by tracing Nietzsche's view of man from his image of man as a predator, through his conception of the antithesis of the genius and the many, all-too-many, to the free spirit and Zarathustra. He shows in each case the tension between the dramatic and the philosophic in these images. Fink then turns to an examination of the images Nietzsche uses to capture the phenomena of life and the world itself. He concludes that Nietzsche's cosmology is anthropomorphic and that his anthropology is cosmomorphic, that individuals are creators who use language to create the "fiction" of world but also that they are themselves mere fictions in the great play of life and are thus dissolved into the universality of the will to power. While Fink accepts the Heideggerian claim that Nietzsche remains entwined in metaphysical categories and that he is often misled by them, he argues that Nietzsche is not fundamentally a metaphysical thinker. As he sees it, what is decisive in Nietzsche is the play of images, the back and forth that seems to defy traditional logic. In Fink's view, it is this Dionysian celebration of the world as a dance or game and not the metaphysical elements that represents Nietzsche's essential thinking.

This element of innocence and play which is central for Strong, Kofman, and Fink is also decisive for Gadamer. Like Harries and Gillespie, however, he tries to show how this element is bound up with the tragic in Nietzsche. In his essay, "The Drama of Zarathustra," Gadamer argues that we must reject the traditional reading of *Zarathustra* as moral philosophy in favor of an interpretation that treats it as a drama that presents us with the tragic answer to the paradox that has troubled German thought since the eighteenth century, the problem of restored immediacy or mediated immediacy. This problem, in his view, arises at the beginning of *Zarathustra,* when the innocent play of the child is posited as the goal of human spirit. This conceptual paradox in Gadamer's view receives a dramatic answer in *Zarathustra* in the doctrine of the eternal recurrence. He argues that this central doctrine of Nietzsche's thought must not be understood conceptually. This is the meaning of Zarathustra's assertion that it cannot be spoken but only sung. It is in truth the dramatic affirmation of the continual renewal of innocence in the face of death, which is an inevitable and therefore tragic infidelity toward life. This dramatic interpretation of Nietzsche's doctrine of the eternal recurrence, and not the later, more metaphysical notion of the will to power, is Nietzsche's definitive teaching for Gadamer. In this respect, he, like Fink, rejects the Heideggerian reading of Nietzsche and sees an ecstatic element in Nietzsche's thought that Heidegger wants to deny.

These essays thus try to chart the course that Nietzsche sets for humanity toward new seas beyond the world bounded by the pillars of Hercules, the world of the Western tradition. They are not the last word on Nietzsche, but we hope they may be part of the first ones. Whether the voyage Nietzsche sends us on can end in the joy and innocence of the blessed isles or in a shipwreck that maroons us on the rocks of nihilism remains an open question.

Perhaps the central claim that unifies these essays is the claim that there is something that one can call the Western philosophical tradition and that thinking in this tradition has been structured in particular ways. In the picture of Nietzsche sketched by these essays, Nietzsche no longer attempts to find a final or definite solution to traditional philosophical problems. Rather, he seeks to show that the problems are themselves problematic:

> *We aeronauts of the spirit!*—All those brave birds which fly out into the distance, into the farthest distance—it is certain! Somewhere or other they will be unable to go on and will perch on a mast or a bare cliff-face—and they will even be thankful for this miserable accommodation! But who could venture to infer from that, that there was *not* an immense open tract before them, that they had flown as far as one *could* fly! All our great teachers and predecessors have at last come to a stop and it is not with the noblest or most graceful of gestures that weariness comes to a stop: it will be the same with you and me too! But what does that matter to you and me! *Other birds will fly farther!* This insight

and faith of ours vies with them in flying up and away; it rises above our heads and above our weakness into the heights and from there surveys the distance and sees before it the flocks of birds which, far stronger than we, still strive whither we have striven, and where everything is sea, sea, sea!—And whither then would we go? Would we *cross* the sea? Whither does this mighty longing draw us, this longing that is worth more to us than any pleasure? Why just in this direction, thither where all the suns of humanity have hitherto *gone down?* Will it perhaps sometime be said of us that we too, *steering westward, hoped to reach an India*—but that it was our fate to be wrecked against infinity? Or, my brothers. Or?— (V 2, 335)

PART I

Beyond Philosophy and Poetry:
Sailing a Sunless Sea

CHAPTER 1

■ # The Philosopher at Sea

Karsten Harries

■ ## 1. THE SEAFARER

In his preface to *Nietzsche as Philosopher,* Arthur Danto writes, appropriately enough given Nietzsche's understanding of himself as a seafaring discoverer, a new Columbus setting sail for uncharted seas: "His language would have been less colorful had he known what he was trying to say, but then he would not have been the original thinker he was, working through a set of problems which had hardly been charted before. Small wonder his maps are illustrated, so to speak, with all sorts of monsters and fearful indications and boastful cartographic embellishments!"[1] This suggests that the special color of Nietzsche's discourse is inseparable from his failure to know what he was trying to say, a failure Danto links to Nietzsche's originality as a thinker.

Writing from the perspective of contemporary analytical philosophy, Danto insists that "we know a great deal more philosophy today."[2] The seas Nietzsche first explored and sought to chart have apparently become much more familiar. Danto also suggests that we have a better understanding of what a philosophical sea chart should look like: such charts have no room for "monsters and fearful indications and boastful cartographic embellishments." The color of Nietzsche's prose is here tied to what makes it nonphilosophical.

But do we in fact know our way by now in the seas Nietzsche was trying to chart? And do we know what makes a discourse philosophical? Danto admits that his way of reading Nietzsche from a contemporary perspective "may precipitate some anachronisms"[3] but claims that the progress of philosophy places us in a position to understand what is philosophically important in Nietzsche better than he himself was able to do; that to read Nietzsche as a philosopher, we may have to do violence to his texts, where such violence would be the price we have to pay if we are to grasp what in Nietzsche's work remains philosophically alive. But what sort of life is this?

Nietzsche himself insisted on the untimeliness of his writings. "The time for me hasn't come yet: some are born posthumously. . . . It would contradict my character entirely if I expected ears and hands for my truths today: that today one doesn't accept my ideas is not only understandable, it even seems right to me" (VI 3, 296).[4]

Do we now have ears and hands for Nietzsche's truths? Nietzsche remarks on the innocence of some professor in Berlin who "suggested very amiably that I ought to try another form: nobody read such things" (VI 3, 297). Since then, taking up this professor's amiable challenge, countless interpreters have tried to recast what Nietzsche wrote into a more readily understood idiom, to make what he was trying to express more accessible. But, before we engage in such exercise in translation, we would do well to consider Nietzsche's insistence on the gap that separates the kind of reader he demanded from the readers available to him. Having understood six sentences of Zarathustra, Nietzsche claims, "would raise one to a higher level of existence than 'modern' man could attain" (III 3, 311). Nietzsche demands "postmodern" readers. Can we claim to be those readers? Should we even want to be such readers?

It is easy to reply that, when Nietzsche speaks of the untimeliness of his books, he is speaking in boastful hyperbole, especially in *Ecce Homo,* written on the edge of madness. And does he not go on to insist that he was speaking only of Germany? "Everywhere else I have readers—nothing but first-rate intellects and proven characters, trained in high positions and duties" (VI 3, 299). He even mentions New York as one of the places where he has been discovered. Pain and irony are difficult to overhear.

But what kind of readers was Nietzsche looking for? His answer deserves our careful attention:

> When I imagine a perfect reader, he always turns into a monster of courage and curiosity; moreover, supple, cunning, cautious; a born adventurer and discoverer. In the end, I could say no better to whom alone I am speaking at bottom than Zarathustra said it: to *whom* alone will he relate his riddle?
> "To you, the bold searchers, researchers, and whoever embarks with cunning sails on terrible seas—to you, drunk with riddles, glad of the twilight, whose soul flutes lure astray to every whirlpool, because you do not want to grope

along a thread with cowardly hand; and where you can *guess,*
you hate to *deduce. . . ."* (VI 3, 301–2)

Such reading is difficult to reconcile with the kind of exploration and
cartography Danto has in mind. This seafarer's monstrous texts demand monstrous readers, fearless sailors.

It is of course possible and instructive to read Nietzsche very differently, for example, from the perspective of contemporary analytical philosophy. But its style cannot do justice to Nietzsche's style,
which must call the analytical approach into question. Not that other
approaches, say a neo-Kantian approach or one indebted to Heidegger's fundamental ontology, are more likely to prove adequate. The
difficulty is bound up rather with the very attempt to domesticate
Nietzsche's monstrous texts by translating them into a philosophical
idiom with which we are more at home and therefore more comfort-
able. Such translation may well help us to appropriate what Nietzsche
has written, but we should ask ourselves whether such appropriation
is not also a defense against a style and a thinking that puts the philosophy guarded by professional philosophers into question.

Just this, I want to suggest, makes Nietzsche a philosopher. In the
Philosophical Investigations, Wittgenstein remarks that philosophical
problems have the form "I don't know my way about."[5] To be sure,
not all problems having this form are therefore philosophical—to
have lost one's way in some unfamiliar city hardly suffices to make
one a philosopher. But in such cases our disorientation is only superficial. To reorient ourselves, we can fall back on a deeper and un-
challenged understanding of where we are and what is to be done.
Philosophy cannot fall back on such an understanding. The fundamental question of philosophy is, Where is man's place? Philosophy
is born of a sense of homelessness that is inseparable from the insistence that man act and think for himself. At the center of philosophy
thus lies an ethical concern born of the demand that we assume re-
sponsibility for our actions and the consequent refusal to rest content with what has come to be established, accepted, and taken for
granted. Man's claim to autonomy forces him to put into question the
authority of history and the place it has assigned to him. Philosophy
is thus a critical enterprise. Not that this critique can rely on firmly
established criteria. Quite the contrary—philosophy remains alive
only as long as the question, What is man's place, his *ethos?* continues to be asked, because that place remains questionable, because
man's vocation remains ambiguous. Once this ground of philosophy
in radical questioning is recognized, the "monsters" and "carto-

graphic embellishments" that are so much part of Nietzsche's maps will no longer seem eliminable ornaments that, born of fear and narcissistic boasting, only obscure what is philosophically significant. They challenge not only all philosophers who feel confident of their place and way, but also, and more important, our common sense. Measured by that common sense, what Nietzsche has to tell us may often seem nonsense. But this is a risk someone who would challenge common sense has to run. We serve Nietzsche ill when, refusing his challenge, we try to show that there is a quite acceptable sense behind such apparent nonsense. His teaching of the eternal recurrence, whose first statement in *Zarathustra* the lines cited in *Ecce Homo* serve to introduce, provides a key example. Citing these lines as he does to describe his perfect reader, Nietzsche suggests that, like that questionable doctrine, in some sense all he has written is a riddle demanding to be read by sailors.

The following remarks examine only that brief introduction in the hope that such an examination will shed some light on the profoundly questionable and, just because of this, philosophical character of Nietzsche's texts and of the demands this places on his readers.

■ 2. THE GREAT HEALTH

Hermeneutics has taught us that we cannot really understand the meaning of a part until we have grasped its place in the whole to which it belongs. As Heidegger insists, interpretation (*Erläuterung*) cannot be separated from consideration of the place of what is being interpreted (*Erörterung*).[6] Such consideration is especially important when we are seeking to understand a writer as preoccupied with the importance of setting and point of view, as fond of masks and self-dramatization, as aware of the importance of style and mood as Nietzsche. What then is the place of these introductory words?

The narrative of *Zarathustra* gives a first answer: the words are spoken by Zarathustra on a ship that is carrying him from the blessed isles back to the land of his mountain and his cave.

The words are spoken by Zarathustra. But who is Zarathustra? In *Ecce Homo*, Nietzsche tells his readers that to understand the Zarathustra type "one must first become clear about his physiological presupposition: this is what I call the *great health*" (VI 3, 335). This suggests that the place from which these introductory words are spoken is defined by "the great health."

There is an obvious objection: the words are spoken, after all, not just by Zarathustra, but by Zarathustra at a particular stage of his development, a Zarathustra who is coming home, still sick, still struggling to cure himself of the spirit of revenge, of "the will's ill will against time and its 'it was'" (VI 1, 176), still troubled by the soothsayer's "all is empty, all is the same, all has been" (VI 1, 169), still resisting the thought of the eternal recurrence that, while still unspoken, yet haunts him, not yet "The Convalescent" ready to affirm himself as its teacher—a Zarathustra, in short, who is not only literally but spiritually at sea, bearing "riddles and bitternesses in his heart," a voyager in search of himself (VI 1, 199).

How then are we to understand the suggestion that the place from which these words are spoken is "the great health"? In just what sense is this great health the presupposition of the Zarathustra type? Was that type born of such health? It would seem not, for, as Nietzsche tells us in the immediately preceding section, the Zarathustra type overtook him when he felt not at all well, in that cold and rainy winter of 1882–83 he spent in Rapallo, on walks he took whenever his frail health permitted. Like the words Zarathustra addresses to his sailors, all *Zarathustra,* and perhaps all Nietzsche's writings, are the work of a sick man. And yet, does this mean that their place may not also be that state of being Nietzsche calls "the great health"? "Health and sickliness: one should be careful! The standard remains the efflorescence of the body, the agility, courage, and cheerfulness of spirit— but also, of course, *how much of the sickly it can take upon itself and overcome*—how much it can *make* healthy. That of which more delicate men would perish belongs to the stimulants of the *great* health" (VII 1, 106).

To explain this "great health," *Ecce Homo* quotes in its entirety the penultimate section of *The Gay Science,* which carries that phrase as its title. This section, too, is spoken by someone who needs and desires rather than possesses health: "Being new, nameless, difficult to understand, we premature births of an as yet unproven future, we need for a new goal also a new means—namely, a new health, stronger, more seasoned, tougher, more audacious, and gayer than any previous health" (VI 3, 335). "Premature births of an as yet unproven future" once more suggests not health but a precarious state of being, precarious because that world in which it could thrive has yet to arrive, and may indeed never arrive. Presupposed is a dissatisfaction with the present age that is inseparable from a still worldless call to a different way of being issuing from beyond that age. He who heeds that call becomes "new, nameless, difficult to understand." Once again Nietzsche invokes the image of the sailor:

> And now, after we have long been on our way in this manner, we argonauts of the ideal, with more daring perhaps than is prudent, and have suffered shipwreck and damage often enough, but are, to repeat it, healthier than one likes to permit us, dangerously healthy, ever again healthy—it will seem to us as if, as a reward, we now confronted an as yet undiscovered country, whose boundaries nobody has surveyed yet, something beyond all the lands and nooks of the ideal so far, a world overrich in what is beautiful, strange, questionable, terrible, and divine that our curiosity as well as our craving to possess it has got beside itself— alas, now nothing will sate us any more! (VI 3, 336)

Nietzsche's great health is the health required of a Jason, an Odysseus, or a Columbus, of a seafarer who, for the sake of the promise of some not yet discovered country is eager to surrender the comfort and the security of the familiar, ready to risk pain and even death, and who will not be sated. This refusal of satisfaction, of the old ideal of being at one with oneself, whole, entire, helps to define the great health.

The above discussion of the great health ends with the words "the tragedy *begins,*" referring the reader back to section 342 of *The Gay Science,* which is virtually identical with the opening paragraphs of "Zarathustra's Prologue." The beginning of *Zarathustra* is the beginning of tragedy, where we should keep in mind the hopes associated with tragedy in *The Birth of Tragedy,* the place of this book, which sought to locate the roots of the ills of our age in Socrates' optimistic embrace of both reason and the ideal of satisfaction and looked both backward and forward to tragedy as to a cure. Nietzsche's great health does not exclude suffering, disease, and death. Just the opposite, it affirms and appropriates them.

We learn more about the state of being Nietzsche calls the great health in *The Genealogy of Morals,* where he opposes it to the "evil eye" man has had all too long for his natural inclinations, for life, for the world, aspiring instead "to the beyond, to that which runs counter to sense, instinct, nature, animal." If this evil eye has supported "all ideals hitherto, which are one and all hostile to life and ideals that slander the world," Nietzsche would have us reverse this millennia-old tradition of self-torture in the name of "higher" values (VI 2, 351).

The attainment of this goal would require a *different* kind of spirit from that likely to appear in the present age: spirits strengthened by war and victory, for whom conquest, adventure, danger, and even pain have become needs; it would require habituation to the keen air of the heights, to winter journeys, to ice and mountains in every sense [the image of the mountain climber replaces here that of the seafaring discoverer]; it would require even a kind of sublime wickedness, an ultimate, supremely confident mischievousness in knowledge that goes with great health; it would require, in brief and alas, precisely this *great health!* (VI 2, 352)

Nietzsche goes on to call for the person with great health as a redeemer not only from the reigning ethics of satisfaction but also from what was bound to grow out of it, the great nausea, the will to nothingness, nihilism, and identifies him with Zarathustra. Redemption here should be understood in the light of Zarathustra's understanding of redemption as an overcoming of the spirit of revenge. The great health is understood in opposition to the spirit of revenge, to "the will's ill will against time and its 'it was'" (VI 1, 176), in opposition to the evil eye that has determined the shape of our culture and alienated us from ourselves.

The power that the spirit of revenge has over us is rooted in the temporality that constitutes our being, shadowing it with sad thoughts of losing all that we can call our own, even ourselves. Cast into a world that we have not chosen, vulnerable, mortal, too weak to secure even our own being, we find it difficult to accept ourselves as we are, especially difficult to accept what most insistently reminds us of our temporality, our corporality, and what is most intimately tied to it, such as sexual desire, hunger, disease, death. Willing power, lacking power, we find it hard to forgive ourselves that lack. So we turn against the reality that denies us power and that means also against ourselves. Seeking to escape the tyranny of time, which denies us what we so deeply desire, the spirit of revenge gives birth to another reality, a reality over which time has no power. Here, if Nietzsche is right, we must locate the origin of most religion and most philosophy.

Consider how Schopenhauer, represented by the soothsayer, whose gloomy pronouncements cast Zarathustra into such profound despondency, speaks of time:

> In time each moment is, only is so far as it has effaced its father, the preceding moment, to be again effaced just as quickly itself. Past and future (apart from the consequences

of their content) are as empty and unreal as any dream; but present is only the boundary between the two, having neither extension nor duration. In just the same way, we shall also recognize the same emptiness in all the other forms of the principle of sufficient reason, and shall see that, like time, space also, and like this, everything that exists simultaneously in space and time, and hence everything that proceeds from causes and motives, has only a relative existence, is only through and for another like itself, i.e., only just as enduring.[7]

Lack is constitutive of what we call realiy. Reality knows no genuine plenitude. There is no presence we can really possess, no satisfaction that is not eroded and overtaken by time. What we so deeply want, to be at one with ourselves, is denied to us by what we are:

Essentially, it is all the same whether we pursue or flee, fear harm or aspire to enjoyment; care for the constantly demanding will, no matter in what form, continually fills and moves consciousness; but without peace and calm, true well-being is absolutely impossible. Thus the subject of willing is constantly lying on the revolving wheel of Ixion, is always drawing water in the sieve of the Danaids, and is the eternally thirsting Tantalus.[8]

To slake this thirst, the spirit of revenge gives birth to another reality that invites dreams of superhuman happiness, constructs "afterworlds," realms of being beyond becoming that promise the plenitude and presence that this world denies, a security not subject to the terror of time, that allow for genuine satisfaction, be it only the satisfaction of really knowing something. But the ideal of a satisfaction that stills care and desire has to turn against the very condition of our being. On reflection, all such ideals turn out to be metaphors of death, directed against life. Here, we have the source of that sickness which the great health would overcome. The great health names a mode of existing that has renounced the ideal of satisfaction, a mode in which it is important to keep in mind the way this ideal has shaped not only religion but philosophy, and not only moral philosophy but metaphysics and the theory of knowledge, to the extent that these have thought being and truth to be against time.

The very language of philosophy is governed by the spirit of revenge. Consider once more Danto's suggestion that Nietzsche's language would have been less colorful had he known what he was trying to say. What do we mean when we say that someone knows what he is trying to say? Presupposed is a distinction between thought and its linguistic expression. To know something is to have grasped the truth of some thought. Inseparable from such knowledge is the knowledge that what I know does not need to be expressed in just this way. The special color of a discourse comes to be understood as an at best dispensable, more often distracting, ornament. Knowledge is best served by a discourse not so tied to the particular perspective of an individual or a group that, without it, it loses its meaning. So understood, knowledge demands objectivity, and objectivity demands translatability. Ideally, the medium of words should become totally transparent; language should be like clear glass so that it offers no resistance to the understanding as it appropriates what is to be understood. The "whiteness" of scientific discourse answers to this ideal.

Nietzsche could have replied that this ideal of a transparent language that does not contaminate the purity of our thoughts is just as much a chimera as the ideal of a transparent body that would not contaminate the chaste purity of our spirit. Both ideals prevent us from doing justice, to language in one case, to human being in the other. And in both cases the desire for purity presupposes that evil eye of which the great health is to cure us.

To say that the place from which Zarathustra tells his riddle is the great health is not to deny that the speaker is still fighting the poison left in him by the tarantula's bite, still struggling with the spirit of revenge, still trying to shake off the soothsayer's gloomy teaching; but it is to say that this struggle is illuminated by the possibility of a yes to time and all that is temporal, of a yes to the body, to hunger and disease, even to death. By choosing just this passage to describe his relationship to his perfect reader, Nietzsche invites us to understand him as someone still sick with revenge, still trying to renounce the ideal of satisfaction and the nihilism which is the unmasking of that ideal, but also haunted by another, still unnamed ideal as by a riddle, in love with life and full of hope.

■   3. THE SAILORS

As he likens himself to a seafaring explorer, Nietzsche likens his perfect reader to a sailor. Like his Zarathustra, he addresses his words to "bold searchers, researchers, and whoever embarks with cunning sails on terrible seas," who "drunk with riddles, glad of the twilight," are lured astray by flutes "to every whirlpool."

Kaufmann's "searchers, researchers" fails to capture the challenge of the word play *Sucher, Versucher,* which calls attention to the prefix *ver* and helps to interpret the nature of the search Nietzsche would have his reader be engaged in. *Versuchen* means first of all "to attempt." To make a *Versuch* is to try something, uncertain of whether such trial will prove a success. A scientific experiment is a *Versuch* in this sense. We engage in experiments to test our conjectures; such testing presupposes a readiness to retract one's presuppositions and to rethink one's assumptions. Nietzsche's texts invite such hermeneutic experimentation.

But *Versucher* means first of all not a scientific researcher but a tempter. The devil, who tempted Adam and Eve with the promise that their eyes would be opened and they would be like God, knowing good and evil, is *the Versucher.* Nietzsche's sailors, it would seem, are of the devil's party, tempted by and tempting with the promise of truth. But the devil is only the mask in which Dionysus presents himself to Christians subject to the spirit of revenge, this "tempter god and born pied piper of consciences whose voice knows how to descend into the netherworld of every soul," this god of explorers and philosophers to whom Nietzsche offered his firstborn as "a *sacrifice*" (VI 2, 247–48).

Called by Dionysus, Nietzsche's sailors, too, are possessed of "that sublime inclination of the seeker after knowledge who insists on profundity, multiplicity, and thoroughness, with a *will* which is a kind of cruelty of the intellectual conscience and taste" and which counters the "will to mere appearance, to simplification, to masks, to cloaks, in short to the surface." Better than perhaps any other philosopher, Nietzsche knows about the importance of being superficial: "Anyone who has looked deeply into the world may guess how much wisdom lies in the superficiality of men. The instinct that preserves them teaches them to be flighty, light, and false" (VI 2, 174). But if there is a superficiality in the service of life, and our ordinary concern for truth is superficial in this sense, there is also a superficiality born of a fear of life, a pursuit of truth born of fear of a deeper truth.

Already in *The Birth of Tragedy* Nietzsche had located in just such a fear the origin of our culture, a culture shaped by the "sublime metaphysical illusion" that "thought, using the thread of logic, can penetrate the deepest abysses of being, and that thought is capable not only of knowing being but even of *correcting* it" (III 1, 95). Man's will to power here blinds him to the lack of power constitutive of his being and thus alienates him from his own reality, from his life. Such a Socratic-Cartesian culture needs "to translate man back into nature;

to become master over the many vain and overly enthusiastic interpretations and connotations that have so far been scrawled and
painted over the eternal basic text of *Homo natura;* to see to it that
man henceforth stands before man as even today, hardened in the
discipline of science, he stands before the *rest* of nature, with intrepid
Oedipus eyes and sealed Odysseus ears, deaf to the siren songs of old
metaphysical bird catchers who have been piping at him all too long,
'you are more, you are higher, you are of different origin!'" (VI 2, 169).

The basic text Nietzsche would have us interpret is *Homo natura.*
His own texts serve such interpretation first of all as a restorer's sol-
vents would, which help to "translate" a painting disfigured by what
later generations have painted and scrawled over it back into its
original state. Such "translation" is fraught with danger. Instead of
allowing us to recover the original, it may only destroy it. And can we
even be sure that there is an original to be recovered?

How are we to understand Nietzsche's expression "the eternal
basic text of *Homo natura*"? This suggests that in principle it is possible to read human nature as one reads a text, even if countless
translations have so obscured the original that our interpretation has
to be at the same time an archeological excavation. But will such excavation yield a *Grundtext?* Has not Nietzsche himself taught us to be
wary of any philosopher who would base his teaching on such a
Grund?

Nietzsche knows that there is something profoundly unnatural
about the refusal to remain with superficial appearance, about the insistence to descend to the *Grund,* the claim to a wisdom deeper than
common sense. In *The Birth of Tragedy,* Nietzsche thus says of Oedipus that, precisely because he possessed such wisdom, because he
was able to solve the riddle of the Sphinx, he had to fall into a whirlpool of unnatural deeds (III 1, 36). Nietzsche knows that to want to
solve the riddle of the Sphinx is already to have fallen out of the natural order. But just Oedipus's refusal to remain on the surface, a refusal
that subverts the natural order and the moral world and lets Oedipus
blind himself, issues in a more profound vision that prepares the
foundation of a new world on the ruins of the old.

Nietzsche demands such courage of his readers. This courage requires us to be deaf to the siren song that places man's essence beyond nature and time. Nietzsche's reference to the seafaring Odysseus
in this place would appear to involve a misreading, for Odysseus did
not seal his own ears with wax but those of his fellow sailors. Lashed
to the mast, he listened to the siren's songs, as Nietzsche himself listened all too eagerly to the siren song of eternity, as his teaching of

the eternal recurrence demonstrates; and it is tempting to link the disaster that overtook him to the absence of those who would tie him to some mast. But, like Odysseus, Nietzsche would seal the ears of his fellow sailors to this siren song, as he would seal his own ears were he only able to do so. We should not forget that, when Nietzsche speaks of standing before the riddle that is man with intrepid Oedipus eyes and sealed Odysseus ears, he is stating a task. Thus, he would also want his readers open to what lies beneath the surface of his texts, its ambiguities, its multivalence, open to the absence of a single unspoken meaning that could gather this text into a whole, to a chaos of affects only superficially gathered into a whole.

Sich versuchen can also mean to lose one's way while searching, as the wise Oedipus, searching, loses his place in the natural and moral order—and Nietzsche liked to think of the genuine philosopher in the image of Oedipus (III 4, 48; VII 3, 399, 429). Wittgenstein, as we saw, understands the philosopher as someone who has lost his way; he is, we can say, *einer, der sich versucht hat.* The existence of a method that would provide us with a way of solving all philosophical problems would mean the end of philosophy. Nietzsche's sailors are philosophers precisely because they demand the questionable for their horizon. To open our eyes to this horizon, and this also means to recall us to life, is one goal of Nietzsche's reflections. This goal is quite the opposite of that of Wittgenstein, who tried to show that the philosopher is someone who has allowed himself to become bewitched by language: as the unity "of language and the activities into which it is woven" that organizes ordinary language is destroyed, language begins to "idle" or "go on a holiday." Wittgenstein, too, rejects the metaphysician's promise of a terra firma. The would be terra firma of philosophers is unmasked as no more than a castle in the clouds. But the point of such unmasking is to return us to the language games of the everyday as the only ground given to us: *Wir legen den Grund der Sprache frei* (we are clearing up the ground of language).[9]

If Wittgenstein would recall philosophers from their airy heights back to the earth, Nietzsche would set them afloat by shaking their confidence, not only in metaphysical construction but also in those language games to which Wittgenstein would have us turn as to a ground, not, however, to replace it with some other terra firma but to render the very idea of such a ground questionable. Nietzsche, too, calls words "the seducers of philosophers," who are likened to fish struggling in the nets of language (IV 1, 189). But instead of giving up this struggle, Nietzsche tears at this net to open us to what more immediately claims and moves us than all words, to open us to the sea, to life. Nietzsche's style is a tearing of language in the service of life. If Nietzsche's sailors are impatient with what is generally accepted and taken for granted, this is because they are haunted by the promise of a life richer than all common sense, richer also than philosophy, and haunted also by the possibility of a philosophy that, unlike all philosophy born of the spirit of revenge, would interpret and justify that life. Such a philosophy would not claim to have discovered a new terra firma. It would not be a philosophy for all times, nor would it be for everyone. It would be a necessarily precarious *Versuch* to answer the riddle of life with a discourse that would allow us to interpret it as a meaningful whole while yet aware that all such understanding must do violence to what it seeks to understand and that it therefore should not be dogmatic. Life overflows every interpretation. All the moral philosopher can furnish are precarious perspectives: "The moral earth, too, is round! The moral earth, too, has its antipodes! The antipodes, too, have their right to exist! There still is another world to be discovered—and more than one! Board the ships, you philosophers!" (V 2, 210).

Nietzsche knows that his call challenges the way philosophers have understood their task as one of securing human existence and more especially the project of knowledge by placing them on firm ground. Think of Hegel's famous suggestion that it is only with Descartes's establishment of the *cogito* as an unshakable foundation that "the education, the thinking of our age begins." "Here, we can say, we are at home and like the sailor, after long journeying about the raging sea, call 'land.'" [10] Hegel describes Descartes as the thinker who marks the beginning of the end of philosophy's age of discovery, which, if philosophy requires the horizon of the questionable, heralds the end of philosophy. And, as a lover of truth, must the philosopher not welcome that end? Must he not be impatient with riddles and insist on clearly framed problems that leave no doubt as to what constitutes a satisfactory solution? Must he not be glad of a light that allows us to see things as they are, distrustful of a twilight that renders ambiguous, inviting us to mistake one thing for another, distrustful of that adventurism Nietzsche practices as a writer and demands of his readers? To Nietzsche, we can oppose Kant, who, in the *Critique of Pure Reason,* presents himself not as an adventurous seafarer but as a sober explorer on firm land:

> We have now not merely explored the territory of pure
> understanding, and carefully surveyed every part of it, but
> have also measured its extent, and assigned to everything

in it its rightful place. This domain is an island, enclosed
by nature itself within unalterable limits. It is the land of
truth—enchanting name!—surrounded by a wide and
stormy ocean, the native home of illusion, where many a fog
bank and many a swiftly melting iceberg give the deceptive
appearance of farther shores, deluding the adventurous
seafarer ever anew with empty hopes, and engaging him in
enterprises which he can never abandon and yet is unable
to carry to completion.[11]

The *Critique of Pure Reason* is written against such philosophical adventurism, and Kant was confident that his transcendental recasting
of metaphysics heralded its imminent completion, which he expected
to have been accomplished before the end of his century. Kant knows
about the lure of the sea, about our dissatisfaction with the land given
us to survey and cultivate, about a proud freedom that would have us
seize what our finitude denies us; there is something in us that resists
the completion he promises and insists on the sublimity of the questionable, even on the terrible. Kant, however, would have us resist the
siren songs of the questionable.

But does this island to which Kant gives the "enchanting name"
"the land of truth" deserve that title? Nietzsche might have asked
whether Kant does not allow himself here to be enchanted by our
natural tendency to transform that place where we happen to be, the
way we happen to think, into a terra firma. Does Kant's "land of truth"
even deserve to be called an island? Is it not rather a ship, perhaps
even one whose timbers are beginning to rot and give way? And who
is to say that such a shipwreck would be a disaster?

That immense framework and planking of concepts to
which the needy man clings his whole life long in order to
preserve himself is nothing but a scaffolding and toy for the
most audacious feats of the liberated intellect. And when it
smashes this framework to pieces, throws it into confusion,
and puts it back together again in an ironic fashion, pairing
the most alien things and separating the closest, it is demonstrating that it has no need of these makeshifts of indigence
and that it will now be guided by intuitions rather than by
concepts. (III 2, 383)

What Kant considers firm land is to Nietzsche a floating prison. To
open philosophy to life, to the sea, Nietzsche's discourse challenges
ossified and taken-for-granted ways of speaking; semantic opposi-

tions and collisions deny us the security of what is expected and accepted, opening up the horizon of the questionable.

But is Kant not right to warn us against trying to journey beyond the land of truth? Truth demands the liberation from the rule of perspective and the all-too-subjective; it demands objectivity. Objectivity, again, demands a discourse as free as possible from the colors added to what is thought by care and desire. Forsaking so readily the part of the suitor of truth, does Nietzsche not become "only fool, only poet" (VI 1, 368)? Nietzsche could reply that it is just because he remains a suitor of truth that he has to challenge Kant's claim to have put an end to speculative metaphysics with his Copernican revolution and to have charted the boundaries of the land of truth once and for all. Are Kant's transcendental subject and the correlative idea of a knowledge of objects, which is free from perspectival distortion, not fantastic constructions? Can human thinking free itself from its subjective point of view and inherited prejudice? Herder already had protested both the elision of the concrete person and of language in *The Critique of Pure Reason,* insisting that we are always bound by what happens to be our nature, that we think with words, not concepts, and that we cannot think in a language other than our own. Thought will never become pure or innocent. There is no language unburdened by past prejudice, no intuition free from the distortion of perspective, no presence not hopelessly entangled in what remains concealed, absent, mysterious. Does the pursuit of truth not demand that we open ourselves to this mystery which our understanding vainly seeks to master? Kant's revolution can be charged with having been insufficiently Copernican. The progress of transcendental reflection since Kant, which has sought to bring Kant's transcendental structures down to earth, can be understood as a response to Nietzsche's call: "Board the ships, you philosophers!"

In this connection, it is interesting to note that Copernicus himself, citing Virgil, relies on the metaphor of the seafarer who is oblivious to his ship's movement to explain and thereby disarm his reader's reluctance to acknowledge that it is the earth that moves and revolves around its axis, and not the firmanent: "The relation is similar to that of which Virgil's Aeneas says, 'We sail out of the harbor, and the countries and cities recede.' For when a ship is sailing along quietly, everything which is outside of it will appear to those on board to have a motion corresponding to the movement of the ship; and the voyagers are of the erroneous opinion that they with all they have with them are at rest." [12] Nietzsche's choppy discourse intends to make the reader's sailing less smooth and thus to let him become aware that our language and the conceptual frames we have raised on it are rather like a ship, that with our words and concepts we do not stand on firm land but are indeed at sea.

If Kant is enchanted by the name "land of truth," Zarathustra's sailors, "drunk with riddles, glad of the twilight," have experienced the very different enchantment of flutes that beckon them to every whirlpool. In *The Gay Science,* too, Nietzsche describes himself and those who are of his mind as "born guessers of riddles," who welcome the twilight of the setting of the sun of the old God. But this darkening of our world, with its ever deepening, ever more ominous shadows, does not fill him with dread but with a new cheerfulness. That cheerfulness lets him invert the traditional light metaphor: what to those still bound to the dead God must seem a sad and gloomy twilight will appear to those stretched out between present and future "like a new, scarcely describable kind of light, happiness, relief, exhilaration, encouragement, dawn" (V 2, 256):

> We philosophers and "free spirits" feel as if a new dawn were shining on us when we receive the tidings that "the old god is dead"; our heart overflows with gratitude, amazement, anticipation, expectation. At last the horizon appears free again to us, even granted that it is not bright; at last our ships may venture out again, venture out to face any danger; all the daring of the lover of knowledge is permitted again; the sea, *our* sea, lies open again; perhaps there has never yet been such an "open sea." (V 2, 256)

■   4. THE THREAD OF ARIADNE

Zarathustra tells his vision and riddle to sailors, who, "because they do not want to grope along a thread with cowardly hand" and would rather guess than deduce, are lured astray to every whirlpool. These sailors then are very different from the culture hero Theseus, who, having sailed to Crete and slain the Minotaur, finds his way out of the labyrinth with the help of Ariadne's thread. Theseus and those like him are here condemned as cowards. Zarathustra, of whom Nietzsche says that he is more courageous than all other thinkers taken together, demands a very different audience: "How much truth does a spirit *endure,* how much truth does it *dare?* More and more that became for me the real measure of value. Error (faith in the ideal) is not blindness, error is *cowardice*" (VI 3, 257). Nietzsche links this cowardice to the desire to deduce: deduction is a defense against truth, masking itself by claiming to serve truth.

"Deduce" is Kaufmann's translation of *erschliessen. Erschliessen,* however, means not so much "to deduce," which better translates *schliessen* ("to lock"), as it does "to unlock," "to open up," for example, land for cultivation by cutting roads into what was wilderness so that what was remote and mysterious is made accessible. *Erschliessen* is a first step toward taking possession. Thinking, too, may have that function. Think of Descartes's promise that his method would lead us to "know the force and action of fire, water, air, the stars, heavens and all bodies that environ us, as distinctly as we know the different crafts of the artisans" and thus render us "the masters and possessors of nature." [13] Descartes presents himself to his readers as the Theseus of a culture founded on technology.

Zarathustra's sailors have come to question this culture. Inseparable from their questioning is a longing for the sea, for the labyrinth. Just as Zarathustra's sailors are lured by the whirlpool's abyss, so Nietzsche, in an earlier draft of *Ecce Homo,* speaks of the fascinated curiosity that draws him to the labyrinth, a curiosity, he suggests, that not only delights in the friendship of Ariadne but is also not afraid to make the acquaintance of the Minotaur, presumably not to slay it, as the culture hero Theseus did.[14] Another passage makes the opposition to Theseus even clearer: "There are cases where what is needed is an Ariadne's thread leading into the labyrinth. He who has the task to bring on the great war, the war against the virtuous (—the good and virtuous Zarathustra calls them, also 'last men,' also 'beginning of the end'—) has to be willing to buy some experiences almost at any price; the price could even be the danger of losing oneself." [15] What makes it so difficult for us to endure the truth about reality is the desire to hold on to ourselves. To hold on to ourselves, we also have to hold on to the world in which we exist, to comprehend it. Nietzsche grounds the desire for knowledge as this has been traditionally understood in the need for security. Security demands stability and order. This demand has to turn against all that is fleeting and confusing. So understood, the demand for knowledge has its telos in the defeat of chaos and time, of labyrinth and Minotaur.

The question is whether there is a reality beyond chaos and time that answers to what is here demanded or whether all such "realities" are only fictions born of cowardice, of an inability to affirm reality as it is.

Just as Nietzsche inverts the traditional valuation implied by the metaphors of land and sea, so he reverses the direction traditionally associated with Ariadne's thread, which he would have us follow back into the labyrinth. The significance of this reversal becomes clear when we compare Nietzsche's use of this figure with that of Descartes, who in the *Rules* offers the reader his newfound method as an Ariadne's thread that would lead him out of the labyrinth of fleeting appearance, where appearance is thought relative to the point in space and even more in time that the knowing subject is assigned by the perceiving body.[16] To find our way out of this labyrinth we have to free ourselves from the rule of perspective. Reflection serves such liberation. To gain a more adequate grasp of nature, we must withdraw from the world that usually claims and moves us; to gain a more certain ground, we have to be willing to surrender the "ground" offered by common sense. Cartesian doubt is such a surrender which brackets our ordinary ways of knowing the world only in order to gain a more complete mastery over it.

If we are to master the world, we must discover in the world's heterogeneous multiplicity homogeneity and simplicity. To reflect is already to take a first step in this direction. By transforming the world of everyday experience into a collection of objects for a thinking subject, we establish that subject as the common measure of all these objects. As the subject comes to resemble a pure, disembodied, and dispassionate eye, the world comes to be like a picture. As long as this picture is seen or sensed, it remains relative to the sensing body and subject to the accident of its location in space and time: no more than a superficial appearance. To penetrate beneath that surface and to ensure access to reality, Descartes insists on a second reduction of experience. Now the thinking subject, not the "eye," is made the measure of what is. Reality is now equated with what presents itself to thought. So understood, reality is essentially without colors or sounds, tastes or smells. These belong only to its appearance, to the surface. Even subjected to this twofold reduction, reality might still prove too complex to be mastered by us. The demand for mastery leads thus inevitably to the transformation of what is to be mastered into a kind of mosaic: the world is to be analyzed into simple parts and then to be reconstructed out of these parts. Science may be understood as such reconstruction.

Descartes's statement of his method is an attempt to lay down the conditions that must be met if such reconstruction is to be possible. It has a counterpart in Wittgenstein's *Tractatus,* which brings out one consequence of such reconstruction; subjected to the requirements of such cognitive mastery, the world turns out to have no room for value: "In the world everything is as it is and happens as it does happen. *In* it there is no value—and if there were, it would be of no value."[17] This loss of value has its foundation in the very first reduction I have sketched, in the transformation of the self engaged in the world by care and desire into a subject that stands before a world of now mute facts, as before a picture. We begin to understand what is at issue when Nietzsche challenges, both as thinker and as writer, the pursuit of truth and the commitment to objectivity that is inseparable from it, as is the "whiteness" of scientific discourse. At issue is the meaning of human existence. Nihilism and the pursuit of truth, understood as the correspondence of our thoughts or propositions to the objects themselves, that is, as they are thought to exist independent of the colors and values with which desire and love, distaste and hatred have endowed them, are inextricably intertwined. Both have their foundation in a will to power that, to secure itself, has to so master its world that it renders it mute and colorless.

It is easy to challenge Descartes's confidence in his method, his faith that human beings are capable of the truth and able to fashion themselves into the masters and possessors of nature. Descartes himself raised the question of whether even his simple natures or clear and distinct ideas might not prove deceptive, and he tried to defeat such doubts with his proofs of the existence of a God who is not a deceiver, proofs that were to establish once and for all that our understanding is indeed attuned to reality and thus were to secure the cognitive anthropocentrism presupposed by the new science. However, all such proofs are inescapably circular. Either we are already convinced of the understanding's ability to discipline itself so that there is no need for a God to shore up such conviction, or such conviction is lacking, and then no argument can be found that will make up for that lack. Nietzsche not only lacks such conviction and dismisses the truth Descartes would have us pursue as a fiction born of a cowardice that refuses to admit how profoundly we are at sea; more important, he also would not welcome such a truth, although, or perhaps precisely because, he knows about the very real power the Cartesian project has given us over nature, even our own nature. Descartes's promise of mastery was not an idle *Ver-sprechen,* an empty promise that sacrificed reality for a fantastic fiction. But just this forces us to share Nietzsche's concern about the price that has to be paid for the power gained: the very success of the attempt to secure human existence threatens to allow us to lose touch with the chaos we bear within ourselves, which is the source of our creativity and of our ability to love. Insisting on security, for lack of courage, we deny the labyrinth of Ariadne.

Who is Nietzsche's Ariadne? In keeping with Ariadne's labyrinthine character, different interpretations can be supported: Ariadne as Cosima Wagner;[18] Ariadne as Arachne, the spider woman, the monster in the web of language;[19] Ariadne as Jung's anima.[20] The last interpretation can appeal to the fact that "On the Great Longing," Zarathustra's hymn to his soul, was originally called "Ariadne." Zarathustra there speaks of having freed his soul, of having nourished it, of having made it overfull, readying it for him who, still nameless, awaits the naming of future song, and of having bid his soul sing. Nietzsche's perfect reader should listen to this song beneath the surface of the words, just as the reader of Plato's dialogues should open himself to the unspoken words graven in his soul. Nietzsche, however, has a very different understanding of the soul. "Soul" is for him "only a word for something about the body" (VI 1, 35). Thus, he speaks of the *Leitfaden des Leibes,* the guiding thread of the body (VII 3, 304). When Nietzsche calls on us to follow the thread of Ariadne back into the labyrinth, he is calling on us to return to our own corporeal soul, to its silent labyrinthine discourse, which finally supports all we care about and value. Nietzsche bids us descend into this labyrinth, even if such descent threatens destructions, bids us leave the terra firma of what has come to be expected and taken for granted for the open sea, even if such seafaring must end in shipwreck.

■   5. THE SHIPWRECK

In the *Inferno,* Dante says of Ulysses that neither fondness for his son nor reverence for his father nor love of Penelope could keep him from sailing beyond the landlocked Mediterranean, through the warning markers Hercules had set up so that no man would pass beyond; longing to gain experience of the world, he sailed west with those few companions who had not deserted him, only to be shipwrecked before that dark, monstrous mountain which lies furthest from Jerusalem.

Nietzsche's description of the great health recalls this passage, although we are referred not not Dante's Ulysses but to the Argonauts. Nietzsche, too, describes himself and his companions as craving "to have experienced the whole range of values and desiderata to date," and, having "sailed around all the coasts of this ideal 'Mediterranean,'" still curious, still undeterred by shipwreck and suffering, eager to sail on, dreaming of "an as yet undiscovered country, whose boundaries nobody has surveyed yet, something beyond all the lands and the nooks of the ideal so far, a world overrich in what is beautiful, strange, questionable, terrible, and divine," daring, for the sake of that dream, a shipwreck from which there may be no return (VI 3, 305).

Nietzsche demands of those who would follow him courage in the face of the constant possibility and final inevitability of shipwreck. Those who evade that possibility, who think themselves secure on firm land of one sort or another and are unwilling to recognize that we are all at sea and that there is no ship not threatened by shipwreck, also have to refuse the abysmal depth of reality, that is to say, have to refuse life.

This has special significance for philosophy. If Nietzsche is right, almost always philosophy has been an evasion of life born of the spirit of revenge. The image of the dying Socrates presides over this evasion—as the image of "the human being whom knowledge and reason have liberated from the fear of death," it is "the emblem that, above the entrance gate of science, reminds all of its mission—namely, to make existence appear comprehensible and thus justified" (III 1, 195). The spirit of revenge bids us understand being against time, lets us oppose the illusory appearance of being to the sea of changing appearance as a terra firma. It teaches that the soul's true home lies beyond time, that we become most truly ourselves when we transcend ourselves as beings subject to time. This allows Socrates to interpret the true philosopher's death not as a shipwreck but as a homecoming of the self to itself.

Nietzsche, too, would have us come home to our soul, but he understands this homecoming not as an ascent to a timeless realm of pure forms but as a descent into the chaos each individual bears within himself, into his own labyrinth. As there is something inhuman about Socrates' ascent into the light of the forms, so there is something inhuman about Zarathustra's descent into himself: both threaten the destruction of the individual in his being with others. Both Socrates and Zarathustra therefore insist on a compensatory movement that lets the thinker whose pursuit of wisdom leads him beyond all community rejoin those whom he has left behind. In the myth of the cave, Socrates thus has the prisoner who has escaped its darkness return, and similarly Zarathustra must leave the privacy of his cave high upon his mountain—the joining of cave and mountain hints at what joins, but also separates, Zarathustran and Socratic wisdom— and return to those he has left behind in order to become human again (VI 1, 6). Thus descending, Zarathustra must do violence to his private wisdom, just as his attempts to give voice to this wisdom must do violence to ordinary language. As Zarathustra's going is not only his own *Untergang,* or "going under," but also a leaping over those who hesitate and lag behind, which is to be their *Untergang,* so his speaking is not only the *Untergang* of his own wisdom but also a leaping over of common sense that threatens the shipwreck of all sense.

Consider Zarathustra's teaching of the eternal recurrence. This is not the place to review the many attempts to domesticate that doctrine so that it no longer can offend common sense. Here, I only want to call attention to the explosive power of this forcing together of time and eternity, which represents a refusal to keep reason confined within the limits marked out by Kant's antinomies, warning philosophers not to pass beyond. Hans Blumenberg speaks of a *Sprengmetapher,* a metaphor that like dynamite explodes inherited sense to open up our saying to an unsayable depth, and points to the role such metaphors have played in the mystical tradition with its *via negationis.*[21] Particularly suggestive are remarks that invite a comparison of Nietzsche's doctrine of the eternal recurrence with Nicolaus Cusanus's rhetoric of the circle whose circumference becomes a straight line as its radius becomes infinite.[22] Just as the fifteenth-century cardinal offers his readers the coincidence of opposites as a gate to God's infinity, so Nietzsche offers his readers the coincidence of time and eternity as a gate to a reality that is deeper than our reason. Intended in both cases is the shipwreck of common sense.

To be sure, Nietzsche links *Untergang* to *Ubergang,* "going under" to "going over," passing beyond the old to the new. The metaphor of the seafaring discoverer invites such a reading. But while the word "overman" gestures toward the new land that Nietzsche would have us discover, it names no more than an ill-defined hope that remains in the subjunctive. Nietzsche thus writes only *as if* he confronted that still undiscovered, overrich country that lures him (VI 3, 336). He knows that he is in no position to begin surveying its boundaries. He also knows that, like those of Dante's Ulysses, his curiosity and craving will not be sated by any discovery. In the end, what lures him is not so much the promise of a new land as the depth of the sea, the whirlpool that means shipwreck. Like his Zarathustra, Nietzsche wants to go *zu Grunde,* to perish.

To be sure, *zu Grunde gehen* in Zarathustra means not just to perish but to descend to the *Grund,* to the ground of human existence. Once again we are made to think of Plato's Socrates, especially of the *Phaedo,* whose *ars moriendi* similarly links perishing and recovery of what is essential. In wanting to return to the *Grund,* Nietzsche joins all those philosophers who have looked for the ground that would give our existence its measure, even if he looks for this ground not to some Platonic or Christian heaven but to the earth, to nature. Recall Nietzsche's determination of *Homo natura* as the terrifying *ewige Grundtext,* the eternal basic text that we have to free from layers of misinterpretation so that it will once again provide our texts, our interpretations of who we are and should be, with a measure (VI 2, 175). But what right does Nietzsche have to posit such an eternal ground, a ground furthermore that is also said to be a text—a text that has authority precisely because we are not its author? All too readily, Nietzsche's appeal to this *Grundtext* recalls the traditional understanding of the book of nature written by God. What justifies the thought that, once we remove all the misrepresentations of past thinking, something like a *Grund-Text* will appear? Is the very word *Grundtext* not an oxymoron that on reflection plunges us into an abyss. *Grund* and *Text*—how do these belong together? Is not a text necessarily a human product, a conjecture that falsely claims the authority of a *Grund?* Where can we find a *Grund* to speak to us as a text would, presenting our existence with a measure? When we try to descend beneath the surface created by our discourse, strip reality of our fictions, what remains? Something that deserves to be called a *Grundtext?* Will we not stare rather into an *Abgrund,* into an abyss?

There is, to be sure, much in Nietzsche that celebrates superficiality. But Nietzsche is also profoundly impatient with superficiality, especially with the shallowness that has shaped modernity, including its common sense, including especially also the edifices philosophers have raised on that common sense. Against all these, Nietzsche raises his hammer. But such destruction leaves us no place to stand. No longer another Columbus eager to discover a better Europe, another America, Nietzsche now appears as a mad discoverer who, dreaming of a lost continent beneath the waves, begins to break apart the planks of his ship. At this point, one should expect those few sailors who have followed the music of his words to revolt, to stay his hand, to assess the damage that has been done, and, once the ship has been saved, to rethink the goal of the voyage. But perhaps they, too, have become captive to the enchantment of the flutes that lured their captain.

■ NOTES

1. Arthur C. Danto, *Nietzsche as Philosopher* (New York: Columbia University Press, 1980), 13–14.

2. Ibid., 13.

3. Ibid.

4. I have used the translations of Walter Kaufmann for works available in *The Portable Nietzsche* (New York: Viking Press, 1954) and *Basic Writings of Nietzsche* (New York: Modern Library, 1968); also *The Will to Power,* trans. Walter Kaufmann and R. J. Hollingdale (New York: Random House, 1967). For "On Truth and Lie in a Nonmoral Sense," I have used the translation by Daniel Breazeale, in *Philosophy and Truth: Selections from Nietzsche's Notebooks of the Early 1970's* (Atlantic Highlands: Humanities Press, 1979). All other translations from Nietzsche's works are my own.

5. Ludwig Wittgenstein, *Philosophical Investigations,* tr. G. E. M. Anscombe (New York: Macmillan, 1953), par. 123.

6. Martin Heidegger, *Unterwegs zur Sprache* (Pfullingen: Neske, 1959), 37.

7. Arthur Schopenhauer, *The World as Will and Representation,* trans. E. F. J. Payne, 2 vols. (New York: Dover, 1969), 1:7.

8. Ibid., 196.

9. *Philosophical Investigations,* pars. 38, 119, 132.

10. Hegel, *Vorlesungen über die Geschichte der Philosophie, Jubiläumsausgabe,* ed. Hermann Glockner, 19:328.

11. Kant, *The Critique of Pure Reason,* trans. Norman Kemp Smith, A 235–36/B 294–95, (New York: St. Martin's, 1965).

12. Copernicus, *The Revolution of the Celestial Spheres,* I, 9, in *The Portable Renaissance Reader,* ed. James Bruce Ross and Mary Martin McLaughlin (New York: Viking, 1953), 591.

13. Descartes, *Discourse on Method,* VI, in *Philosophical Works,* trans. E. S. Haldane and G. R. T. Ross, 2 vols. (Cambridge: Cambridge University Press, 1972), 1:119.

14. Friedrich Nietzsche, *Sämtliche Werke, Kritische Studienansgabe,* ed. G. Colli and M. Montinari, 15 vols. (Munich: de Gruyter, 1980), 14:484.

15. Ibid., 497.

16. Descartes, *Rules,* V, in *Philosophical Works,* 1:14.

17. Wittgenstein, *Tractatus,* 6. 41. Trans. C. K. Ogden (London: Routledge & Kegan Paul, 1961).

18. Hermann J. Weigand, "Nietzsche's Dionysus-Ariadne Fixation," *The Germanic Review* 48 (March 1973): 99–116.

19. J. Hillis Miller, "Ariadne's Thread: Repetition and the Narrative Line," *Critical Inquiry* 3 (Autumn 1976): 57–77.

20. Kathleen Higgins, "The Night Song's Answer," *International Studies in Philosophy* 17 (Summer 1985): 33–50.

21. Hans Blumenberg, *Schiffbruch mit Zuschauer; Paradigma einer Daseinsmetapher* (Frankfurt: Suhrkamp, 1979), 84.

22. See Karsten Harries, "The Infinite Sphere: Comments on the History of a Metaphor," *Journal of the History of Philosophy* 13 (January 1975): 5–15.

CHAPTER 2

■ Irony and Affirmation in
Nietzsche's
Thus Spoke Zarathustra

Robert B. Pippin

■ I

The importance of Nietzsche's *Thus Spoke Zarathustra* is equaled
only by its relative inaccessibility. It is important because it appears
to be much closer to a single Nietzschean magnum opus than any
rival work. This is especially so given the recent, often compelling
suspicions raised by Bernd Magnus about the overuse of Nietzsche's
"nonbook," *The Will to Power.*[1] *Thus Spoke Zarathustra* would therefore appear to be the single most important, comprehensive work of
the mature Nietzsche of the 1880s. Works written after it often refer to
it without qualification as the principle text of reference and indicate
that it is intended to be deeper and more subtle than works explicitly
said to be mere "popular" counterparts, like *Beyond Good and Evil.*
And what appear to be the topics of the book do include virtually all
the famous themes associated with Nietzsche: the negative side, with
diatribes against post-Socratic philosophy, religion, morality, especially religions and moralities of revenge, modern nihilistic man ("the
last man"), the modern nation state, and so forth; and the positive side, what appear to be Nietzsche's own views about the *Übermensch,* the eternal recurrence, and even the "postmodern" future.

Yet, however often the individual speeches of Zarathustra are
plundered by commentators and quoted as evidence for some general theory about Nietzschean philosophy, one must note immediately that there is, in the surprisingly small amount of literature
devoted chiefly to *Zarathustra,* nothing close to a standard reading of
the work's intention, form, development, resolution, or lack of resolution. (In fact, there are not even standard disagreements.) There is
certainly little enough agreement about these matters to justify the
claim that the work has remained basically inaccessible (or that is

45

commonly taken to be obviously accessible, which amounts to the same thing). Much of this elusiveness is due to a range of problems that could all be grouped together as problems concerning first the "literary" properties of the work, and second the philosophical implications of those properties. My intention in the following is to suggest a broad approach to such an interpretive issue and to argue that the results of such an interpretation are of decisive importance when one tries to attribute to Nietzsche theories, beliefs, or philosophical opinions of the standard sort. In particular, the issue I shall be concerned with is the peculiar irony with which, I think, Zarathustra's fate is presented and the various ways in which that irony qualifies what appear to be the affirmative pronouncements of Zarathustra, his declarations, injunctions, prophecies, and even hopes.

Consider first the most prominent literary and philosophical problem encountered even at first reading. Clearly, the most obvious question raised by the work is simply, "What kind of a book is it? Here, we do not have, as we sometimes do, a literary, or religious, or rhetorical form appropriated by a philosopher. No category whatsoever seems appropriate for this work. Or rather, so many do: epic poem, novel, Old or New "Testament," prophecy, or, as Nietzsche himself suggested, "dithyramb," "music," or "tragedy."[2] To be sure, the work does contain what appears to be a series of philosophic pronouncements. But it also contains deeds as well as words: wanderings, departings, odd adventures, not to mention soothsayers, illnesses, and so on. And this vexing classificatory problem is only the beginning. More familiar is the direct charge that the text is not simply without precedent and so difficult to read but that it is chaotic, that there is not a new principle of unity holding the parts together; there is none. At the very least, even sympathetic commentators complain about the overwritten, rambling quality of the work. Kaufmann complains that it "cries out to be blue-penciled."[3] More typical are Danto's comments, in his writing about *The Birth of Tragedy* and *Zarathustra,* that "the latter acquires a certain external structure by having each segment pose as a homiletic uttered by Zarathustra. In neither book is there an ordered development, however, or a direction of argument or presentation. They may be entered at any point,"[4] and Fink's conclusions about the "fragmentary character" of the work.[5] In fact, in spite of Nietzsche's insistence, after completing the first part, that "it is a poem, and no aphorism collection,"[6] the work is most often read and taught precisely as a collection of aphorisms that Nietzsche, for some reason, put in the mouth of an ancient Persian prophet.[7] Finally, to complete the confusion, there is the compositional problem: the fragmented publication history, confusion about whether the fourth part was really intended as a conclusion, supposed hints about a fifth or sixth part, and so on.[8] In sum, if this is a new philosophic genre, it seems most of all characterized by the absence of any thematic thread that even the most willing Theseus could follow, a rambling series of prophecies, sermons, parables, dreams, allegories, aphorisms, fables, songs, and brief, inconclusive dialogues.[9]

Second, what one could call, if only provisionally, the philosophic context of the work is even more daunting. Zarathustra is introduced to us in the prologue as a figure of potentially epochal philosophic status. The opening image, Zarathustra at home in his cave, that Platonic symbol of the demotic and of enslaving ignorance, suggests that Zarathustra is intended as a self-conscious rival to Plato, as does his opening, arrogant, anti-Platonic speech to the sun, his insistence that the sun would be nothing were it not for those for whom it shines. (Thus, we begin with a reversal of the Platonic claim that we and the world itself would be nothing were it not for the sun, the Idea of the Good.) Moreover, Zarathustra "goes down" full of a sense of his own historical importance. "God is dead" he proclaims; that is, he *has* died, and so *now,* and only now, a new beginning can be made, the *Übermensch* is possible.[10] Thus, the opening passages introduce us with stunning abruptness to what is perhaps Nietzsche's most ambitious claim: his characterization of the fate of the Western tradition itself, his account of why it is as it is, and why, according to Nietzsche, it is coming to a nihilistic end. This is such a large-scale claim, involving as it does both a historical thesis, particularly about the role of post-Socratic philosophy and Christianity in the fate of the Western tradition, and a philosophical claim about the necessary "devaluation" of that tradition's highest values, that there is little that can be said about it that is both brief and fair.[11] However, with respect to *Zarathustra,* Nietzsche's account of the historical fate of post-Socratic value also obliges him to go some of the way in describing for us what "postnihilistic" value would look like. It would only be by means of such a contrast that we could evaluate and possibly come to accept and transcend the internal self-destruction of the modern historical epoch. Without that contrast, the story Nietzsche tells about the Western tradition would have to look like the inheritance of a permanent "unhappy consciousness," tragic in the Faustean sense, as it did to Weber, Freud, and much modernist self-consciousness. But, for Nietzsche, such claims still *express* the modern point of view; they only express regret at what one had to give up to be modern and so do not finally come to terms with modernity. That a postnihilistic, postmodern age is, on the other hand, possible for Nietzsche is signaled often by him in different contexts: by his invocation of a new "aesthetic justification of existence,"[12] and indeed by his use of that term in *Zarathustra* that (tragic moderns that we are) still sounds to us at once so ominous and so juvenile—*Übermensch.*

To be sure, all such issues are so interrelated in Nietzsche that it is difficult to discuss any as a separate topic. Indeed, it is difficult even to begin to discuss Nietzsche's view of what a nonphilosophic but "affirmative" discourse would be like without simply assuming the complicated and quite controversial details of his history of European nihilism. If he is wrong about that tradition, then there is no point in worrying about what follows it. Perhaps there never was a tradition as understood by Nietzsche; perhaps the ancient/modern split within it makes all talk of "post-Socraticism" a gross simplification; perhaps the tradition ended the way Hegel thought, successfully, in triumph; perhaps the tradition, whatever it is, is necessarily perennial; perhaps the way in which various pivotal philosophers have been appropriated by the tradition has little to do with the alternatives they actually represent, so that the Socrates and Plato who emerge after the Christian tradition's influence, are not *the* Socrates and Plato. These are all important questions and ought to be addressed with some care given to Nietzsche and other modernist philosophers who attempt an overview of "philosophy" (such as Heidegger, Wittgenstein, and, most recently, Rorty), but they must be postponed for now. For my purposes, such a sweeping issue can only serve as a scene-setting introduction. The basic problem at issue here is the interpretive one: how to read *Zarathustra.*

■   II

The "plot" of the book is as good a place as any to begin. *Zarathustra* is the story of a forty-year-old man who, after ten years of solitude on a mountain begins to descend to rejoin the human community. On the way down, he meets and has a conversation with an old hermit, who questions his motives in returning to mankind. He then comes upon a town, where people are waiting to see a tightrope walker perform. Zarathustra immediately and confidently begins, in a sermonizing language, to teach the people about the *Übermensch,* but, after a strange accident with the tightrope walker, Zarathustra is jeered at and leaves. His public teaching career looks to be a complete failure, and this failure completes most of the action of the prologue. In the rest of the first part, his audience changes; it is now not public but more restricted, apparently disciples, and his language is more parabolic. His speeches in this part, as he wanders around the city called "The Motley Cow," cover a variety of topics but generally concern various human virtues. On the one hand, Zarathustra indicts many of the old virtues of Christian humanism and modern liberalism. According to him, they promote "sleep," even death, divide the self against the body, deny the passions, create "pale" criminals who cannot own up to their own deeds, and promote a worship of a new idol, the state, the institution appropriate for "flies in the marketplace." On the other hand, he briefly suggests "a new way . . . to will this way which man has walked blindly," and this way has its own virtues: courage, friendship, "the way of the creator," a "free death," and "the gift-giving virtue." In sum, the first part establishes Zarathustra as "the annihilator of morals" (as "morals" have been understood by "the good and the just") and offers some vague suggestions about what human life would look like without the self-hatred and resentment of the last man. Moreover, while the doctrine of the *Übermensch* had insistently begun the prologue, Zarathustra does not mention it again until the very last speech. In that speech, he again expresses deep disappointment with the effect of his teaching, leaves the city altogether, and returns to the mountains.

In the second part, Zarathustra again descends from his mountain, but now anxiously not joyously, worried that his teaching is in danger. He visits a number of islands, The Blessed Islands, the Island of Tombs, the Island with the Smoking Mountain (as if to emphasize how much more isolated he and his disciples are becoming). His speeches in this part are largely focused more on individual types than on individual virtues, this in keeping with Nietzsche's general tendency to deny that the attraction and legitimacy of individual virtues can be understood unless we see the whole "type" that would like this or that virtue, or the whole type that would result from such a virtue. So here his teaching is somewhat deeper than in part 1, somewhat more isolated from what the last men could understand, and is still primarily negative or critical (although occasionally resonant with redemptive and transformative imagery). In this part, he goes after priests, the virtuous in general, the rabble, the preachers of equality, famous wise men, immaculate perceivers, scholars, and even poets ("I have grown weary of the poets . . . their thoughts have not penetrated deeply enough"). At the end of part 2, a shocking series of events occur, which I shall discuss in a moment, and, shaken, Zara-thustra leaves his disciples again (now called friends) to wander alone back to his mountain.

In the third part, the action begins with Zarathustra still on his way back to his mountain, crossing the Blessed Island to look for a ship to take him to land. Part 3 is unique in that, for the most part, Zarathus-tra is alone and talks often to himself, or to various emanations of himself. Moreover, this loneliness is a great burden to Zarathustra, who had begun the book "overflowing" with love of man. At the start of part 3, in contrast, he is convinced that "in the end, one experi-ences only oneself," and this appears to be a major cause of his "mel-ancholy and bitterness." When Zarathustra reaches land, he still does not journey straight to his mountain but continues to wander "among many peoples and through many towns" before his "homecoming."

For most of the third part, his monologues are either straightfor-ward internal reflections or dialogues with what appear to be aspects of himself, most specifically a dwarf called his "spirit of gravity," later something called "Zarathustra's ape." That reflection is everywhere troubled by a variety of worries concerning an "abysmal thought" Zarathustra cannot quite face. The whole section is pervaded by a doubt caused by this thought and by a skepticism about the wisdom of trying to teach the *Übermensch* ("down there . . . all speech is in vain") and seems to approve the wisdom of "passing by" and soli-tude. At the end of the section, with Zarathustra "home," he again has an audience, his animals, but they are not of much help to Zarathus-tra, who calls them "buffoons" and accuses them of making a "hurdy-gurdy" song of his "abysmal thought."

The fourth part, with Zarathustra still on his mountain, reads like some parody of allegorical literature. His audience here is the most bizarre yet: an array of so-called higher men (e.g., a king, a magician, a retired pope, the ugliest man in the world), who all end up par-ticipating in an even more bizarre "ass festival." (The action of the fourth part thus represents a reversal; the denizens of the town "go up," Zarathustra does not "go under.")[13] At the conclusion of the fourth part, Zarathustra repeats the first words of the prologue, de-cides that his "children" are near, and again leaves his cave.

Several issues emerge immediately from this brief summary of the dramatic action. First, the center of that drama is clearly Zarathus-tra's wandering, his inability to rest content in any one place, and his dissatisfaction either in solitude or within the human community. This dissatisfaction is tied to his constant, openly expressed search for an audience, or, more properly, to his own inner search for a proper understanding of his audience. (In that sense, it could be said that the basic dilemma in the book is "political," one that calls to mind again the classic Platonic political dilemma—how to establish a relation between the philosopher and the city, how to reconcile the wise and not wise.)

Further, Zarathustra's "journey" is not at all like familiar attempts at philosophic enlightenment. In keeping with the above suggestions about Zarathustra as a "post-" or even "anti-" philosophic image, he does not seek a knowledge he does not have, his conversations are not dialectical or interrogative, nor are they (despite early appearances) attempts to transmit an already achieved "wisdom" (he is upset when his disciples act as if that were his function). Whatever the "reception" of his gift is supposed to involve, it clearly involves much more than simply coming to believe what Zarathustra says. Zarathustra never does find a proper recipient for his "gift," not the many, his disciples, animals, not even the so-called higher men of part 4. Indeed, in a number of contexts, Zarathustra himself, supposedly some sort of spokesman for Nietzsche on many accounts, is portrayed as a personal failure, an almost comic figure in his lack of resolution, his self-pity, confusion, self-doubt, and misperception. (Whatever the nature of this failure, it seems a prominent aspect of Nietzsche's own view of the work, one signaled by his famous claim, harking all the way back to his first explosive book, that, with Zarathustra, *"Incipit tragoedia."*)[14]

Moreover, Zarathustra's constant wandering is not portrayed as a result of his inability to find some destination, some context where his gift can be properly understood and accepted. Rather, as begins to dawn on him, there is no such destination. This theme alone allows one to see that *Zarathustra* is as much in two major parts as four: the first two, where Zarathustra still attempts to speak publicly (and looks like a teacher), and the latter two, where he does not. These two divisions are separated by one of the most important sections, "The Stillest Hour," which occurs in the exact middle of the book.[15]

There are several other indications that this "break" in Zarathustra's enterprise is the decisive event in the book. Besides the dramatic break (his withdrawal from teaching and his much less clear or confident relation to his audience), there is a noticeable thematic shift (i.e., a change in what Zarathustra thinks and talks about) and a corresponding reinforcement of this shift by means of a complex pattern of recurrent, cross-referenced images.

Thematically, the great issue of the book, the central event that divides his wanderings, is Zarathustra's attempt to understand what the

Soothsayer first tells him toward the end of the second part, the eternal recurrence of the same. This realization provokes the central crisis in the book, and all that Zarathustra says before he encounters it, and after, is decisively influenced by the realization. In the images of the book, it provokes a great illness in Zarathustra (the illness itself is a "disgust" with man, the very man for whom Zarathustra had been full of overflowing love at the beginning of his journey). Zarathustra's confidence in the possibility of a new *kind* of human being, his celebration of the power of the will, his faith in his core of elite, new leaders, indeed, his confidence in the possibility of a transformative teaching at all, are all shattered by this new revelation, and he is never the same again. (The fact that Zarathustra is *immediately* affected by the soothsayer's speech, that he never opposes the eternal return with an insistence on the epochal possibilities of the new "age of the *Übermensch*," appears to indicate that Zarathustra immediately realizes that the very assumptions that make the *Übermensch* possible—the death of God, or transcendent authority, etc.—also entail the radical contingency, antiteleology, and deflationary animus of the eternal return image.) The plot of the narrative thus concerns not only Zarathustra's apparent failure to establish a satisfactory relation to an audience (and so a failure to understand how he could be a "teacher") but an even deeper crisis, one based on the realization that this failure is not simply the result of the corruption and deformity he had encountered in the modern bourgeois culture of the city of the Motley Cow, but that his own teaching *could* not have been accepted, that his destructive attack on the culmination of the modern idea of virtue had not, as he had thought, led to a new "teaching" about a possible state permanently beyond or "over" the "man" we had known. The "best" grow weary of their work ("too weary even to die") when they realize that even the *Übermensch*, full of honesty and courage about his nontranscendent, self-created status is *not* a permanent self-transformation but only what *we* now might want to be, given what we see we have become. (That is, it is a radically temporal, contingent "ideal"; it answers *only* the specific, practical incoherence of the ideals of late bourgeois culture.) Since Zarathustra had been teaching the *Übermensch* as if it were such a transformative "solution," he is shocked to consider that it too might one day seem like the pontifications of last men, that, in another time, later, it might not appear as the final "bridge" it now appears to be; or that *all*, including the last men, recurs eternally. At any rate, it appears to be this realization that "touched Zarathustra's heart and changed him.

He walked about sad and weary; and he became like those of whom the soothsayer had spoken" (VI 1, 168–69).

The same kind of realization is represented imagistically. In the prologue, after Zarathustra had convinced himself that his failure as a teacher was due to the denseness and corruption of his audience, he accepts what he calls "a new truth" and states it metaphorically, "No shepherd shall I be, nor gravedigger" (VI 1, 20). He declines to offer himself as a new shepherd to these sheep, and he sees the futility of merely "tending the graves" of their highest values. In the midst of the crisis, or illness, caused by his realization of the eternal recurrence, these images return. In "The Soothsayer," he has a terrifying nightmare in which, despite his earlier resolve, he is *still* a "guardian of tombs," and he watches as a coffin bursts open, full of the "grimaces of children, angels, owls, fools and butterflies as big as children" (VI 1, 170). In his resolution to free himself from the last men and proclaim the *Übermensch* as an act of will, Zarathustra had assumed he could free himself of time and face only the future. The soothsayer's doctrine reminds him that he is seriously self-deceived. A "dead" tradition is, paradoxically, never finally dead, and Zarathustra's "conscious" resolve to overcome it is still haunted by these unconscious, nightmarish reminders. Zarathustra's dream-interpreting disciple gets all this exactly wrong when he ignores Zarathustra's explanation that *he* had been the guardian of tombs, and claims that Zarathustra is instead the coffin, mocking death and finitude, an "advocate of life," full of "new starts" and "new wonders" triumphing over "the weariness of death." Zarathustra "looked a long time into the face of the disciple who had played the dream interpreter and he shook his head" (VI 1, 171–72).

Likewise, Nietzsche completes this imagistic echo of the prologue in what is easily the most gruesome passage in the book, "Of the Vision and the Riddle," in part 3. Zarathustra there recounts meeting a "shepherd," one who was "writhing, gagging, in spasms, his face distorted, and a heavy, black snake hung out of his mouth" (VI 1, 197). Later in the third part ("The Convalescent"), Zarathustra offers his own interpretation of that vision and admits that, again despite his earlier decision, *he* had been that shepherd but "choking," it now appears, on his own doctrine. As we saw, after the prologue, he had not intended to be another "teacher of virtue" and instead tried to act as if the doctrine could be wholly his, or only for those few with the resolve to act likewise. Now he sees that, despite that individualist, or at least apolitical, stance, he is still a "shepherd" of sorts, tied somehow to what others have become, although now he "chokes" on his own doctrine, chokes, I would suggest, on the fact that he has not come to terms yet with the historical contingency of his own idea. (Later in this section, he makes even clearer the centrality of both the tomb/corpse/gravedigger images and the shepherd's "choking": "My sighing sat on all human tombs and could no longer get up; my sighing and questioning croaked and gagged and wailed day and night: Alas, man recurs eternally! The small man recurs eternally" [VI 1, 270].)

To be sure, at one level, the introduction to the eternal recurrence seems only to convince Zarathustra that the last man, modern, bourgeois, self-hating, resentful man, *cannot* be historically overcome; he will recur eternally, prompting Zarathustra's disgust with man himself. However, at another level, Zarathustra also seems to realize that he cannot affirm his own doctrine without affirming everything—all the contingent, self-deluded, ascetic, resentful aspects of modern culture that make the *Übermensch* possible and valuable in the first place. A clear implication of this would be an acceptance of the necessary connection between the limitations and delusions of those criticized in the first two parts and the *Übermensch* that the modern crisis calls for. (That is, it is the *image* of the last man recurring eternally that helps to express the impossibility of a finally *redemptive* historical moment; the claim itself depends on no literally cosmological theory about the return of just these men. In this context, the image, and the disgust it causes, decisively alters Zarathustra's perception of what the "possibility of an *Übermensch*" means; it forces him to try to separate any affirmation of such a new type of man from reliance on a hope for historical redemption. Hence, the notion of the "historical contingency" of the *Übermensch* doctrine.)

The eternal recurrence image, in other words, suggests to Zarathustra a radical deflating of the *Übermensch* ideal, and much of Zarathustra's later struggle involves his attempt to reconstrue that ideal, given that deflation. That image suggests that any hoped-for postmodern age, supposedly free of the self-deluded optimism of the Enlightenment and the resentment of Socratic-Christian morality, cannot be understood eschatologically, and certainly not as man's final goal, his ultimate self-overcoming. Thus, Zarathustra's expressions of disgust that the last men will recur eternally is not merely an expression of sadness that his redemptive project cannot succeed, that the ideal is too difficult ever truly to take hold. The soothsayer does not merely announce that Zarathustra's hopes are exaggerated, too optimistic for the pitiable creature, man. He announces instead a kind of ontological myth, that all recurs eternally, not because of the last man inherent in all of us, but because all returns eternally. There is no privileged or decisive moment in history, and Zarathustra must give up his Hegelian pretension. There is only the "longing" for man that *this* community, for all its "cow-like" faults, has produced. Even if that longing is satisfied, the satisfaction is *no more* historically decisive or redemptive than its origins. (*It* ends and recurs as well.)

This deflationary impact is partly captured by the animals' summation in "The Convalescent." Speaking in Zarathustra's voice, they announce, "But the knot of causes in which I am entangled recurs and will create me again. I myself belong to the causes of the eternal recurrence. I come again, with this sun, with this earth, with this eagle, with this serpent—not to a new life, or better life, or a similar life: I come back eternally to this same, self-same life, in what is greatest as in what is smallest . . . to proclaim the *Übermensch* again to man" (VI 1, 272). This does appear to express and expand on what Zarathustra himself had just proclaimed, that, to him, "the greatest man" and "the smallest man" are "all too similar to each other."

Of course, Zarathustra (and Nietzsche) leaves out a great deal here. There is no satisfactory explanation by Zarathustra of the sickening impact of this vision, only incomplete explanations by disciples and animals. There is no explicit admission by Zarathustra of the contingent and historically bounded character of his hopes for man. There is only the indirect, negative realization that his earlier hopes for "redemption" were based on a secret hatred of time, an attempt to will backward, to will away the past, and there is the rather indirect evidence about this change obvious in how differently Zarathustra acts in the last two parts. And there are certainly no details here, as elsewhere, that would help us see what aspects of the culture of the last men would necessitate a hope for a "higher type," or even what the specific qualities of that higher type might be. However, there are indications throughout that Zarathustra must come to realize that he too is motivated by a kind of revenge, a resentment against the past and other men, and that this must be overcome. The narrative itself strongly implies that Zarathustra is fated eternally to go "up" or beyond man and "down" into the human community. He can neither accept nor fully transcend the context that produced him.[16] And there are frequent images that "tie" Zarathustra's speeches to time, particularly images of sun and shadow, and time of day. (Indeed, it turns out that what Zarathustra most appears to want, as his temporal moment, is impossible, a "great noon," when there is no shadow stretching backward or forward, a timeless present, and so a genuinely new beginning for man.)[17] And there is this decisive passage (in "On Human Prudence") right after the soothsayer's revelation:

> Not the height but the precipice is terrible. That precipice where the glance plunges *down* and the hand reaches *up*. There the heart becomes giddy confronted with its double will. Alas, friends, can you guess what is my heart's double will?
>
> This, this is *my* precipice and my danger, that my glance plunges into the height, and that my hand would grasp and hold on to the depth. My will clings to man; with fetters I bind myself to man because I am swept up toward the overman; for that way my other will wants to go. And therefore I live blind among men as if I did not know them, that my hand might not lose its faith in what is firm. (VI 1, 179)[18]

This is all, of course, only the beginning of Zarathustra's crisis. His "convalescence" from it has yet to be presented. However, even at this point some preliminary conclusions can be drawn about the themes introduced in the first part of this paper. The most obvious "literary" qualification to the speeches of the first two parts stems directly from the simple narrative fact that there is such a profound schism in the narrative, that Zarathustra undergoes such a crisis and that the nature of the crisis is self-reflective, that it involves a great self-doubt. Zarathustra, it turns out, has been deceived about himself, the possibility of his gift giving, about the correct implications to draw from the nihilistic collapse of the European tradition, and even about his own *Übermensch*. Stated more simply, given what happens at the end of part 2 and the beginning of part 3, Nietzsche must be said to be at some substantial ironic distance from the Zarathustra of the first two parts. The *Übermensch* "resolution" of the crisis signaled by the prologue's famous "God is dead" is, in more fashionable language, a solution that deconstructs itself, but what is responsible for the deconstruction is not "textuality" itself but Nietzsche.

There is another kind of irony in such a result. First, introduced directly into the text, as a kind of disease Zarathustra must recover from, is one version of the standard relativist paradox Nietzsche is, according to some critics, supposed to have ignored, that is, "If the will to truth is an illusion, whence the alleged superiority of the Nietzschean ideal? Can Nietzsche affirm without inconsistency?" Zarathustra's recovery may not provide a standard, discursive answer to such a question, but it is clearly some kind of explicit attempt to overcome the enervating self-doubt such an experience can create.[19] Moreover, there is a historical irony in Nietzsche's name being so closely associated in many corners of intellectual culture with the *Übermensch* doctrine. An infrequent and somewhat marginal aspect of the published works before *Zarathustra,* it virtually drops out afterward. It would appear that the major source for ascribing it to Nietzsche as a doctrine is the first half of *Zarathustra.* As we have seen, however, Nietzsche introduces the "Nietzschean" theme ironically, as a "moment" in his persona's *Bildung.*

■   III

The central images of part 3 confirm the preceding claims about a fundamental alteration in Zarathustra, one fundamental enough to prompt a rethinking of his entire self-understanding. Those images are Zarathustra's "homecoming" and his "convalescence." Thematically, these images should suggest to us how Zarathustra returns to his "original position" in order to begin again, returns to his sense of what is possible if a continued reliance on traditional values is impossible. With an emphasis on solitude, internal discourse, self-questioning, doubt, and eventual recovery, the drama of this part is clearly designed to suggest, however obliquely, a kind of return to Zarathustra's intellectual origins that will take into account what he has now suffered. And his convalescence should suggest how he comes to terms with the central experience of that suffering, his "abysmal thought," the profoundly antiredemptive thought of the eternal recurrence. Also, Zarathustra is much concerned in this recovery with how easily what he says can be misinterpreted, particularly by low-minded popularizers, his ape, and by insensitive epigones, his animals. So, *how* one is supposed to affirm, or even "long" for, a new goal without repeating the traditional stance of revenge, and without Zarathustra's own self-delusions, looms large on the agenda.

As with the prologue, the introduction of these issues relates directly to the deepest aspects of Nietzsche's more accessible project. In the more prosaic terms of *Beyond Good and Evil* and *The Genealogy of Morals,* we should expect that the self-appointed "legislative" function of a character like Zarathustra would be difficult to come to terms with directly (for him and for us). That is, once the so-called will to truth is supposedly exposed as an illusion, once the self-delusions of a desire for the "highest" good and an unconditional moral code are presented ("truth is a woman," morality is essentially either master or slave morality), we might expect that Zarathustra's own self-understanding of such things as a "virtue" that *does not* "make small," of his *own* great longing, his *own* sense of "apostates," sins, and old and new tablets, would have to be very carefully presented, at least much more carefully than in parts 1 and 2. Even more prosaically, suppose that Nietzsche's direct attempts to expose the "prejudices" of morality and philosophy succeeded. We would then realize that it is impossible to ask straightforwardly and simply about the truth of claims like "No one does evil knowingly" or "All human behavior should be explained by reference to alterations in brain states." On Nietzsche's account, we do not properly understand the claims being made unless we understand the "moral agenda," for want of a better term, in which it plays, and must play, a role unless we understand what is sought, what value is being affirmed (and one always is) in making the claim. Now, what I am suggesting is that Zarathustra begins to undertake a "genealogy," in similar fashion, of his own pronouncements, one that is as initially destructive and enervating as Nietzsche's straightforward genealogies can be.

Thus, again, the contrast between the two major parts of *Zarathustra* is crucial. In this part (and in a different way in part 4), in contrast to what one might call the "politics" of redemption, the rhetoric of sermon and prophecy, expressions of resentment, and the collection of disciples, we have the "politics of self-knowledge." Zarathustra has come to realize that much of his own desire for man requires a self-knowledge he does not have, and one that would be quite difficult to attain, particularly without reliance on traditional notions of "self" or "knowledge." When he is exposed by the soothsayer to the consequences of this lack, to his own inconsistent teleological hope that man can be completely overcome, then Zarathustra's incomplete self-knowledge becomes prominent and decisive. (Or, Zarathustra begins to realize that any collective self-transformation of man, the great hope throughout *Zarathustra,* is not simply a matter of collective action, or resolve, or even just a matter of an educated insight into past self-delusions. The way in which such a realization comes to be and how one speaks in the "light" of it look now to be far more elusive, difficult issues than in the first two parts.)

Zarathustra realizes that man cannot be "overcome" (that his desire for man is "dual") and that to want to overcome man finally is to be guilty of the Nietzschean sins of pity and resentment. He must now try to understand what *that* realization entails, especially with respect to a wide range of public or political issues: What should he say? How? To whom? When? Why? To what end? Thus, I think, parts 3 and 4. (And I note again that, however Zarathustra confronts and comes to terms with these questions, there is no reason to think that the ironic distance between Zarathustra and Nietzsche has been overcome.) One might even suspect that Nietzsche's "resolution" of the above questions, in writing and publishing a book about Zarathustra, a work in which the ironic mask is never dropped, would be quite different indeed from Zarathustra's self-understanding. As we shall see, Zarathustra does not resolve his crisis by deciding to write about it, and the work is everywhere silent about the identity of the narrator.

For the most part, this struggle to overcome resentment, the attempt to resolve the tension created by Zarathustra's "double will," at once attached to man and contemptuous of the last men, occurs in the third part, in his conversations with a dwarf, his "spirit of gravity," Zarathustra's "devil and arch enemy" (VI 1, 194, 239). This spirit taunts Zarathustra that he had thrown himself up high, assumed a kind of historical transcendence, and that he will, like all else, fall back on himself, a clear reference to the break in Zarathustra's confidence about the *Übermensch* that signals the division between the second and third parts. The dwarf makes use of the eternal recurrence in a wholly skeptical, critical way, insisting that there is no point in "climbing high," in overcoming and transcending, if one will always be dragged down again. In effect, he represents the gravity of reason itself and serves as a spokesman for all those who think that Nietzsche's own attacks on the hidden, amoral, contingent origins of traditional virtues and values make impossible any "new" will to virtue (or for those who think that Zarathustra's illness is the relativism paradox sketched above). In his first response to this challenge, Zarathustra admits, in an odd, hermetic phrase, that the two paths of past and future, when they face each other, in a "moment . . . offend each other . . . contradict each other eternally" (VI 1, 196).

However, as Zarathustra responds more extensively to the dwarf, it becomes clear his response finally involves a complete rejection of the dwarf's *assumption:* only if the future *could* be transformed into a permanent present would action be worthwhile. That is the premise of resentment, of revenge against time, and when Zarathustra, in his next vision, counsels the shepherd to "bite off" the head of the snake that is choking him, he is encouraging him not to accept the premises of those who, like the spirit of gravity, would counsel resignation or cynicism as a result of the eternal recurrence.

Later in the third part, in the section explicitly called "The Spirit of Gravity," Zarathustra returns to this theme and is more explicit about

rejecting the assumptions that some sort of finality or historical redemption (some *replacement* for the moral tradition) is necessary for
the will to will powerfully and confidently.

> "Yes, life is a grave burden." But only man is a grave burden
> for himself! That is because he carries on his shoulders too
> much that is alien to him. Like a camel he kneels down and
> lets himself be well loaded. Especially, the strong, reverent
> spirit that would bear much: he loads too many grave words
> and values on himself, and then life seems a desert to him.
> (VI 1, 239)

It is such a rejection of this burden that allows one to say, as
Zarathustra does in "Before Sunrise,"

> "By Chance"—that is the most ancient nobility of the world,
> and this I restored to all things: I delivered them from their
> bondage under Purpose.

And,

> O heaven over me, pure and high! That is what your purity
> is to me now that there is no eternal spider or spider web of
> reason; that you are to me a dance floor for divine acci-
> dents, that you are to me a divine table for divine dice and
> dice players. (VI 1, 205–6)

Finally, it is at the end of this section that Zarathustra answers the
dwarf with the oft-quoted lines,

> "This is *my* way; where is yours?"—thus I answered those
> who asked me "the way." For *the* way—that does not exist.
> (VI 1, 241)

But, from the context now developed, it is clear that Zarathustra is
not advocating a simple, individualist relativism. What he is denying
and approving must be seen in the context of his struggle with the
spirit of gravity throughout. That is, he is denying that, because he
cannot defend the virtues of the *Übermensch* as "the way," he cannot
defend the *Übermensch* at all. The spirit of gravity "and all that he
created: constraint, statute, necessity, and consequence and purpose
and will and good and evil" (VI 1, 244) assumes a perspective from
the start that Zarathustra will not accept. As has become clear
throughout the third part, Zarathustra cannot simply deny "resent-
fully" the culture of the last men and will a new ideal ex nihilo. His
hopes for man are tied to that past in its origin and possible success.
The Zarathustra, then, of "my way" is not just one individual among

many others who each have individual, equally worthwhile ways. The way Zarathustra points to throughout, and that he has been encouraging others to follow, still depends on a claim to have offered a correct diagnosis of the self-delusions of modern culture and a correct denial that these virtues can provide a coherent "ideal" in life. The ideal that emerges from these problems is a specific ideal, the *Übermensch*, but it is now understood to be *only* the ideal that emerges from *these* problems. The alternative to Zarathustra's earlier pronouncements of "the" *Übermensch* way is not an invitation to moral anarchy ("no way"), but a historically specific ideal, a way that can be defended only *within* a historical epoch. That realization is what Zarathustra comes to accept in the central epiphany of the book.

Not only does such an interpretation make more sense of Zarathustra's "struggle" with his "abysmal thought," and how that struggle changes his own view of the *Übermensch* and the context of modern will and action, it makes more sense of Zarathustra's *practice.* If, that is, Zarathustra had concluded that his way was his alone, it would be hard to see why the "loneliness" that results from that position bothers him so much, why he thinks it must be overcome, or in general why Zarathustra remains so involved in the affairs of those whom he often despises. Rather, since he realizes the *Übermensch* is not a new "god" who will reign forever over the future, he also realizes that this ideal has no transcendent or independent legitimacy. It is an ideal only if it *does* actually offer a way out of the practical contradictions and dead ends of traditional virtue. Zarathustra must, therefore, offer this ideal (as a "gift") to those whose virtues are promoting a permanent "sleep," or, as suggested earlier, his will *must* be "double," tied to man and beyond man, since, after the death of all the old gods, there is only man. Zarathustra cannot become a hermit, like the one he meets in the prologue, *because* "God is dead," including finally (after the second part) the new god Zarathustra was prophesying.[20]

Now, none of this settles finally the issue of *how* this *Ubermensch* should be offered and exactly what this ideal entails. And it certainly has not broached the question of whether Zarathustra'a criticisms, and Nietzsche's analysis elsewhere, do amount to a powerful rejection of that web of virtues, values, and assumptions about human being and agency that constitute our tradition. It does, however, suggest that Nietzsche's views about a "postmodern" culture contain within it an involved self-consciousness about its own potential problems and misinterpretations. Zarathustra comes to adopt a far more historical, secular view of his ideal and realizes that his advice about "revenge" against temporality and finitude applies to him as well.

Moreover, he also learns that there is no possibility of a permanent break with modern culture, that his fate is linked to that culture, if only because there *is* only that world, into which Zarathustra is continually "thrown."

However, it is also true that all this leaves Zarathustra in a dilemma whose dimensions Nietzsche frequently refers to as "tragic." To understand that tragedy, one can first note how many of Zarathustra's expectations at various points have been frustrated. For all his convalescence, it is still true that he has failed with all his proposed audiences, with the city, with his disciples, with his animals, and with the higher men; even his speeches with emanations of himself are often tense and unresolved. In the face of this, it is even more significant that Zarathustra does not seem to accept his animals' view of his convalescence, their counsel of resignation, that Zarathustra should just "bless himself" and resign himself to that fact that his doctrine will perish (VI 1, 272–73).[21] Zarathustra is silent when he hears this, but signals his disagreement by, in the next speech, explaining to his "soul" "The Great Longing." That is, Zarathustra appears now unwilling either to assert his will against time (as if he could create the age of the overman) or to pursue the goal of his "great longing" while resigned (pessimistically?) to his failure, or by trying to "forget" this finitude. Now, this may seem to leave the problem of "public discourse" in the "post-philosophic" age simply unresolved.

And, indeed, that lack of resolution does help explain much of the tragic tone of part 4, for all its low comedy.[22] This tragedy though, appears to be a "tragedy of discourse," a necessity to "speak," proclaim, even to "long for a goal," all without denying the radical historicity of all will (as embodied in the thought of eternal recurrence); that is, a tragedy without private consolation in a new "god," or without the new god of most historical views of human existence—an apocalyptic, decisive, "posthistorical" *future.* Zarathustra's tragic dilemma in part 4 involves not denying himself an audience, and so not trying to will *away* what the past has created (no new revenge against man), and yet not submitting himself to that audience. (Hence, again, the work's "motion," an eternally necessary going under and return home.)

Even without attention to the details of Zarathustra's complicated relation to the "higher men" in part 4 (at once flattered, contemptuous, gently ironic, hopeful, and finally disappointed), one can see the dimensions of this tragic position in a decisive transformation of Zarathustra's view of his "project." White-haired, "yellowing," he has returned to his mountain, and now, rather than preach, teach, sing, wander, or examine himself, the implications of his own insights and his own defeats have led him to a different "stance," one already announced in "On the Great Longing."

> O my soul, overrich and heavy you now stand there, like a vine with swelling udders and crowded brown-gold grapes—crowded and pressed by your happiness, *waiting* in superabundance and still bashful about waiting. (VI 1, 275; my emphasis).

And, in the first speech of part 4,

> Thus men may now come *up* to me; for I am still waiting for the sign that the time has come for my descent; I still do not myself go under, as I must do, under the eyes of men. That is why I wait here . . . . (VI 1, 293)

This remark about a "sign" is critical, because part 4, and the entire work, ends with "The Sign." In that passage, the sign (the appearance of the lion mentioned in Zarathustra's very first speech) signals that "my children are near, my children." This sign is what persuades Zarathustra that he is free of his "final sin," "pity" for the higher men, and can leave his cave again "glowing and strong as a morning sun" (VI 1, 401–4). But this final, decisive sign still seems deeply ironic. Zarathustra is persuaded that he must "wait," presumably until the time is right, until his children *can* appear (until he has the audience he cannot create). But we hear nothing about how or when these children have been created, whether they are taken to be children of the body or spirit.[23] To make matters worse, Zarathustra's speech about the metamorphosis that produces these children deliberately prohibits any natural, metaphorical understanding of how a "lion" could be transformed into a "child." Finally, only Zarathustra says he sees his children; "we" only have his word for it (the narrator of *Zarathustra* does not acknowledge them, as he does the lion). And, while we can understand what he is waiting for—a historical moment and a historical community that Zarathustra cannot create but cannot do without—a moment when the fate of the philosophic age is experienced, rather than avoided, when the *Übermensch* becomes possible, we see no evidence that either has occurred. It would seem that the dramatic and philosophic resolution of *Zarathustra* is that Zarathustra can *only* wait for the "age" of his children, that, tragically, he can do little to help propagate or even prepare for such children, and that he cannot protect himself from the kind of constant mistakes about his audiences that he has made so frequently before. (Zarathustra's fate is thus the same as that of the work *Zarathustra.* Its potential "authority," and so the limitations of its "power," mirror Zarathustra's, as Nietzsche himself states in *Ecce Homo* [VI 3, 302]).

All of which makes for quite a complicated ending, with a dazed Zarathustra alternately forgetting where he is, laughing angrily at himself, and leaving his cave again, alone, "glowing and strong as a morning sun." The complications stem from a double set of ambiguities concerning Zarathustra's fate and Nietzsche's intentions. In the first place, Zarathustra is now likened to the sun itself, almost as if he has become the icon he first addressed. This suggests, though, that, like the sun, he too would be nothing had he not those for whom he shines. He realizes the "knot of causes that produced him" and does not now try to deny them by, vengefully, willing away the past. Nothing of what he can become is possible without some collective accomplishment. Hermits have only their own gods and private, now untenable religions. But the tone of even this insightful revelation about himself is tinged with the comedy of his hopes for and then disappointments with the "higher men" and his mysterious, sudden decision that he no longer pities them. One senses that Zarathustra, after this encounter, needs these wholly new, unspoiled children with whom to begin this collective self-transformation of man, needs them so badly that he rather hopes they are present than knows they are. And, while this hope is certainly not parodied, it has a touch of the misplaced confidence of the prologue, and it looks as if the cyclical structure of the work will be cyclical in that sense too, that Zarathustra has returned to a hope for man that will face again the problems he encountered there and throughout parts 1 and 2. And what will Zarathustra say to these children? How will he alter the "gift" he wants to give them? What reason do we have to believe that anything will be different, that Zarathustra's attempt at a genuinely new kind of affirmative discourse will be any better received or the complications of his own self-knowledge any more resolvable? And these ambiguities seem deliberately left open. It indeed looks as if Zarathustra's fate consists of irreconcilable options, neither a final going over nor a resigned going under, that Zarathustra's self-knowledge cannot be completed either alone or publicly. Or, that Zarathustra's fate is what Nietzsche claims it is, tragic.

I realize that all this is far from the standard picture of Nietzschean swagger, but the situation with respect to Nietzsche is even more complicated yet. At the very least, a broad conclusion that can be drawn, if we keep in mind Nietzsche's role as the teller of Zarathustra's tale, is this. The literary element of that relation most significant

for the issue of "Nietzsche's position" is the fact of that literary relation itself or the fact of Nietzschean irony, that Zarathustra's pronouncements and hopes are both affirmed and ironically qualified.
Or, Nietzsche both portrays himself as Zarathustra (obviously a large
number of Zarathustra's remarks in the first two parts repeat "Nietzschean claims") and as behind the "mask" of Zarathustra, as creator
of the mask and so other than it. In this context, then, it cannot be
incidental to Nietzsche's possible affirmation that it is ironic. The
irony Nietzsche clearly creates in his presentation of Zarathustra is
complex, though. Most straightforwardly, that irony simply involves a
lack of identity between the self-understanding of a character and
that of the author and, by virtue of that difference, a potential negative qualification of what is said or done by that character, however
elusive (because unspoken) such an ironic qualification might be.

However, Nietzsche's "negativity" is not a version of modernist
irony, of the nearly self-cancelling sort visible, say, in T. S. Eliot's
bitterly ironic references to classical and Christian mythology in *The
Wasteland,* and, while similar, is also different from the sublime, divine irony of the ever-silent, ever-wary Plato. But Nietzsche's involved rhetorical stance does seem to suggest a kind of inherent
"tentativeness" in any supposed Nietzschean position, a yes to Zarathustra and yet a no to him as well, a stance we might well expect
from a thinker who defined himself in opposition to what he called
"dogmatism." If this is so, then the admittedly speculative inference
that could be drawn about Nietzsche's alternative to dogmatism
("perspectivism") is that it could not be the sort of willful, individualist, anomic creation ex nihilo sometimes attributed to Nietzsche. As
Nietzsche puts it in his more direct moments, such a perspectivism is
a love of masks or, as here, a realization of the appropriately ironic
nature of affirmation.[24]

In this setting, that means that the affirmative and negative relation
between Nietzsche and Zarathustra does not derive from some partial
Nietzschean "criticism" of Zarathustra but is itself much like Zarathustra's "tragic" realization of his inability either to define himself
and the meaning of his gift or to become again a "shepherd" to the
"herd animal," modern man. (Again, unlike Plato's refusal to appear in
the dialogues, this ironic stance is not based on a sense of the limits
of human possibility but rather on a realization of the radical muta-
bility of the human, on, if you like, its limitlessness.)

Such suggestions about the literary elements of *Zarathustra,* if
they could be pursued, might also allow one to take quite seriously
the relevance of frequent, otherwise puzzling remarks by Nietzsche

about his own discourse. For one thing, while Nietzsche remarks often that he shares none of the traditional assumptions about intentionality, consciousness, ego, will, and so on, and that what we now *value* is the "*un*intentional," he rarely tells us what it would be like to speak and affirm in the light of such a realization. Obviously, much of what we regard as persuasion, argument, rhetoric, and the like would be affected by such Nietzschean revaluations, and the most self-conscious attempt to speak in the light of such revaluation would appear to be *Zarathustra*. Although this introduces a much longer story, one can at least note that attending to the indirection, obliquity, irony, and so always contextually qualified nature of Zarathustra's affirmation could well begin a discussion of how Nietzsche deliberately means to address the "moral *sensibility*" (for want of a better term) of his audience, rather than what they think they believe, a sensibility so deep and unnoticed that it can be called forth and addressed *only* "aesthetically," as in Nietzsche's famous claim to have provided an "aesthetic justification" of existence. Such a project could also begin to take seriously Nietzsche's claim that he *always* speaks in "masks," that great souls must speak in such a way.[25] This would introduce the Zarathustran possibility that many of the famous works contain a self-conscious, ironic dimension, a Nietzschean personna: Nietzsche as, and *only as,* a "free spirit" philosopher of the future, a moral genealogist, a gay scientist, a philosophizer with hammer, an anti-Christ, or even as what "Nietzsche" has become in *Ecce Homo.*[26]

But these are highly speculative suggestions. There are problems enough with *Zarathustra.* Most prominently, "tentativeness" is obviously an inaccurate word to describe the results of such ironic qualification.[27] A further account of what would be more accurate, though, would clearly have to range over a number of issues that can only be introduced: the kind of self-knowledge that makes an appropriately self-conscious affirmation possible, the kind of modern audience and collaborators one needs and could have in effecting such self-knowledge, and the consequences of any such self-knowledge's being itself wholly provisional, itself a kind of mask. My claim here is that the exploration of all these and similar issues would do well to take its bearings from this paradigmatic example of Nietzsche and his essentially ironic affirmation, Nietzsche and his paradigmatic mask—Zarathustra.

Of course, Nietzsche does not make such an exploration easy. He is quite capable of multiplying endlessly the levels of irony involved in his relation to this strange book. In the 1887 preface to *The Gay Science,* for example, in a passage that is, I would hope, finally instructive to those who would read every pronouncement of Zarathustra's as Nietzsche's, and as clearly indicative of the self-conscious, elliptical, and unresolved nature of *Zarathustra* as anything else Nietzsche wrote:

> "Incipit tragoedia" we read at the end of this awesomely aweless book. Beware! Something downright wicked and malicious is announced here: *incipit parodia,* no doubt! (V 2, 14).[28]

■ NOTES

1. Bernd Magnus has made these claims in a series of lectures, beginning with an April 1984 address to the Western APA, "Nietzsche and Schacht's Nietzsche," an address to the Nietzsche Society in October 1984, and in an unpublished later version of that talk, "Nietzsche's Philosophy in 1888: The Will to Power and the *Übermensch.*"

2. For a sampling of Nietzsche's own remarks on *Zarathustra,* see his comments in *Ecce Homo,* VI 3, 343 (on "inventing the dithyramb"), 310 (on being the first tragic philosopher), 333 (on the whole of *Zarathustra* as "music"). On the language of "acts" and "drama," see his letter to Rohde, 22 February 1884. For a general discussion of these and other important passages, see the extremely helpful work by Anke Bennholdt-Thomsen, *Nietzsches "Also Sprach Zarathustra" als literarisches Phänomen* (Frankfurt: Athenäum, 1974), 5, fn. 13. Another rare example of an attempt at an integration of the literary and philosophical elements of *Zarathustra* is Harold Alderman's *Nietzsche's Gift* (Athens: Ohio University Press, 1977).

3. Preface to his translation of *Thus Spoke Zarathustra* (New York: Viking, 1966), xvii.

4. Arthur C. Danto, *Nietzsche as Philosopher* (New York: Macmillan, 1965), 19–20.

5. Eugen Fink, *Nietzsches Philosophie* (Stuttgart: Urban, 1960), 64.

6. Letter to Overbeck, 11 February 1883, *Nietzsches Briefwechsel,* ed. G. Colli and M. Montinari (Berlin: de Gruyter, 1985), III 1, 326.

7. The most familiar explanation for the choice of Zarathustra as protagonist is that given in VI 3, 365. This explanation stresses that since Zarathustra invented the "error" of "morality," he must be the first to recognize that error. However in *Twilight of the Idols* Nietzsche claims something somewhat broader, that it is when the "apparent" world is abolished along with the "true world" that "INCIPIT ZARATHUSTRA" (VI 3, 75).

8. Nietzsche's own explanation for why he had misleadingly suggested that there might be further adventures of Zarathustra seems to me convincing, i.e., that he was trying to attract a publisher and had no intention of altering what had always been his plan for a four-part work. See the following letters in *Nietzsches Briefwechsel:* 14 February 1885, III 3, 11–12; 20 February 20, 1885, III 3, 13–14; and the discussion in Daniel Conway's doctoral disser-

tation, *Nietzsche's Oblique Promotion of Moral Excellence* (University of California, San Diego, 1985), 14–15.

9. For an important attempt at offering a unified interpretation of the "tropological" shifts in the work (from an emphasis on metaphor to metonymy to synecdoche to irony), see Gary Shapiro, "The Rhetoric of Nietzsche's *Zarathustra,*" in *Philosophical Style,* ed. Berel Lang (Chicago: Nelson-Hall, 1980), 347–85. As will be apparent in what follows, I believe that a focus on the dramatic structure of the work can help explain what an emphasis on its polytropic character cannot—*why* there are specific shifts in rhetorical style. However, I agree with many of the general conclusions Shapiro draws from his different approach. See especially 366–67, 373, and 378–80. For a different approach to the problem of language in *Zarathustra,* see Fritz Martini, *Das Wagnis der Sprache: Interpretation deutscher Prosa von Nietzsche bis Benn* (Stuttgart: Klett, 1961), 1–55.

10. For a further discussion of the prologue, see my "Nietzsche and The Origin of The Idea of Modernism," *Inquiry* 26 (1983): 151–80.

11. Many of Nietzsche's major texts almost stridently call attention to the centrality of this historical or epochal self-consciousness in all his accounts of virtue, perspective, nihilism, and what we would call ideology. *The* Birth *of Tragedy,* Untimely *Meditations, The* Dawn, Beyond *Good and Evil, The* Twilight *of the Gods.* Even so, it is still the case that most of the literature on Nietzsche emphasizes the individualist, psychological, and metatheoretical elements, often as if these themes could be separated from Nietzsche's frequent reliance on this historical self-consciousness. My intention in this article and in the article cited in n. 10 is to argue that this separation creates a misleading picture of Nietzsche's central ideas. My claim is that Nietzsche's sense of a possible epochal change (from the "last men" to the *Übermensch*) is not based on a prior, independent epistemological critique. The situation is, at least roughly, the other way around.

12. The clearest invocation of the notion of aesthetic justification is in Nietzsche's new 1886 preface to *The Birth of Tragedy,* the "Versuch einer Selbstkritik," (III 1, 8, 11), although the notion appears in other works, e.g., VI 2, 420. For just two prominent examples of Nietzsche's awareness of his own moral agenda, see Nietzsche's claim that "we immoralists . . . have been spun into a severe yarn and shirt of duties . . . and in this sense we are 'men of duty,' too" (VI 2, 168), or his even clearer, earlier claim that "It goes without saying—unless I am a fool—that many actions called immoral ought to be avoided and resisted, or that many called moral ought to be done and encouraged—but I think the one should be encouraged and the other avoided *for other reasons than hitherto*" (V 1, 89–90).

13. Zarathustra himself points this out (VI 1, 293).

14. Cf. n. 7.

15. Bennholdt-Thomsen, in *Nietzsches Zarathustra,* makes a great deal of this "break" in the drama of the work, but her reading of why Zarathustra suffers and how he convalesces is different from mine, she declines to pursue

any of the philosophic issues raised by this crisis (see 85), and she has a much more affirmative reading of part 4 than I do (cf. 135ff).

16. In VI 2, 39–40, Nietzsche discusses the appeal of a life in a "citadel," "saved from the crowd," but also notes that such a person "was not predestined for knowledge" and that, if he were, "he would go down, and above all, he would go 'inside.'"

17. Of course, altering the meaning of the *Übermensch* does not alter the need for an overcoming of man, as he has come to be. That is just the "nauseating" temptation of the eternal return image that must be resisted, lest we become, as parodied in part 4, mere "cows," contentedly chewing our cuds (VI 1, 330–31). But such self-overcoming, it begins to be clear, cannot itself be an exercise in resentment; it must be *both* monologic and dialogic, private and public, relying neither on old tablets nor on a "willing ego." In the best summation of much of Zarathustra's fullest self-understanding, "On the Higher Men" in part 4, he expresses this new point of view well:

> Walk in the footprints where your fathers' virtue walked before you. How would you climb high if your fathers' will does not climb with you? But whoever would be a firstling should beware lest he also be a lastling.

18. The alternative reading of this passage, that Zarathustra regrets being still tied to man and longs to be free of this bond, is not borne out by the remainder of the second and all the third parts. Zarathustra does express impatience with man but he still (at the end of part 2) has much to learn (and an illness to convalesce from). He begins to learn in the very next speech, when his "stillest hour" reminds him, in one of the most important lines in the work, "O Zarathustra, he who has to move mountains also moves valleys and hollows" (VI 1, 184). Cf. also the dominant visual image in the work: the sun's *continual* rising and setting.

19. Cf., for example, Stanley Rosen's interpretation of "the dreams of Zarathustra" in *The Limits of Analysis* (New York: Basic Books, 1980), 201–15, and Heidegger's interpretation of the relation between the two doctrines, *Nietzsche* (Pfullingen: Neske, 1961), 2:14–16. I should also mention here that the emphasis below on the "tragic" dimensions of the eternal recurrence idea is, at this point, merely a proposal. To some extent, it follows the suggestion of Bernd Magnus, in *Nietzsche's Existential Imperative* (Bloomington: Indiana University Press, 1978), that the acceptance of the eternal recurrence is what it *would be* for "nihilism" to be overcome, that its main function is its "diagnostic thrust," and its expression of the "being-in-the-world" of the *Übermensch*. But my proposal suggests more of an "internal tension" in that acceptance (see Magnus, 142–43, 156). Alexander Nehamas's account of "The Eternal Recurrence," *Philosophical Review* (1980) is also indispensable to a fuller reading, although his analysis tends to focus on the "self" and its "states" in Nietzsche in a way which isolates such a self-affirmation from the "historical community" that, I am suggesting, plays such a large role in

Zarathustra. My approach also differs from Alderman's in that I think the possibility of the eternal return alters much of the earlier discussion of the will and its possibilities; it does not, I think, extend or enhance that doctrine (cf. Alderman, *Nietzsche's Gift,* 91–92; but see also 111 for slightly different emphasis, and 69–81 for a good statement of the general, uniquely Nietzschean problem of the "will" and its "freedom").

20. This issue obviously touches on Heidegger's famous concern with the "modernity" of the will to power notion and the "classical" resonances of the eternal return. See my "Nietzsche and the Origin of the Idea of Modernism" for a discussion of Heidegger's interpretation. I should also note the important contributions of Wolfgang Müller-Lauter on this issue, many aspects of which I am in sympathy with. See his *Nietzsche: Seine Philosophie der Gegensätze und die Gegensätze seiner Philosophie* (Berlin: de Gruyter, 1971).

21. There is a good deal of dispute in the literature about the role of the animals (creatures who are without history, for whom a cycle of repetition is almost literally true) in *Zarathustra.* See Bennholdt-Thomsen's discussion and notes, *Nietzsches Zarathustra,* 200–201.

22. There are some letters to Peter Gast (from 1885) in which Nietzsche himself remarks on the unusual tone of Part IV. See Bennholdt-Thomsen's discussion in her *Nietzsches Zarathustra,* 15, 210–11, and especially her citation of aphorism #150 from *Beyond Good and Evil.*

23. This supposed discovery of his children also conflicts with Zarathustra's earlier realization, in "Involuntary Bliss," that, with respect to "the children of his hope," "behold, it turned out that he could not find them, unless he first created them himself" (VI 1, 199).

24. To cite only some of the frequent passages where Nietzsche insists on the necessity of masks and connects that rhetorical issue with a land of self-deflating irony, see VI 2, 53–54, especially the claim "Every profound spirit needs a mask: even more, around every profound spirit a mask is growing continually, owing to the constantly false, namely shallow, interpretation of every word, every step, every sign of life he gives"; V 2, 90–91, especially, in this discussion of the "consciousness of *Scheine,*" the remarks on "self-mockery" (*Selbstverspottung*) and the need to "continue the dream" after one realizes one is dreaming; see also V 2, 262. See also the compilation of *Nachlass* remarks (1882–88) on style, language, and expression in Robert Rethy's doctoral dissertation, *An Introduction to the Problem of Affirmation in Nietzsche's Thought* (Pennsylvania State University, 1980). I might also take this opportunity to thank Robert Rethy for a number of helpful suggestions about an earlier draft of this paper.

25. On Nietzsche's use of such masks, see the discussion in Alderman, *Nietzsche's Gift,* 1–17. I also agree with Alderman that Zarathustra undergoes a "transformation" and find his use of the "Camel-lion-child" metamorphoses instructive, but I place much more stress on the difficulties of a "final" metamorphosis, and so stress more the tragic than comic or affirmative elements

of part 4, and do not think we are ever shown a way to be "released" from the "tragedy" of knowledge or experience a "catharsis" (cf. 147).

26. For some further suggestions about the thematic presuppositions of such an approach to Nietzsche, and how the approach might look in practice, see Eckhard Heftrich, *Nietzsches Philosophie: Identität von Welt und Nichts* (Frankfurt: Klostermann, 1962).

27. For another thing, Nietzsche's own understanding of the notion of "irony" is extremely complex and would require an independent study before its use in describing Nietzsche's intentions would be justified. Indispensable in such a discussion would be Ernst Behler's study, "Nietzsches Auffassung der Ironie," *Nietzsche-Studien* 4 (1975): 1–35. See especially his concluding remarks on *"tragische Ironie,"* 32–35.

28. For a helpful discussion of Nietzsche's understanding of parody, and the relevance of that notion for his views on history, historical reception, art and science, see Sander L. Gilman, *Nietzschean Parody: An Introduction to Reading Nietzsche* (Bonn: Bouvier, 1976).

PART II

Toward a New Logic:
Singing the Siren's Song

CHAPTER 3

■ Commentary

Jean-Michel Rey
Translated by Tracy B. Strong[1]

Another century of such readers and the spirit will stink.
                                        —Nietzsche

When attacked, I prefer to respond that my contemporaries
do not know how to read.
                                        —Mallarmé

Writing/Reading: These activities in a text by Nietzsche strike us in a
realm that they order as a new, nonpublic (*inédit*) game. It is played
on a stage where metaphysical discourse, for having been too long
invested with "values," is thwarted in its very beginnings. The major
and most immediate effect of such a displacement is the constantly
reiterated affirmation that the text of metaphysics is only an illusory
mastery of meaning. We see this in its metaphoricity and in the fact
that it always repeats itself to us. On one level, Nietzsche's decoding
of this text articulates what we must call a repeated return of metaphor, analogous to the return (*Wiederkehr*) of the repressed in Freud.
    One of the reasons, therefore, that a simple commentary on
Nietzsche is impossible is that every element of his text is *already* a
signifier;[2] there is no possibility of its delegating, representing, or
expressing something else. In its most systematic form (Plato, Descartes, Kant, and Hegel), the text *of* metaphysics focuses on a network of categories which, in the interpretive field offered by Nietzsche,
can be read as products of the imagination, as a phantasmic system
without autonomous coherence. In a Nietzschean reading, this fan-

Translated by permission of the publisher from Jean-Michel Rey, *L'Enjeu des
signes: Lectures de Nietzsche,* © Les Editions du Seuil, 1971.

tasy is rather the consequence of a set of nonphilosophical agencies. To set these forth, to show how they structure the world, would be to subvert the logic of their text; philosophical discourse would then be placed on another stage where the syntax and structure of each element would be apparent.

Such a multivalent text is in opposition to what it states; it cannot be read in terms of truth and falsehood. Once read, such a text abolishes its own legitimacy, that is, it thwarts (*déjoue*) all questions of origin, of paternity, or of self-possession (*propriété*), everything that seeks to legitimate a foundation. In this revelation of the play of individual particulars (*instances*), any simple will to meaning (*vouloir dire*) is expressed.[3]

Nietzschean interpretation often remains allusive or metaphorical, like descriptions in Freud. It is as if philosophy was only a phantasmic discourse, the discourse of a desire that has been endlessly displaced and idealized and that has returned again and again by unspoken detours. In the *Interpretation of Dreams,* Freud defines thought as a detour toward the accomplishment of a desire—*Umweg zur Wunscherfüllung.*[4] It is the discourse of an unconsciousness that can only be read through the post-hoc interpretations which are the instances which structure it (such as morality and religion). The most important effect that appears in philosophic discourse—that is, the effect whose consequences are the most visible (the most contradictory)— is the predominance that meaning acquires over the mode of its production; it is the usurped mastery of the signified over the signifier.[5] Nietzsche decodes this process as the surest sign of idealism, of which the moral origin is evident.

The "forbidden" and "castration" are the major processes of the economy of political discourse. This discourse consists in a cleavage which continually reappears under different names: good/evil, truth/ error, life/death, and so forth. A consequence of this has been to set aside as laws a number of specially defined terms. To make sense means then to give oneself the "legal" power to use these terms at points across a predetermined horizontal spectrum. In this centered, "theological" space, where the complicity of the signified is established, meaning and value are preestablished even before their own formulation (*inscription*). Philosophical discourse "lives" off this illusory reserve, off the lure of a permanent infinite of which the subject is at the same time the bearer as well as the prime example. Consciousness (*conscience*) is only the effect of the play of displaced forces, the refraction of a "life" or a desire which cannot, as such, appear as itself. In this understanding, a proper noun is the possibility—

a possibility of which philosophical discourse has availed itself—of a signifier becoming the predicate of "truth" or "value." This means that it is a negative inscription awaiting a presence that fills it; it awaits an infinite which displaces it by rendering it as a simple "means of expression" destined to disappear. Thus, a consequence of Platonic discourse was the canceling out of the body in the subject.

The commentary thus always presupposes that any discourse conceals a background which at once offers and refuses access and is present in a manner that always remains incomplete. Commentary takes over this background in a more constraining discourse; it is more neutral, perhaps more pedagogical. It is as if what the text signifies were always more than the signifiers, and one tried to reduce this excess through translation. Commentary is an explicit and implicit game whose goal is to liberate the meaningful "contents." Classically, commentary takes up a series of oppositions (present/absent, manifest/latent, etc.) which have been used by metaphysical discourse. Louis Althusser called this the "religious complicity established between the logos and being"; in his reading of Marx, he sought to "break with the religious myth of reading."[6]

No commentary, unless blind to its own work, can ignore the richness of the signifier (first, as metaphoricity) nor its historical stratification, its sedimentation and overlay. In fact, Freud should have alerted us to this question, as he speaks of a "nodal point" where several vectors intersect, of "changes in expression in the service of condensation," of "changes in verbal expression between thoughts." He gives us a logic of the signifier in its unformulated (*inédit*) syntax, explains to us how each symbolic formulation comes about, attempts to write out (*inscrire*) the "architectonic symbolism of the body and the genital organs," and shows how the "precipitate of the fantasy metaphors" (*der Niederschlag von Phantasievergleichungen*) of the past was created. The signifier always functions as a layered reservoir, as a memory of which one perceives only the traces and the "symptoms." It is a device which allows one to produce the effects and the formal conditions of work. Nietzsche indicates this again and again—in a language loaded with metaphors, but still where the very writing lets us see their markings (*l'écriture laisse voir le tracé*). Nietzsche tells us that all texts are produced by a journey through language such that meaning can acquire body. A text is produced by a perspectivization of speech: translation risks a diminishing or even an erasing of the very body of expression (the historical consequences of this can be seen).

For a number of reasons, metaphysics requires a reading that is not centered on its own categories. It is the field of play of instances that it cannot name without destroying its own ideal coherence; it does not understand the "force" of the desire that sets it in motion; it produces an empty space for signification; it is centered on the absolute value of truth and reduces the powers of discourse to simple expression. For these reasons, metaphysics requires a reading that establishes the game of instances and of the indefinite dismissals that they give rise to. Metaphysical reading works on them without paying attention to its own work and finds the warp in which "metaphysical" concepts are caught.

Commentary is thus committed to a sterile and unproductive repetition, identical to the "diseased" repetition that is the grounding of metaphysical systems:

> The hermit does not believe that any philosopher—
> assuming that every philosopher was first of all a hermit—
> ever expressed his real and ultimate opinions in books:
> Does one not write books precisely to conceal what one
> harbors? Indeed, he will doubt whether a philosopher could
> *possibly* have "ultimate and real" opinions, whether behind
> every one of his caves there is not, must not be, another,
> deeper cave—a more comprehensive, stranger, richer world
> beyond the surface, an abysmally deep ground behind every
> ground, under every attempt to furnish "grounds." Every
> philosophy is a foreground philosophy—that is, a hermit's
> judgment: "There is something arbitrary in his stopping
> *here* to look back and look around, in his not digging deeper
> *here* but laying his spade aside; there is also something
> suspicious about it." Every philosophy also *conceals* a phi-
> losophy; every opinion is also a hideout, every word also
> a mask. (VI 2, 244)

Metaphysical discourse would thus be a complex apparatus, playing on several different keyboards and building itself up on different strata. Its positions mask its absence of grounding. A surface is not so much the effect of a secret depth (be it veiled, darkened, or even forgotten) as a game of incessant re-views, re-covered in the name of a given signified which is set up as "original" or unconditioned. We perceive the effects—as if in negative or filigree—of a permutation and unlimited substitution that takes place in the absence of any original signified. The fundamental lure of discourse about truth—a lure that is a calculated unblocking (*un décalage calculé*)—is the pretense that there is a determinate foundation beyond all metaphoricity and any signifier. This could also be read as a denial that language had any impact, as if the articulation of the signifier and the signified had always been accomplished without fault or remainder. (This, for Nietzsche, was the goal of Platonic dialectic: "Dialectic believes in cause and effect; and thus in the necessary relation between crime and punishment, virtue and happiness: the arithmetical problem must have no remainder.") It is as if the "resources" of the signifier could be mastered without consequence and as if the displacements effectuated in language could be undamaging.

We have not brought into the light this other stage, on which instances incorrectly called philosophical are played out, in order to reestablish on the other side of metaphysical systems and their propositions hidden truths or ontological intuitions that have been covered over.[7] Rather, we have sought to in-scribe the major processes of repetition, of displacement, of abnegation, of the forbidden. It is by means of all these that a rhetoric of truth is encoded. We have tried to produce the syntax which is at work in the subjection of each signifier to a network of the signified which is always deemed "anterior" to it. This is what is set in motion in Nietzschean writing as well as in the reading one makes of it.

At a certain level of Nietzsche's text, a topographical map of philosophical discourse is elaborated to show the spatial relations of the different fundamental concepts of this discourse. We find how these concepts knit themselves around certain stitches of meaning as the reiterated movement of different "interpretations," much in the manner of "secondary elaboration" as given us by Freud. We see the displacement of instances (what we now call the "separation of powers") in the effect of new cleavages, hidden under the apparent regular linkage and systematic articulation of concepts: we see the diverse modalities of abbreviation which are produced in the space of the sign. Thus, for instance, the concept of "being" (given most often by Nietzsche in quotation marks) is resituated in a chain of metaphors from which one can read and decipher the functions that it plays in philosophical systems, the displacements which it engenders and the instances of which it is the "representative." The syntax on which Nietzsche relies shows itself in this new metaphoric space which denounces its own utopia (that is, denounces the transcendental authority with which it finds itself invested).

If metaphysics is made up of moves which are identical, despite the apparent difference in their systematizations, and if these gestures come down to reducing or erasing the powers of the signifier (and of the body) by means of arbitrary separations or cleavages, then this cannot happen without leaving marks. These are lacunae,

for which we must afterward produce their syntax, the different modalities of their inscribing, the "unconscious" logic of their agency.

Even given all the differences that must be retained, this is still
comparable to what Marx says about commodities and value: "Value
does not carry about on its head what it is. Rather it makes of each
product of labor a social hieroglyph. It is only over time that man deciphers the meaning of this hieroglyph, manages to penetrate the
secrets of the social work to which it contributes, and the transformation of use objects into value is a product of society, just as much as
is language."[8]

Nietzsche wants to reinscribe into the failing memory of metaphysics the signifying possibilities which are now returning as different and unseen (*inédit*) figures after having too long been subjected
to a systematic repression. The practice of reading and the practice
of writing express themselves together (*se conjugent*) incessantly,
they exchange places, rely on each other; as philology they produce a
break in the interior of the philosophical text and inaugurate new
modes of philosophizing. Philology permits one to grasp the signifying stratification in all of its detours and elaborations. This is not inscribed in linear history nor in a simple temporality, if only because it
derives from an interpretation after the fact. We thus also apprehend
the space of a significant plurality which has remained obscured, subject to the privileges of a temporal meaning. Whether we understand
philosophical discourse as semiotics or the sign as a process of abbreviation, what is at stake is the same. It is a matter of dis-implicating the
different figures that are sedimented into the concepts and the signs
of the metaphysical text (assuming that they are really different and
not just different names for a repeated identity). It is a matter of pro-
ducing another text that inscribes itself in the lacunae of the first, of
bringing onto the stage the instances that are silently present in the
work, of restarting that which has been shut down. This is a writing
that has no ascertainable origin, no earlier tracing. The sign presents
itself for deciphering as a complex, condensed, and overloaded apparatus, continually displaced and remolded. The sign can never be
read in the field of a logic of identity (what Nietzsche calls the "belief
in identical cases"); it is never simply inscribed as linear history.

It is as if the philosophically signified was a game of diverse moments which mutually implied each other, exchanged their resources,
and thus produced a text that interfered with itself. Commentary, by
focusing exclusively on the "meaning" of statements, must remain
blind to these implications of instances (Freud spoke of a *Trieb-
verschränkung*—a cross-cutting of drives).[9] Only a reading that is re-

inforced by a genealogical "ascent" can make evident the work of reelaboration which has its principal place in the sign. To use Nietzsche's word, a metaphysical text is comparable to a palimpsest whose "original" inscription has forever disappeared and which consists entirely of overlay. The metaphysical reading of a text would thus be an indefinite retreat through the signified and its reinscription in other chains as signifier. In a like manner, Freud read the text of the dream, or of hysteria, showing that "the language of nervous obsession was a dialect of the language of hysteria"; "equivocal" words became the significant relays. Such a reading unveils "conventional" syntax which had placed signifiers on a simple horizontal chain, in a field for which the evidence already exists and which is constituted simply by vision. (The metaphor of the eye is fundamental to Nietzsche's destructive enterprise, in that it concerns the "subject" and in that the conditions of visibility, or perspectivism, define the norm of metaphysical "truth.")

The most elementary formulation of the utopia of the metaphysical standpoint is its atemporal character. Nietzsche analyzes this as the *Ti esti* and in the effects of the presence that it brings about. It supposes a permanent infinite, of which the Cartesian *cogito* is the most explicit form. The evasions of this stance are found in the "complicity" of "philosophical" language and ordinary language, in the dissimulations that such a complicity produces, in the unending metaphoricality that philosophical language unconsciously produces—what Nietzsche calls the "spider's web." The most obvious paradox consequent to this: philosophical discourse uses all the resources of the signifier while attempting to erase its equivocation and to use it simply as a means of expressing that which is "behind" it, as a means of representing something independent. For Nietzsche, a genealogical reading should first demonstrate the polyvalence of the philosophical signifier, in which an unperceived game of masks has been institutionalized and codified, on whose surface one sees only the refraction.

In *The German Ideology,* Marx writes about Stirner: "Synonymy is used by our saint [Stirner] to metamorphose real relations into idealistic ones. He takes a term that has a practical sense and a idealistic sense only in its idealistic sense, develops some formulas from this sense in order later to give himself the air of having criticized the real relations that this term serves to designate. . . . Synonymy, together with apposition, is his essential device."[10]

Any sign is already caught in the undefined network of "interpretation"; any signified can only be read in a stratified space of signifiers.

Any sign is a space in which a whole of negative concepts, of displaced forces, of piled-up interpretations coexists. Any genealogical reading can only be interminable (in the sense that Freud uses
the term—see *Dora*) and can only work by continually returning to
itself. Thus, Nietzschean interpretation always exceeds the question
"What?" and hollows out a space for the question "Who?" Such an
excess can only be found in the field of an unworked-out (*inédit*) writing which removes from the author all power, all property, which
erases his proper name by reading it as a perspective, as an interpretation whose economy is always beyond the question of essence.

All discourse—and first of all philosophical discourse—must inscribe itself in a field constituted by language. It must unfold itself, as
if passive, in a space already worked over by a syntax. "Humanity has
from time immemorial confused the active and passive; this was its
eternal grammatical mistake."

If, at first glance, the difference of the sensuous and the noumenal
(*le sensible et le non-sensible*) allows a definition of the track of metaphor as the tracing (*tracé*) of the proper meaning onto the figurative
meaning, the logic of philosophical discourse would consist in codify-
ing this difference. It would use its powers while concealing its traces.
It would transfer meaning and order reinvestments, none of which
would ever be noted in its practices: "Here an experience that man
has made in the social-political domain has been falsely transferred
to the farthest metaphysical domain: there the strong man is also the
free man, there the living feeling of joy and sorrow, and high hope,
boldness in desire, the power of hatred, is the property of the rulers
and the independent, while the subjected man, the slave, lives op-
pressed and dull.—The theory of the freedom of the will is an invention of the *ruling* classes" (IV 3, 183).[11]

Philosophical texts are ruled, as if from outside, by a logic of identity, the postulate of an order already given; they are ruled by the belief in a "truth" inscribed from the beginning in words, the effect of an
imaginary causality which works as a principle of individuation.
Freud, we remember, spoke of a "tardy interpretation." Here, the impact of a grammar and of a logic deciphers itself tardily in *beliefs*
(also called "procedures") which are at work in the cloth of the philosophical text. Concepts and values are subjected to the same expression and their syntax is revealed at the same time, as they are
elements of a same system, the stake of the same displacements:

> We praise and censure, however, only under this false pre-
> supposition that there are *identical* facts, that there exists a
> graduated order of *classes* of facts which corresponds to a

graduated world order; thus we *isolate* not only the individual fact, but also again groups of supposedly identical facts.
. . . The word and the concept are the most manifest ground for our belief in this isolation of groups of actions: we do not only *designate* things with them, we think originally that through them we grasp the essence of things. We are still continually misled by words and concepts into imagining things simpler than they are, separate from one another, indivisible, each existing in and for itself. A philosophical mythology lies concealed in *language* which breaks out again at every moment, however careful one may be. Belief in the freedom of will—that is to say in *identical* facts and in *isolated* facts—has in language its constant evangelist and advocate. (IV 3, 184–85)[12]

The identity of being and discourse which is postulated by metaphysics (which as we indicate below finds its realization in the space of the book) has its correlation in the determination of language as the order of expression or of designation. It allows itself to be read as a hierarchy of the signified and requires that an origin be assigned to it. In this space, it is the signifier that is closed out, crossed out and struck out, subjected and displaced. This is done in the name of a complicity between "seeing" and "reading," in the name of the determination of the sign as a transparency to itself, in the name of an "evidence" whose perspectival character is never noted, in the name of a fascination and of a "seduction" (*Verführung*) exercised by the word and the concept. This can only work if the "lacunae" left by this imaginary causality are filled in with large strokes (one of the tactics of idealism, according to Nietzsche).

Genealogy—which works on the body of definition itself—thus works on these principles: a reading of the effects of this misreading which is constitutive of metaphysics: a grasping of the "silent" returning of the signifier in the lacunae of the text; a constituting of metaphoricity as the "basis" of concepts and condensations which are at work in the web (*la trame*) of the text. It is—to use Freud's terms—to execute a "reversal for the chain of effects" (*Umkehrung der Reihenfolge*), a "regressive analysis" (*Ruckverfolgung*).

Working in a speculative dialectic which takes over the "perceptible" (*le sensible*), Hegel has noted this "equivocality" of the signifier. In order to be justified, any borrowing from ordinary language must be recast in a repetition and reinscribed as the rule-bound alternation of positive and negative. Thus, can its use value acquire the civic right[13] of citation:[14]

To transcend (*aufheben*) has this double meaning, that it signifies to keep or to preserve and also to make to cease, to finish. To preserve includes this negative element, that something is removed from its immediacy and therefore from a determinate being [*Dasein*] exposed to external influences, in order that it may be preserved.—Thus, what is transcended is also preserved; it has only its immediacy and is not on that account annihilated.—In the dictionary the two determinations of transcending may be cited as two meanings of this word. But it should appear as remarkable that a language should have come to use one and the same word for two opposite determinations. It is a joy for speculative meaning: the German language has served as such.[15]

This dialectical lifting up (*relève*), as contained in the term *Aufhebung* (which for Hegel defines the progression of the history of meaning), contains in short form all the occultation gestures of metaphoricity as well as all the procedures by which meaning institutes itself beyond the proceeding of signifiers. It defines the overcoming of facticity into the "juridical" order (which Hegel elaborates as the equivalence of absolute knowledge and the universal state, as well as the parallelism of rationality and the system of law). In the field of the speculative, the concept always has the force of law.

Leibniz also notes the difference between the "civil use" of language and its philosophical usage, defined as "that to which one must give words to have a precise meaning and to *express* certain truths as general propositions. . . . The first use of signs is civil and the second is philosophical."

Univocality can only be constructed and elaborated, decided and agreed upon after the fact: "For it depends on us to determine the significations, at least in some scientific language, and to agree on them in order to destroy this Tower of Babel."[16]

The eighteenth century played a fundamental role in bringing to light the process[17] by which metaphor is the material basis of the concept.[18] Even if this takes place in the perspective of an empiricist questioning, it is not without connection to the political problematic. The question of the sign is, most often, inseparable from another question, that about the basis of law and right (*droit*), about the state, the legitimacy of power, about political "representation." All these elements are present, in differing manners, in Vico, Rousseau, Condillac, but also in Diderot, Hume, or Locke.[19]

Leibnitz also writes in the *New Essays*: "Observe how the words which one employs to formulate actions and notions quite distant from the senses have their origin in sensuous ideas, from which they are transferred to more abstruse significations. . . . It would be important to consider this analogy of sensuous and nonsensuous things, which serves as the basis for tropes" (III, 1). "Understand how metaphors, synedoches and metonymies had moved words from one signification to another, without it always being possible to follow the track" (III, 2).

To think the world in the plural mode would be to conceive of it most centrally as metaphorical space and as the model for all fiction; the drawing of the analogy between the visible "world" and the invisible "world" (as is done in Platonism) remains the "postulate," still beyond all question. It is only through the detour of metaphor that this analogy can utter its own syntax. If metaphor is the possibility of speaking of an "unknown" thing in the very terms that make this thing possible, metaphor is then inscribed, as a filigree, in the text of metaphysics. It is in the service of an investment of meaning that is never named in its outline nor in its production. The reactivation of metaphor (particularly in its "poetic" function) renders ineffective any "original" position; it marks, that is, the inexhaustible character of the play of signifiers, except to index them on a value of truth, on an original signified. It is to return all forms of presence or of the infinite to their own arbitrariness. It is the displacement of a "desire" and its subjection to a hierarchy of the signified or of values. It is thus first of all the metaphoric quality of "truth" that is targeted in Nietzsche's text.

From a completely different point of view, Spinoza has noted this metaphoricity:[20]

> It is for him who seeks the first meaning of a word to ask himself what it first meant in the vulgar; this is especially true given the absence of other causes which might be adduced from the nature of language to undertake this research. The first meaning, thus, of "true" and "false" seems to be derived from stories. A story was called true when what it was about really happened; false, when it never happened anywhere. Only later did philosophers use the word to designate the accordance or nonaccordance of an idea with its object. Thus, a "true idea" is one that shows an object as it is in itself; false, when it shows a thing other than it is in reality. Ideas are nothing other than accounts or stories of nature in the spirit. And from there one came to designate inert things as metaphor, as when we speak of true or false gold, as if gold which is presented to us was

telling us something about itself, something which was or was not in itself.[21]

The world as "fable"; the "true world" as the production of the imaginary (world), as the effect of a desire which does not understand itself and is self-alluring, of a desire to decipher in its refractions in the theoretical field (*de déchiffrer par ses contrecoups dans le champ du théorique*). This "syntax," expressed in its most elementary form by Nietzsche, takes the field of philosophy over into that of fiction. It is the space of an imaginary doubling which goes beyond the logic of identity and of simple causality. It is the speculative space of an indefinite repetition where metaphor is without direction or origin.

Hegel makes philosophy appear constituted by its own history; he inscribes the "permanent" identity of logic and ontology. In the relations knit together by the dialectic as an immaculate memory and in the relations between history and consciousness, he produces a repetition of the same in the perspective of a history that is linear and teleological, completely present to itself and transparent to itself. (These are qualities that Nietzsche designates as "theological.") The Hegelian system gives an account of itself (*se récite*) in the future, but a future that is nothing other than the other name of presence, its realization and its suppression in the figure of eternity.

Nietzsche's text is written in the conditional mode. It deciphers another text that does not exist as such before being read, and produces a text whose effects have not been controlled but always censured by philosophy. He does not write to uncover depth, which is only a fold (*un pli*) and a surface attraction, an effect of censure or the place of mystification. Rather, he wishes to inscribe instances on the vertical plane of writing, in the plural space of interpretation. "*Deep explanations.*—He who explains a passage of an author "more deeply" than the passage was meant has not explained the author but *obscured* him. This is how our metaphysicians tend in regard to the text of nature: indeed, much worse. For in order to apply their deep explanations they frequently first adjust the text in such a way that will facilitate it: in other words, they corrupt it" (IV 3, 189–90).[22]

Philosophizing (*le philosophique*) is a chain (the "horizontality" of the concept and of vision) of interpretations which each cover the other. It is a chain at whose beginning one can note in Plato the concept of the metaphorized and divided "world." Any "discovery" of a simple origin introduces a theological perspective (that is, the erasing of all perspectivism) under the name of unconditional and absolute. The history of philosophizing can be read as a chain of disavowals, of abnegations, of displacements. These are all practices which for an important reason—the "maintenance" of this discourse—hide themselves in the thickness of the text, in the networking of multiple signs. This is the source of Nietzsche's insistence that philosophy has only prospered by ignoring philology (the opposite case would be the conjunction of a genealogical reading and a vertical or scenic writing). The death of philosophy is prefigured in this absence; to draw the consequences all that we have left to do is to decipher the actual effects, the refractions in the field of discourse:

> With almost all *philosophers,* the use of precursors and attacks on the same is not vigorous, and unjust. Such attacks show that they have not learned to *read* and interpret properly; philosophers underestimate the difficulty of really understanding what another has said, and do not concern themselves with it. Thus Schopenhauer completely misunderstood both Kant and Plato. Artists, too, read poorly, with a penchant for allegoric and pneumatological explanations. (IV 2, 507; cf. IV 2, 24–25)

Metaphysical texts are produced by a succession of "forgettings" (Nietzsche speaks in the *Genealogy* of an "active faculty of forgetfulness"), a repeated foreclosing of the space of the signifier (and of the "body"). They set to work an economy whose major components are inscribed in the "postulate" of identity and presence. This fundamental economy, which makes up the cloth of philosophy and articulates its "proper" logic, can be deciphered from what it most significantly lacks, from its lacunae. This will be read in the network of signifiers, in the "loss" of the very body of expression in translation, the scission of the symbolic field and the subjection of the text to the imperative of the original signified.[23]

> The degree of the historical sense of any age may be inferred from the manner in which this age makes translations and tries to absorb former ages and books. . . . They did not know the delights of the historical sense; what was past and alien was an embarrassment for them; and being Romans, they saw it as an incentive for a Roman conquest. Indeed, translation was a form of conquest. Not only did one omit what was historical; one also added allusions to the present and, above all, struck out the name of the poet and replaced it with one's own—not with any sense of theft but with the very best conscience of the *imperium Romanum.*[24]

The articulation of the letter and the body, the incarnatability (*le devenir-corps*) of the text: the same question is at stake in each. In the field of theory (metaphysical idealism), it had found itself disqualified and foreclosed, subjected from the outside to a "logic" which precedes it and gives it its law. In the end, it is through the same processing that the signifier is thwarted as well as hidden and that the body (as the form of a plurality without law) is disavowed and denied. This repeated disavowal, this constantly renewed abnegation can be read in the effects which are inferred *aus den nachfolgenden Vorgängen* (from the successive predecessors)—to adopt an expression of Freud's that could be applied perfectly to the reading of Nietzsche. Philology can only begin by first bringing to light this "logic" of abnegation, of which the first consequence is to hold the body as a dead letter. (This is the primary characteristic of the intangible position of an ideal signified, of a refractionless mastery of language and thus of metaphor; of the assignation of a stable hierarchy of values.) Philology, as well as interpretation, cannot do without a genealogical perspectivization.

It is thus not accidental that for Nietzsche religion is responsible in part for the disqualification of the letter and the body. Religion practices a form of decoding (transcendental or theological in its nature), which was most often taken over without modification by philosophy. It is a "symbolic" or "pneumatological" decoding, in which the sign becomes transparent to itself, becomes the simple correlate of a consciousness completely present to itself, simply the respondent to the sign. The sign is, at one level, the space in which theology (re-)takes its rights, all the while masking and disguising itself while extending its powers. This happens because of the bias of the subject. It is as if philosophy actively forgot the materiality of the sign (this is its "idealism") as well as hid its "historical" overlay by postulating a "history" of a pure and simple linearity. This "repression," once read after the fact in its effects and in the different types of "return" that produce it, displaces the philosophical field in its entirety. It produces it as the "representative" of another plurality, as a network of symptoms that cannot call upon its own genealogy. (It is basic to Nietzsche that symptoms are always articulated, in a "secondary" elaboration.) In Freud, on a similar basis, in the text of the dream or of the neurosis, it is a question of decoding the inversions of the grammatical subject, the permutations of "persons," the covering up of different fragments and the ceaseless transformation of the principle statements. In an unblocked (*décalée*) Nietzsche reading, any signified can only appear as a signifier.[25] From this point of view, it is important not to neglect the medical aspect of Nietzsche's vocabulary, of the impact of "sickness" in his text, as well as the whole problem of "physiology." "A practiced eye, to be able to read the past clearly out of the manifold superimposed handwriting of human features (expressions) and gestures" (IV 2, 496).

This is a fundamental aphorism which defines what one might call the "method" (in fact, it is something quite other) of Nietzsche: a practice which is realized as "linguistics" or philology, and which must constantly call upon a forbidden in order to get started, which must design (contourner) a disavowal (méconaissance) to produce itself in an unedited space:[26] "Linguistics helps show that man has completely failed to recognize and falsely named nature: we are the heirs of these names (this naming of things), the human spirit has grown up in these errors which nourished it and gave it its strength" (IV 2, 508).

Bringing to light the investment of meaning can only be accomplished by taking the signifier back to its "equivocality," only by grasping the effects of a "desire" that everywhere exceeds the bounds of a metaphysical text. To decode these effects is only to mark out a missing place (une place manquante), an active absence, a consequential lacuna. Something is preparing itself quietly on this side of the difference between good and evil, between "truth" and "error," on this side of the fissure in the symbolic field, itself a consequence of the metaphorization of the eye and the complicity of "seeing" and "saying." It is on this side of all the symbolic or imaginary figures of a renewed castration in the field of theory or metaphysics. For Nietzsche, it is a question of putting an end to the autonomy of philosophy, or even to the autonomy and "sufficiency" of consciousness: "After having looked long enough between the philosopher's lines and fingers, I say to myself; by far the greater part of conscious thinking must still be included among instinctive activities, and that goes even for philosophical thinking" (VI 2, 11).

To put an end to this privilege by revealing its "syntax" is to demonstrate that a utopia is at work in the logic of identity that is in the very matter of philosophical questioning. Or, we might say that it is to show this philosophical question as a facade, as the rationalization of a completely different want, as an avoidance and detour around a nonphilosophical moment. Nietzsche will substitute for this philosophical question what he calls the "response of comedy," an articulated play of instances:

> . . . it is high time to replace the Kantian question, "How are synthetic judgments *a priori* possible?" by another question, "Why is belief in such judgments *necessary?*"—and to comprehend that such judgments must be *believed* to be true, for the sake of the preservation of creatures like ourselves; though they might, of course, be *false* judgments for all that! Or to speak more clearly and coarsely: synthetic judgments a priori should not "be possible" at all; we have no right to them; in our mouths they are nothing but false judgments. Only, of course, the belief in their truth is necessary, as a foreground belief and visual evidence belonging to the perspective optics of life. (VI 2, 19–20)

Synthetic judgments a priori are "foreground belief." In aphorism 289 of *Beyond Good and Evil* (cited above), Nietzsche characterized *philosophy* as "foreground philosophy."

The visible stage—the manifest content—rules the text as a whole. It is a facade whose function is to hide the staging, the production of the "philosophical" syntax. Everything that presents itself as "depth," "ultimate ground," "master word" turns out to simply be a superficial fold. "Depth," "background," the "real world" are all a world of fiction, compromise formulations whose syntax must be revealed, whose economy must be inscribed in the space that communicates the play of moments and the networking of symptoms. The aphorism cited above ends thus: "And one must still speak of the prodigious activity which 'German philosophy'—I hope that one understands why that is in quotes—has exercised over Europe. A certain *virtus dormitiva,* let us not doubt it, has helped."

For Nietzsche, the use of quotation marks to scratch out the fundamental concepts of philosophy was a necessary practice. He could thus play with them, reinscribing them in other chains and turning them against the place of an origin. He practices a symptomatic and genealogical reading, accomplished in repeated slidings in writing (*glissements de l'écriture*), by the vertical traverse of the space of the sign. He throws the resources of metaphor back to us again and again. Nietzsche tried this fragmentary, discontinuous, and aphoristic writing at the same time that he was trying to formulate "theory." This is the stage for a new infinity, that of "interpretation," which goes beyond the name of any author, beyond all symbolic property:

> But I should think that today we are at least far from the ridiculous immodesty that would be involved in decreeing from our corner that perspectives are permitted only from this corner. Rather has the world become "infinite" for us

all over again, inasmuch as we cannot reject the possibility
that *it may include infinite interpretations.* Once more we
are seized by a great shudder; but who would feel inclined
immediately to deify again after the old manner this monster of an unknown world? And to worship the unknown
henceforth as "the Unknown one"? Alas, too many *ungodly*
possibilities of interpretation are included in the unknown,
too much deviltry, stupidity, and foolishness of interpretation—even our own human, all-too-human folly, which we
know. (V 2, 309)

Interpretation cannot have an "original"; it is articulated in the
plural mode by the bias of "representatives" (*Vertreter*) who play a
fundamental role in Nietzschean reading. In a like manner, genealogy
always resolves itself in typology.

To bring to light new modalities of reading (and of writing) is at the
same time to produce the schema of a stratified history of which the
sign is the initial and not continuing form.

■ NOTES

1. Rey writes in contemporary French philosophical style which seeks to
lessen the distance between the form of writing and the content of the essay.
Since that is the topic of this essay, translation is especially difficult. Most
problematic has been finding English grammatical forms that correspond to
the way Rey's text slides from subject to predicate. His text is built like a series of Chinese boxes or Russian dolls, where the core is almost nonexistent
and is surrounded by predicates, which often have subpredicates (and sub-
sub . . .) attached to them. At times—too often, perhaps—in the interest of
clarity I have broken these boxes down into planks.

Another aspect of this writing style is an attention to all the resonances
that a word may have, as if the "meaning" were merely a sort of indefinite
nucleus surrounded by aura and penumbra. For instance, in the title, "*enjeu*"
means literally "ante" or "stake." It is also "*en jeu*"—"in play." The word carries then both the resonance of the activity and what the activity is about. I
have tried (not very successfully) to give this as "the game." Unless noted, all
subsequent notes are Rey's.—Trans.

2. It is a question here of a reading that must reflect on itself at the same
time that it produces itself. Nietzsche's text requires such a reading, if only
because he insists on philology as the art of reading and writing well. As such,
his is a multivalent text that cannot be reduced into thematic snippets such
as the "will of power," "eternal return," the "death of God," and the "overman" (categories which according to Fink are the fourfold articulation of the
metaphysical question). Nor can it be reduced to a network of themes:
Nietzsche's is a text that introduces a break (*rupture*) into philosophical dis-

course and that, as such, cannot be subject to a classical "commentary." This is what our work has trying to bring together by saying that we are crossing Nietzsche on the diagonal. See M. Serrès's introduction to his *Le Système de Leibnitz* (Paris: Presses universitaires françaises, 1968), where the question of commentary is exposed and unfolded in all its dimensions.

3. The *"vouloir-dire,"* as will to meaning, is doubtless a notion that cannot subsist in the movement of Nietzschean destruction. As a will which wills itself, it comes under the whole critique that Nietzsche makes of the concept of the will as well as all that such a concept controls. It is a simple variant of a will to power that is always turned aside and subjected to the task of meaning, to the "horizontality" of the concept. This is central to Nietzsche's critique of Socratism; that is, it is absent from tragedy.

4. Sigmund Freud, *Gesammelte Werke* (London: Imago, 1943), II 3, 572.

5. The use made here of the categories of linguistics (notably, the difference between the signifier and the signified) remains ambiguous. Overall, Nietzsche's text comes down to the demonstration that the space of the distinction is unreal; signifier/signified is a metaphysical distinction. By using them in our reading, we are trying to make them play inside the Nietzschean text, showing their application at the same time as their limits. More generally this is the problem of putting to use scientific concepts on the inside of a reading for which their theory is missing and of the slippage undergone by concepts so used (here we know the importance of the work of Jacques Derrida, especially in *On Grammatology*). [Rey here somewhat apologetically invokes the classic Saussurean distinction between *le signifiant* and *le signifié*, between the "signifier" (that which one makes sense of by a sign) and the "signified" (the sense that the sign makes, with reference to that which sense was being made of). Translation is awkward since one can easily say in French *les signifiés,* which does not work well in English.—TRANS.]

7. Fink, among others, following the path traced by Heidegger, wants to constitute Nietzsche's thought as an ontology, albeit a negative one. This misses in Nietzsche the continual slippage (*glissement*) of being as soon as it comes into play, a slippage due to the bias of the metaphor and the trace of a writing which continually retraces itself. The same can be said of any interpretation which attempts to reactivate an "original" intuition of truth which would be, as it were, hidden in metaphysics. Such interpretations, it seems to us, derive from the separation of Nietzsche into various themes, without asking about the status of a work such as his, without raising the question of the modalities by which it is produced. In Nietzsche, all the critique and all the destruction ignite (*s'entament*) in writing and in its conjoined practice, reading. It appears that any thematic reading of Nietzsche, with all of its metaphysical presuppositions, is an obstacle to a productive reading of Nietzsche.

8. Karl Marx, "Commodity Fetishism," *Capital,* I 1, iv.

9. *Triebe* is the word Freud uses for which we in English usually give "instincts." "Instincts" is less than accurate, as *Triebe* means simply "drives" and does not carry the sense of a goal or particular activity that "instinct" does.—TRANS.

10. Karl Marx, *The German Ideology* (New York: International Publishers, 1964).

11. An essential text which shows politics as one of the essential referents of metaphysics, just as transference exists between the different moments which are at work in metaphysical discourse (politics, ethics, religion, even "biology"). In Nietzsche, we see the unpacking of these different moments from the signs into which they have been condensed. All this raises the question of the status of Nietzschean politics, since Nietzsche speaks several times of "ideology" and since the procedures which metaphysics puts into operation do not call upon the subject but upon a collectivity which is known by a typology (the priest, the man of knowledge, the philosopher, the moralist, all these are representatives [*Vertreter*] of certain moments and social practices). Thus, Nietzsche emphasizes the code (linguistic and moral) by making precise its social impact. One cannot then read the particular political affirmations of Nietzsche without circumscribing their political function as a referent or a moment. Failing this, one remains at the level of a postulated analogy. (There is the same problem with Artaud in terms of the apparently reactionary quality of his political statements.) If there is a certain open space (*blanc*) in Nietzschean discourse about politics, one must still know how to find the boundaries of this space. We know how completely contradictory Nietzsche's political heritage has been.

12. A strict separation of powers is at work in the production of metaphysical conceptions. They operate in a metaphysical orientation in which a hierarchy is inscribed. This separation is the central principle of identity and presence; it equally permits one to inscribe the subject in absolute, unmeasured autonomy.

13. "Civic right of citation" is a rendering of *droit de cité*, with its play on "city" and "citing."—TRANS.

14. In Hegel, equivocality is taken up in the dialectical logic of identity and is the movement of the concept in its regulated displacements. It is thus always a matter of the linguistic mastery of the transcription (which operates without loss or residue) and of the logic of borrowing which is itself proscribed. This move is not without relation to Hegelian politics and to the problem of the concrete universal. This matter takes place in the book; see here my article "Kojève; ou, le fin de l'histoire," *Critique* (May 1969). In the preface to the second edition of the *Science of Logic*, Hegel writes:

> It is a great advantage to a language when it has a wealth of logical expressions—that is, expressions characteristic and set apart for the determinations of thought: of prepositions and articles, many belong to those relationships which depend upon thinking. . . . It is much more important that in a language the determinations of thought should be manifested in substantives and verbs and thus receive the stamp of objective form; the German language has here many advantages over other modern languages; indeed, many of its words have the further peculiarity that they have not only various, but even opposed, meanings, so that we must recognize here

a speculative spirit in the language; it is a joy to thought to stumble upon such words, and to meet with the union of opposites (a result of speculative thought which seems senseless to human understanding) in the naive shape of one word with opposite meanings registered in a dictionary. For this reason [in German] philosophy for the most part requires no peculiar terminology. Of course some words from foreign languages (which indeed have already acquired by prescription the right of citizenship in the philosophic realm) [have to be adopted in German]." [Cited from G. W. F. Hegel, *Science of Logic,* trans. W. H. Johnson and L. G. Struthers (New York: Humanities Press, 1966), 1:40. Rey omits the material in brackets.—TRANS.]

On this problem one could also compare Hegel with the reduction of equivocality in Husserl and the whole question of "pure grammar" and of formalization at the level of a general epistemology. One could also bring in here the parallel to what Hegel says about the material function of reason as a remedy to *Entzweiung.* . . . The mother is a figure of conciliation and of reduction of differences (as in what Nietzsche says about *Versöhnung* in several places). In Nietzsche, the corresponding image is that of truth/woman, whose central activity is the dissimulation of self, "modesty." [See the essay by Sarah Kofman in this volume.—TRANS.]

15. Hegel, *Logic,* 1:119–20.

16. Leibnitz, *New Essays,* 3:9.

17. *Le procès* has the double meaning of "process" and "lawsuit" or "trial" and calls to mind the German *Prozess,* which carries the additional meaning of procession.—TRANS.

18. The empiricist and "materialist" moves in metaphysical space must be made more precise, if only because Nietzsche while making those moves on one level rejects them on another. To determine that empiricism is non-philosophy is not to resolve the problem but to dissolve it. What is at stake is in essence the status of empirical and "materialist" discourse, and the relation that it establishes to a scientific reference (or one thought to be such), or in other places the status of the metaphor (which is tied to the problem of origin). One should also ask what the place of Sade is in such a space, beyond a doubt a bloody axis [*charnière fondamentale; charnière* means hinge or joint but calls to mind *charnier,* which means "charnel-house," "ossuary"].

19. Vico, whose close links to Rousseau are known, is certainly the one who best laid out the problematic of the metaphor in a style which is not that of empiricism. Nietzsche cites him, but only in relation to the historical schema he proposes: "The first poets, who saw objects as substances with spirit, attributed to them in fact all the effects they felt in themselves; this is, meanings and passions such as those from which they created their stories. This is why any metaphor can be taken as a short fable. . . . All metaphors founded on analogies between material objects and the products of mental activity must be contemporaneous with the beginnings of the formation of philosophy" (*La Scienza nuova,* par. 404).

20. The link with Spinoza has other aspects: the critique of finality, of "humanism." Nietzsche especially radicalizes the theme of the control or expropriation of fiction. "For man to experience pleasure or pain, he must be dominated by one of two illusions: either he believes in the identity of certain facts . . . or he believes himself to be a free judge" (IV 3, 185). That which Spinoza calls "illusion" finds itself in Nietzsche as "snare" (of which the economy needs to be laid out).

21. Spinoza, *Metaphysical Thoughts,* I.

22. This is exactly what Spinoza says in the *Tractatus Theologico-Politicus,* especially in chap. 7: "The proper method to follow in the interpretation of Scripture is in no ways different from that which one makes of nature." Only philology permits us to undo "illusions." Nietzsche repeats this, with a few nuances, and adds physiology (or medicine). The body is in some manner a "text," at least the anchor for any text. But a body is never a nature (Nietzsche thus attacks empiricism) nor even an essence: the body is historical. The *Gewohnheit* and the *Trieb* are always affected by a historical index. Thus it is difficult to express clearly what Nietzsche means in his text by "biology"; this is the central problem of force, of the difference between active and reactive forces which has been clearly set out by G. Deleuze, *Nietzsche et la philosophie* (Paris: Presses universitaires françaises, 1962).

23. It is this "project" which we are trying to bring about in this work, by means of a diagonal reading of Nietzsche's text. By means of a productive reading, we want to reconstruct a problematic from elements and scattered fragments. It is thus that Nietzsche's text can be read parallel to other great texts of modernity, specifically those of Freud (whose proximity we have tried to indicate) and to Marx (whose exemplary rigorousness is noted in important works by Althusser). What is perhaps common to all three is a modality of reading, a certain sinking into the thickness of the signs that are inscribed in these texts (despite all their differences) outside a theological space of which they are themselves the limits.

24. In the second *Untimely Meditation,* whose topic is history (and to which Heidegger refers in *Being and Time,* pars. 74, 75, and especially 76, in order to elaborate his own concept of historicity), Nietzsche writes: "In order to define the degree and to fix the limit at which one must absolutely forget the past, without which it would become the gravedigger of the present, one would have to know exactly the exact measure of the plastic force of a man, a nation, a civilization. I mean the faculty to grow of oneself, to transform [*umzubilden*] and assimilate [*einzuverleiben*] the past and the foreign, . . . to reconstruct broken forms" (III 1, 247). *Einzuverleiben:* as a "carnal" taking up of a text and of that which is alienating in history. The problem of "translation" and of "philology" is of the same order as that of the "diversion" of instincts. "Body," "text": these are equally traversed by history, and in history they are lost, erased, covered over by "beliefs" of a theological origin. It is Nietzsche's achievement to have noted this "same" process at work in the censure (by diversion and displacement) of the body and of the text to the

profit of an abstract "subject." This subject is the double of the theological figure, if not his grimacing imitation ("the ape of God"). This process also profits a humanism which is only the exact counterweight of theology and its imaginary undoing [*dédommagement*]. Text, body: they have no relation to a proper name, be it that of an "author" or a "proprietor": once they are around the censor of which they are the "object" and once they have escaped from "ideological" networks in which they are taken and circumscribed, they give themselves as a signifying plurality, which requires a practice of deciphering of the signs for which the text and the body are the support and the arena. If the body is the anchoring point of any text, it is also, as signifier, that which takes place in the text. This is what Nietzsche saw when he announced the necessity for *Wissen sich einzuverleiben*—to incorporate knowledge into oneself—or when he asks the question, "To what degree can truth support embodiment?" (V 1, 56). He asks this because we carry inscribed in our body all the procedures of censure and diversion (the "errors") for which metaphysics has been the place of growth. Here Nietzsche's text multiply intersects that of Freud: inscription is the becoming-body (*le devenir-corps*) of the letter. What is it in us that refuses the Christian, the moralist, the ascetic priest? What is in the text that comes to interrupt the theological privilege of a truth already signified? This is the same question, played on the same stage; or, What in us wants truth, wants the hierarchy of values? (It is thus not a matter of a "biological myth" which is only an unheard-of diversion of Nietzsche's text itself, to what purpose we know.)

25. Cf. esp. "The dream of the yellow rays" as analyzed by Freud in *The Wolfman*. The reversal of wordings, the substitution of personal pronouns; all this grammatical work labors in unconscious productions. All the procedures that appear in Freud's texts are also in those of Nietzsche, sometimes with different names.

26. G. Deleuze is one of the only commentators on Nietzsche to have placed the accent on linguistics, which he properly names "active" (*Nietzsche et la philosophie,* 83ff). It is at once symptomatological, typological, and genealogical.

CHAPTER 4

■ The Form-Content Problem in Friedrich Nietzsche's Conception of Music

Curt Paul Janz

Translated by Thomas Heilke

The phenomenon of music occupied and indeed fascinated Friedrich Nietzsche his entire life. If one were to compile all the remarks concerning music from his works, notes, and letters, one would have two imposing volumes, in which, naturally, the specifically "musical" writings, including *The Birth of Tragedy out of the Spirit of Music, Richard Wagner in Bayreuth, The Case of Wagner, Nietzsche contra Wagner,* and the posthumous *Bayreuth Meditations at the Horizon* would constitute the focal points. One could nearly add *Thus Spoke Zarathustra,* the work that Nietzsche signified as his "symphony," a music in words that leads to the extensive volume of Nietzsche's compositions and experimental compositions.[1] The quantity of this work alone justifies the question about Nietzsche's relationship to music, which undoubtedly lies far above the ordinary musical enjoyment of enthusiastic dilettantes and is supported in its philosophical grasp by an incomparably wide knowledge and a nearly professional competence, perhaps on a level with Kierkegaard's.[2]

The meaningful and stimulating importance that the experience of music had for Nietzsche has been referred to repeatedly with roughly the same prominent quotations. We may forgo their renewed recitation: they are easily found through the indexes of Oehler and Schlechta.[3] That no emanation of the human spirit captivated Nietzsche for even nearly so long a time—from the earliest days of youth until far into his madness—has also been sufficiently set forth as biographical fact.[4] However the question of the *depth* of meaning of

Translated by permission of the publisher from *Philosophische Tradition im Dialog mit der Gegenwart: Festschrift für Hansjörg A. Salmony (zum 65. Geburtstag),* ed. Andreas Cesana and Olga Rubitschon (Basel, Boston, and Stuttgart: Birkhäuser Verlag AG, 1985).

Nietzsche's practical and intellectual-critical preoccupation with music has not yet been posed, let alone answered.

Despite its attested duration, its human relevance, and its emotional and intellectual intensity, one may assert that his preoccupation with music never reaches the depth and, above all, the decisiveness of his philosophical dispute with Plato "and his consequences" or the Paulinian dogmatic "and its consequences," or with their common denominator in the ground of metaphysics. The relationship, particularly between compositional practice and philosophical determination, remains ambivalent. In this relationship, however, Nietzsche's fundamental preoccupation with music touches directly on the determination of its nature, especially on a basic question concerning all artistic expression, the *question of the relationship between form and content,* that is, of the meaning of the aesthetic garb and the intent that is to be transmitted in this aesthetic garb from an "author" to the recipient(s). Georg Simmel seems to have achieved the most precise formulation of this question when he asks "whether the presentation of this *content* or the *presentation* of the content determines the sense and the worth of the work of art."[5] He summarizes the proposition of Schopenhauer "that the work of art exists for the sake of its content, namely its idea, that everything which one could name as the functional in art, that all interest in this, receives its tenure only from the interest in the idea that constitutes the respective content of the work"—a conception that Nietzsche will absolutely oppose.

Comprehended more narrowly, because it is related solely to music and has the tendency to restrict music to dogmatics, is the question, "Is music heteronomous or autonomous?" The Zurich music scholar Hans Conradin used the question as the title for his dissertation in 1939. He defines "autonomous" in the following manner: "Music has no foreign rules, and is connected to a datum that (1) cannot occur outside and without music and tones; and (2) is thus maximally different than nonmusical data."[6] This is the *l'art pour l'art* view of post-Romantic aesthetics. One must still consider, however, a "heteronomous" element: the composer, the person making use of acoustic signals, the "author," or in Nietzsche's terminology "the creator" (that with time becomes for him a *theourgos*). There can be hardly a doubt that in his contemporary, Richard Wagner, Nietzsche saw the prototype of this vision, a vision that intensified with the years. For Nietzsche the classicist, Wagner's retreat in Tribschen, near Lucerne, was in fact the "Isle of the Blessed."[7] Here, as he notes in a letter of 19 July 1870 to Cosima von Bülow, he feels the presence, "the existence of the gods in the house of the genius," and consciously (and pointedly) compares Wagner to Aeschylus. An additional heteronomous element is added thereby: the forming artist becomes a medium, a herald of transcendence. Nietzsche is still standing in the ancient tradition of the "heavenly singer" who is inspired by the muses (Apollo), and at the same time he betrays himself as a Romantic, an adept of the Schopenhauerian metaphysics of art, or, more particularly, of music, which he will surmount as philosopher but not as musician. Nietzsche's "creator" is not yet a free, arbitrarily creating artist—the road from Wagner to Zarathustra has not yet been traversed—and, moreover, he is subject to the rules of the orthography and syntax of his art. "As letters merely lumped together cannot form a proper word, let alone a good sentence, so the simple combination of tones cannot form a proper hymn." This is the position taken toward the meaning of form in a *musica enchiridion* of the late ninth century, mistakenly ascribed to Hucbald.[8] "Proper" form as the precondition of comprehensible formation, appearance of a content: is this *physei* or *nomoi*, by nature or by convention? If it were convention, acquired knowledge and ability, then Nietzsche would have to question it because of his philosophical method. But in the case of music he does not do so; on the contrary, in the development of his aesthetic of music he increasingly insists on the rigidity of the conventional forms—of which, as composer, he is not the master.

The question of the relationship between the form and content of music, within the purview of the question of the nature of music, appears to be as old as musical expression itself. From the very beginning of his experience, man has been impressed—and irritated—by the finely distinguished psychic reactions that acoustic signals—particular tones *and* sounds (drums)—are able to evoke, and this all the more so as these acoustic signals appear in a particular, recognizable order, be it rhythmic or melodic arrangements with dynamic enhancements. The form, the aesthetic appearance, is therefore inseparably bound up with the intelligibility of a "content," of an intent to arouse certain emotions or to awaken mystical notions. The oldest comprehensibly musical forms occur conspicuously in the service of religion, work, and (by instilling courage) battle.

The clear spirit of Greek philosophy soon took hold of the problem and developed the foundations for a theory of music that are still basic today (we still extensively use the Greek terms). Greek philosophy, however, also lost its way in the unfruitful speculations of numerology that are likewise continued here and there even today. In principle, two contrary conceptions stand opposed to one another: the noetic, which recognizes musical forms as something created and, for example, designates specially formed cultic songs as *nomoi,* or laws (just like the laws that are the foundations of a state), and the mystical, which conceives of the tonal relationships as images or representations of cosmic proportions in whole numbers, beginning with the ratios 1:2 (octave), 2:3 (fifth), 3:4 (fourth equals a tetrachord; and two tetrachords, a scale), whereby the numbers $1 + 2 + 3 + 4 = 10$, and so on.

The Middle Ages inherited much of this legacy, and the church, because of its dominance in spiritual matters, succeeded both in using music completely for its own purposes and in determining its content as well as its appropriate form. The church thereby was able to appeal to all five senses: holy water for the sense of touch, incense for the sense of smell, the host for the sense of taste, magnificent furnishings for the eye, and music for the ear; thus, the entire instrumentarium. In the Reformation, Swiss Protestantism thoroughly did away with all this. Not only the icons but also the organs disappeared from the church; instrumentally aided singing—at first accompanied only with string bass—was able gradually to reestablish itself again only in the early nineteenth century (Waedenswil, for example, obtained an organ again in 1826; in Basel, there were organs again somewhat earlier; and in Bernbiet, cornets and trombones took their place).[9] The musical Luther thought otherwise. As a composer of church, that is, religious, battle songs (his chorale "A Mighty Fortress" is decidedly a battle song), he remained closer to music than the Swiss, even if he justified it only as a vehicle of proclamation, as is clear from his preface to the *Little Book of Spiritual Songs* of Johann Walter.[10] Thus, even in the post-Reformation church, music remained an *ancillia ecclesiae,* as it had since the time of Augustine. However, even in this context the great spirit of Johann Sebastian Bach was able to give it a greatness and an independent formal and substantive development that lifted it far above the limits imposed on it by dogma. Even in his "wordly" instrumental works, however, he never had to take the large step across into the pagan arts that had been flowering since the Renaissance. The same could not be said for his contemporary (in time, age, and nationality), Georg Friedrich Handel (born in Sachsen-Thüringen, 1685), with his operas and concerts. The entire, rapidly ascending development of classical and romantic European music of the eighteenth and nineteenth centuries that followed was based upon the work of these two greats: they were followed by Haydn, Mozart, Beethoven, and, in Nietzsche's time, by Wagner and Brahms.

This was the intellectual situation, the position of music into which Nietzsche was born and that he first experienced in Lutheran-

Reformed Naumburg as the child of a young pastor's widow. In addition, his earliest and formative musical impression is closely interwoven with an event that pervades Nietzsche's entire being, feeling, and thinking: the early death of his revered father as a result of a brain disorder. Even nine years after the event, he writes, concerning the funeral ceremony: "At one o'clock in the afternoon, the ceremony began with a great ringing of bells. Oh, their hollow pealing will never fade from my ears, never will I forget the somberly thundering melody of the song 'Jesu meine Zuversicht!' The tones of the organ echoed through the halls of the church." In December of the same year, 1858, he attempts a choral arrangement in four voices of this hymn.[11] The musical impression thus deeply penetrated the child who was not yet five years old, a remarkable fact which certainly presupposes an unusual impressionability and receptivity to music. In ordinary terms, Nietzsche was "deeply musical."

He describes another musical impression, no doubt from the autumn of 1857, in the same recollections. It is of Mozart's *Requiem,* Handel's *Messiah* and *Judas Maccabeus,* and Haydn's *Creation.* These he experienced not only as externally resplendent productions, but to some degree as an "intruder," quietly, for himself, turning inward, somewhere in the dark, anonymous space of the Naumburg cathedral into which he was able to steal during rehearsals. A curious passion for a thirteen year old! At the same time, he received lessons on the piano. He demonstrated ability; although the actual lessons did not last long and therefore could not have progressed very far, Nietzsche developed into a better than average pianist whose rich imagination in improvisation and whose unusual talent for tonal nuances were particularly noted. The piano became one of his most important means of expression in his relations with himself and his surroundings. It also afforded him an immediate access to composers, particularly Haydn, Mozart, Beethoven, Schubert, and especially Schumann.

Soon, he felt compelled to express what had been so intensively experienced. It could not be put into words. Musical things already now proved to be adequately expressible only in music. Thus, he himself seized upon music as the genuine medium, and he began to compose. In rapid succession, we find attempts at motets, then a requiem, a mass, and extensive sections for a Christmas oratorio, until, finally, on July 4, 1860, he succeeds with a "Miserere" in a notable arrangement for five voices, a capella, in the style of Palestrina. These early efforts were all undertaken along the lines of sacred music.

With these works, Nietzsche now came upon the problem that is inherent in all art: the meaning of form and its "technical" mastery.

How does one write for piano, orchestra, or choir voices? How do tension and resolution come into being in the course of the harmonies, how are the voices to be employed against and with one another? All these questions of orthography, theory of harmony, art of composition, and syntax now presented themselves.

Even in youth, Nietzsche's drive to get to the root of a matter reveals itself. He does not merely take note of Beethoven as a pianist but also concerns himself with the man and his life. Thus, he discovers Beethoven's teacher, Johann Georg Albrechtsberger (1736–1809) and Albrechtsberger's *Concise Method for Learning the Figured Bass* (1792). Nietzsche procured the work and with it taught himself the fundamentals of harmonic phrases and counterpoint. The effect of the newly won knowledge is immediately clear in his sporadically overpowering inclination toward formal constructions and four-part fugues in his drafts for the Christmas oratorio. The religious motivation for his composition, which involved the presentation of predetermined content, thus wanes, and he departs in the direction of an independent music, developed from its own laws of form. Soon after his confirmation, which he experiences as an aesthetic intoxication, he turns to these earlier drafts and arranges them in a fantasia for four-hand piano under the motto "Pain is the Keynote of Nature." The piece is in three parts, following the Italian schema of the overture, fast/slow/fast, in which the slow middle piece is composed from the scene "The Death of the Kings" from the drafts for the Christmas oratorio. It is a piece that Nietzsche later (summer 1882) calls "parsifalesque." The phenomenon of "death" appears forebodingly on the horizon; an elegiacal keynote pervades Nietzsche's compositions—including the later ones, and in particular his songs. With the "conversion" of these segments of the Christmas oratorio into a free piano fantasy, he similarly overcomes his attachment to the piety of his closest circle. And later, much later, in the *Twilight of the Idols,* we read: "Nowhere have the two great European narcotics, alcohol and Christianity, been abused more dissolutely [than in Germany]."

Nietzsche had already taken a preparatory step beforehand with his "Miserere." It was indeed a "Miserere," but in the style of Palestrina. Here, as in much of his understanding of music at this time, the influence of his friend, Gustav Krug, was essential. Krug was pursuing comprehensive studies of music, at this time of Palestrina (Giovanni Pierluigi da Palestrina, 1525–94). Palestrina has passed into the history of music as one of the great reformers and rescuers of music (Hans Pfitzner dedicated an opera to him in this capacity in 1917), who, through his simple and artful musical style, succeeded in securing for music an important structure and development peculiar to it and in giving it its genuine forms, even within its role as a servant to congregational singing, governed by the Gregorian style.

It was Gustav Krug who in April 1861 confronted Nietzsche with the newly published piano arrangement of Wagner's *Tristan,* and thereby with Wagner as such. Nietzsche let himself be drawn by Krug into a veritable frenzy of agitated musical passion and possession. With their simple, rudimentary musical training, neither one recognizes or, indeed, is able to recognize that Wagner adheres throughout to the classical rules of orthography and syntax, that he manipulates them with greatest precision and virtuosity. Thus, Nietzsche develops the impression that only expression, unbridled passion, or naked content rule here, and he reacts with timidly expressed skepticism, without ever again being able to free himself entirely from the spell of this intoxication. There is much bitterness contained in what follows the sentence quoted above from *The Twilight of the Idols,* where he continues: "Recently even a third has been added—one that alone would be sufficient to dispatch all fine and bold flexibility of the spirit—music, our constipated, constipating German music." This remark is aimed not only at Wagner but also at Brahms. It is a defense against his own disposition; as a musician, he himself was and remained a Romantic, indeed a German Romantic. This is shown in a number of compositions of his youth, the short piano pieces, "Album Pages" or "Songs without Words," and the songs, whose musical expression and content must be attributed throughout to the imitation of Schumann—not Wagner. As a composer, Nietzsche was never a Wagnerian. They are Nietzsche's best pieces because he had no problems of form to master here. The form was given by the pattern of the text, poems, most often taken from contemporary authors, predominantly in stanza form. Yet, in their musical inspiration the pieces are independent throughout, certainly not recitations of texts. The musical consideration is demonstrably primary, although certainly prompted by the mood given in the content of the poem, yet in its rhythmic and melodic structure often directly contradicting the words or the meter of the verse. He was successful in the musical presentation of the deeper content but not in the formal agreement with the textual pattern, which he treated freely and altered in translation (Petoefi, Pushkin), while employing the German originals untouched.

During this time, two compositions were also brought into being that were decidedly heteronomous, that is, determined by a non-musical program. After Easter 1861 at Pforta, Nietzsche was to deal with the legendary Gothic King, Ermanarich. The character and fate of this brutal tyrant excites him; Ermanarich receives features of Etzel and becomes nearly a Hun. At this time, Nietzsche must have become acquainted with Franz Liszt's symphonic poem *Hungaria,* perhaps interpreting it himself from the piano arrangement. In September, he decides upon a composition. In this regard, he writes in *Germania,* the chronicle of his student union, for 1862:

> I was still too moved to write poetry, and not yet distanced enough to produce an objective drama; but in music I successfully expressed my mood, in which the saga of Ermanarich has fully incarnated itself. . . . However, I have depicted neither Goths nor Germans: they are—I dare assert it—Hungarians. The material is borne from the Germanic world into the Hungarian Pusztes, into the fiery Hungarian soul.

The music is of an unbridled passion that slavishly follows the given dramatic program that provides the background for scene after scene—it could serve as cinematic music—and dispenses with every genuine musical structure or form; in large portions the musical meter is not even correct. (Nietzsche heard and conceived this music for a full orchestra, but since he was unable to write the orchestration, he wrote a piano version for four instruments in the first draft—a so-called particell—and its second, final form was for two-hand piano, a "piano reduction," as it were.) It is Nietzsche's most extreme contribution to contemporary program music (with which Richard Strauss is also associated). He feels only too distinctly that with this composition he has distanced himself considerably from his classical models and forthwith attaches to his explanations the most important beginnings of a critique: "The pressure and drive of the passions, ending with their sudden transitions and stormy outbursts, brims over with harmonic monstrosities, concerning which I dare not judge." Here, something external to music, that which is to be presented, an event, dominates as "content."

At the end of December 1863, a decidedly melancholic mood finds expression in "New Year's Eve," a fantasia for violin and piano, which is then followed at the beginning of 1864 with melancholic poems. But no "program" or dramatic action underlies this composition; it is exhausted in the painting of moods. A year later, shortly before Christmas 1864, he writes home to his mother and sister—he is a lonely student sitting in his room in Bonn—in a similar mood:

> Do you still remember how we passed last Christmas together in Gorenzen? Did I not say then, that we would

probably not be together again for over a year? Now it has happened. It was beautiful in Gorenzen; the house and the village in the snowfall, the evening church services, the profusion of melodies in my head, Uncle Oskar, the muskrat pelt, the wedding, and me in my nightgown, the cold, and many gay and serious things. All these things together bring on a pleasant mood. When I play my "New Year's Eve," I perceive this mood in the music.

In the introductory section, which has the effect of a prelude, Nietzsche succeeded with a head-theme that was suited to the beginnings of a study of motif and to which he would return twice more in later years ("Reminiscence of a New Year's Eve," 1871, and "Manfred Meditation," 1872). After 1865, Nietzsche the composer is silent for years, because now Nietzsche the thinker begins to reflect on music, and he becomes aware of the form-content problem. He begins to move away from the Romantic conception of music, emerging as a philosophical pioneer of a formal aesthetic of music that finally, decades after Nietzsche, is completed in the serial constructions of Joseph Matthias Hauer and Arnold Schoenberg.

The speculative basis of this transformation in his relation to music is certainly in part his newly developing knowledge of the relevant literature of antiquity, including the pre-Socratics and, most important, Plato, but also Aristotle and Quintilian, to name only a few.[12] However, the intractable contemporary debates concerning the "new Germans" (Wagner and Liszt), who were cited—nearly dogmatically—by the Viennese music critic Eduard Hanslick, with whose basic booklet *On the Musically Beautiful* Nietzsche became acquainted in 1865 (possibly already in 1862), may have had a more decisive effect.[13] When Nietzsche finally entered into a close personal relationship with Wagner (the word "friendship" misses the mark here), he was fully caught up in the whirlpool of wild and hateful partisan battles. The Romantic aesthetic of music emphasizes the value of symbols and the effect of music on the emotions, psyche, and subconscious; this is the antithesis to the preceding "classical" aesthetic, whose understanding of music was trenchantly characterized by Georg Christian Weitzler (1739–75) in his tract "Thought on Tones": "Music has no higher purpose than to be music."[14]

Knowledge of Schopenhauer's metaphysic of art, that is, of music, may be presumed here. The definition of Wilhelm Heinrich Wackenroder (1773–98) may be less well known: "The darker and more mysterious its language, the more powerfully does musical art affect us, and the more fully does it bring all the forces of our being into turmoil."[15]

Various concepts that Nietzsche, sparked by the precise remarks of Hanslick, had to clarify for himself become confused with one another. What is the essence of music, and what is its purpose? Is the excitation of emotions truly its essence? Hardly—it is one of its possible purposes. Is the presentation of a content the purpose or the essence of music? In part—since it can present a variety of contents. Further, what is content, what can be the content of music? Here Hanslick separates clearly genuine musical content from an "object," that is, something nonmusical, which he categorically excludes. But in his rigor, Hanslick overlooks the possibility of music's awakening specific ideas (of a pictorial nature) through associative elements. To be sure, these associative elements rest on convention and tradition, but they are present and usable. One may think, among others, of the use made of Gregorian melismas or Protestant chorales, bells (Parsifal), the "kingly" trumpets, hunting horns, war drums (shepherds') flutes and shawms (oboes), folk styles, and so on. (Trombones, for example, were long used only in sacred music, and Mozart first brings them to opera in *The Magic Flute* in the scenes with priests to create a sacral mood.) Hanslick passes over these possibilities, used even by "classical" composers such as Beethoven and even Johann Sebastian Bach, possibilities through which the young Nietzsche could feel himself justified in his illustrative musical efforts, to say nothing of the spreading contemporary "program music" of Liszt or Berlioz. Nietzsche held the latter in high honor and let himself be introduced to him in 1876 in Geneva by the conductor Hugo von Senger, who had been fond of Nietzsche. Hanslick's dogmatic assertion, "Art must before all things present a *thing of beauty*," must have left little impression on him, yet it confronted him with the demand for a definition of the "beautiful," which no one has yet satisfactorily and finally been able to provide (Kant's *Critique of Judgment*, too, does not answer the question in the end).[16] For example, can an artistically complete presentation of the crucified Christ, grippingly realistic in its effect, therefore also be called "beautiful"? Here, the reception of the aesthetic form (the presentation) and that which is presented clearly part.

The same thing may also appear in music, even if the ideal of the balancing harmony, of the culminating beauty of the euphony, was held the longest and most tenaciously, particularly in music. An example of how Nietzsche broke through this ideal may be found in his "Manfred Meditation" of 1872, about which the conductor Hans von Bülow wrote him on 24 July 1872:

Your Manfred Meditation is a most extreme exemplar of fantastic extravagance, the most unpleasant and antimusical of writings on music sheets that has come before my eyes in a long time. . . . Do you consciously mock uninterruptedly all the rules of linking notes, from higher syntax down to ordinary orthography? If you truly have a passionate desire to express yourself in the language of sound, then it is imperative to acquire the primary elements of this language. . . . If you . . . really intended your aberration in the field of composition in earnest . . . then at least compose only vocal music, and allow the words to steer the boat that drives you about the wild tonal sea.

Nietzsche replied three months later (rough draft of a letter from the end of October 1872):

I have been writing music of my own since childhood, I possess theory through the study of Albrechtsberger, I have written fugues (en masse), and I am capable of pure style—to a certain degree of purity. However, such a barbaric and excessive desire, a mixture of defiance and irony overcame me from time to time, that I—as little as you—could not clearly discern what was meant to be serious, caricature, or mockery in the last music. I have given it to my closest housemates . . . as a pamphlet of the best program music. And the original directions for the character of the mood were "cannibalido" . . . of my music I know only one thing: with it I become master of a mood, which, if left unappeased, would perhaps be more harmful.

And in the letter of 29 October 1872:

Various things likely were put to paper in such a confused manner because of technical ineptitude, that every sense of propriety and purity of a true musician must thereby be offended. Remember that since my earliest youth until now . . . I have always found great joy in my music. . . . It has always been a problem for me, whence this originates. There is something so irrational in it. . . . Precisely in this Manfred music I had such a grim, indeed mockingly pathetical feeling; it was like the pleasure of an infernal irony! My other "music" is . . . more human, gentler and also purer. Even the title was ironic—I am hardly able to think of the Byronic *Manfred*, which I marveled at as a boy as nearly my favourite poem, as anything other than a raving formless and monotone absurdity.

107

Nietzsche's clearly documented aversion to Byron is a part of his attempt to overcome the Romantic in himself, and for this he calls upon music—the art in which Romanticism realized itself most purely—as a means to pour himself out with unrestrained ferocity. He will do it again in the days of the breakdown in Turin. That this is not a "sympton of illness" is indicated by the existence of the same phenomenon in the *Ermanarich Symphony* of the seventeen year old. The apologies and protestations directed at Bülow indicate that, as a musician, Nietzsche was taken aback by the critiques and theories of Hanslick, whose tract he evidently studied again with lasting effect during this "physical," although not yet "spiritual," separation from Wagner as a result of Wagner's definitive move from Tribschen to Bayreuth. This is particularly so for Hanslick's treatment of opera. He maintains:

> Opera is primarily music, not drama. One can easily assess this by the particular, greatly varying intentions with which one attends a drama in contrast to an opera of the same plot. The neglect of the musical part will always affect us far more deeply.

And further:

> The greatest cultural-historical significance for us of the well-known dispute between the Gluckists and Piccinists lies in the fact that through the antagonism of its two elements, the musical and the dramatic, the inner conflict of opera is comprehensively articulated for the first time.[17]

Hanslick extensively cites Grillparzer's discussions of the relationship between text and music in opera, and Nietzsche also takes up these suggestions. In a letter of 7 December 1872, he strongly and with praise refers his friend, Rohde, to Grillparzer's *Studies of Aesthetics:* "He is nearly one of ours!" He can no longer free himself from the fundamental dispute between Gluck and Piccini, and when Heinrich Köselitz (Peter Gast) comes to Basel in the autumn of 1875 to study with Nietzsche, the first topic of their discussions is this Parisian operatic quarrel of 1780.[18] In the winter of 1887–88, he returns to this theme in connection with his rejection of Wagner, under the influence of Bizet's *Carmen,* and with an unequivocal preference for Piccini over Gluck.[19] 1872 is a decisive year in general for Nietzsche's understanding of music. At the beginning of January, his first philosophical work and last contribution to Romantic aesthetics, *The Birth of Tragedy out of the Spirit of Music,* appeared. In April, he completes the questionable "Manfred Meditation" (in a setting for four-hand piano but intended for a full orchestra), with which he provokes Bülow's sobering critique; at the end of April, the Wagners (Richard and Cosima) leave Tribschen, and as a result the personal contacts and the fascination diminish; the query of the composer, Hugo von Senger, the conductor in Geneva, whether Nietzsche would compose a text for a cantata for him, causes Nietzsche for the first time to take a clear position concerning Wagner's significance in the history of music, a question that never again left him and that still in 1888 in his short work, *The Case of Wagner,* would find an unusual answer, which itself had effects far into the future. To Hugo von Senger he wrote:

> With regard to this . . . in my capacity as a philosopher who considers the contemporary development of music in connection with a culture to which we should aspire, I have a few personal thoughts concerning contemporary composition in great dramatic musical styles. I am well aware that in the professional musical journals Wagner's significance is attributed to his having destroyed the old forms of sonata, symphony, quartet, etc., and that, indeed, the end as such of pure instrumental music is supposed to have come with him. If from this we are to draw the conclusion that the composer must now necessarily change over to theatrical music, then I am always very apprehensive and suspect a confusion. Everyone must speak in the manner that befits him. . . . Therefore, I am delighted that you have the courage to take seriously the form of the sonata, which has been held under such suspicion of late.

In 1873, the *Bayreuth Meditations at the Horizon* revealed the still-intense personal ties to Wagner and the future of his works. At the same time, Nietzsche finally completes his efforts at expression through the medium of music with a new composition. If "Reminiscence of a New Year's Eve" (1871) and the "Manfred Meditation" rested thematically (head-theme) on a recourse to the "New Year's Eve" of 1863, then this new "Hymn to Friendship" offers, both formally and substantively, a completely new discovery. Outwardly, the "symphonic poem" (again drafted in a setting for four-hand piano and arranged in a piano setting but intended for orchestra and chorus) is clearly divided into well-proportioned sections: prelude, hymn (a chorale), first interlude, second verse of hymn, second interlude (same time signature as the first), third verse of hymn. Particularly in the second interlude, Nietzsche works at developing the musical techniques of a motif, variation, and the figured chorale under a quasi-*cantus firmus* of the hymnodic melody. He attempts to fulfill Hanslick's definition: "The content of music is the tonally moved forms"; or "tonal formation" is the free "creation of the spirit from intellectually accessible forms."[20] This alone was not sufficient for Nietzsche; he gives the parts "programmatic" titles: to the prelude, he affixes "Procession of the Friends to the Temple of Friendship"; to the first interlude, "As in Happy-Sorrowful Remembrance"; to the second interlude, "Like a Divination Concerning the Future"; and concerning the hymn, he still says in 1887 (in the edition for chorus and orchestra in the arrangement by Peter Gast of the text of Lou Salomé's "Prayer to Life" of 1882): "May this piece of music serve as a completion where the word of the philosophers, by the nature of words, must necessarily remain unclear: the affect of my philosophy expresses itself in this hymn" (draft of a letter to Felix Mottl). The original text of the hymn from 1873 appears to have been lost.

Nietzsche acknowledges the primacy of music: it is not clarified through the word but clarifies the word, leading beyond words into realms of experience that are no longer rationally accessible, but it does not thereby attain formal and musical-substantive independence, "autonomy." In this respect, Nietzsche remains, as musician and composer, a Romantic; musically, he remains close to Wagner but fundamentally rejects his aesthetic of music and even more his intensity and realm of expression, the unconscious, or the "intuition" ("logic of the lower levels of consciousness," in Baumgarten). (In *The Case of Wagner,* he mockingly comments on all the things that "Wagnerian initiates" must "intuit" and are able "to intuit" through Wagner's technique of leitmotif, that is, through music.) But with this rejection he must at the same time take a position against himself. The struggle against Wagner is tied to the struggle against himself, against his own musical heritage and home. If one sees this conflict, one can understand that which is unpleasantly screeching, caustic, and cynical in *The Case of Wagner,* a work that ranks among the most important steps in the intellectual-historical development of music from Romanticism to modernity. Naturally, it would be inappropriate to see Wagner's work and conception of the arts as "false" or "exposed" through this work. Today, we can and must assume the position of the historian. Wagner's work was as right in his own time as, for example, Johann Sebastian Bach's *St. Matthew Passion* was in his. Wagner represents an important aspect of the musical conception of Romanticism in a nearly exemplary manner.

One must also recognize in the total picture of the nineteenth century the flowering of Germanic studies, of a sort that would no longer be possible today since it would come under suspicion of nationalism or indeed chauvinism. (The various national styles of music also arise at this time.) Wagner let himself be stimulated and sustained precisely by this concern with German culture; indeed, he dedicated his work to it. He created his mythical cosmos, a cosmos sui generis beyond our reality, out of the *spirit* of Romanticism, and it is therefore a complete misunderstanding, a forgetting of the premises, when recent editors attempt to turn this mythical world into an allegory of the *society* of the nineteenth century and psychologically to classify the mythical figures. This is more appropriate to the other great musical dramatist of that time, Guiseppe Verdi (born in the same year as Wagner and Nietzsche's father: 1813), whose protagonists never operate "on principle" nor are led by a transcendent force (as with Wagner), but always from human passions or dispositions (Leonora is purely love, the Duke only a playboy, etc.). And it is precisely this that the "modern" psychologist, Nietzsche, seeks and praises in Bizet's opera *Carmen.* But he also finds something else: the comprehensive musical form, which is also present in Wagner, but in greater dimensions. *Carmen* is once again a "number opera" in accordance with the classical model. Every musical aria and ensemble is formally and thematically self-contained, independent. The musical numbers occur where, basically, there is nothing to compose, tied together with dialogues that were only subsequently composed by E. Giraud as recitatives. In *The Case of Wagner,* we read in this regard: "This music is . . . rich. It is precise. It builds, organizes, finishes: thus it constitutes the opposite of the polyp in music, the 'infinite melody.'" Above all, this is directed at Wagner's acts that are through-composed, that is, that have new music for each stanza. As a historian—even if of his own stamp—Nietzsche knows nevertheless that Wagner is a symptom, a shining representative of a time, that he, Nietzsche, is preparing to leave behind him. In sections 10 and 11 of the same work, we find:

> Hegel is a taste—and not merely a German, but a European taste. A taste Wagner comprehended—to which he felt equal—which he immortalized.—He merely applied it to music—he invented a style for himself charged with "infinite meaning"—he became *heir of Hegel.*—Music as "idea." . . . The same human type that raved about Hegel, today raves about Wagner, in his school they even *write* Hegelian. . . . I have explained where Wagner belongs—*not* in the history of music. What does he signify nevertheless in that history? *The emergence of the actor in music.* . . . Never

yet has the integrity of musicians, their "authenticity" been put to the test so dangerously.

His motherly friend, Malwida von Meysenbug, reacted violently to *The Case of Wagner.* Nietzsche replied equally violently on 20 October 1888:

> Have you not noticed at all that for ten years I have been a kind of court of conscience for German musicians, that in every possible place I have planted artistic integrity, refined taste, and the deepest hatred against the repulsive sexuality of Wagnerian music?

Thereupon follows a praise for the music of his friend Heinrich Köselitz, alias Peter Gast, whose clean technical work is sufficient for him. He does not perceive it as a shortcoming that Köselitz has nothing to say. In contrast to the actor, the incident, a "heteronomous" element; for "authenticity," the purely musical substance of the music, worked with "artistic integrity"; we may signify it as "faultless in the artificial." Whither does this lead?

If we consider generally the development of the concept of art in the past decades, we see everywhere the aspiration toward the artificial postulated by Nietzsche, an aspiration toward artistically autonomous arrangements in rigid forms with a neglect of content—reaching a complete absence of content, pure form play, indeed, aleatory music, in which the artist finally gives up the construction of his work to chance.

Free-form sculptures do not represent someone or something, nor do they have any historical or human references: they are "accents"— for example, in a park—or they play with a principle of form. Painting no longer serves the presentation of something recognizable, it passes through forms and chromatic contrasts—they are "autonomous." Melchior Berri could still say of his teacher, Hayot (Paris): "He knew how to give the appropriate character to every detail, so that one could see from the single parts to what kind of building they belonged."[21] This embodiment of intention is hardly represented any longer in functional architecture, or at least, is covered over by principles of form, as, for example, the City Theater in St. Gallen, which is dominated by the hexagon to the last detail.

Music is no longer a medium of communication with which the composer conveys or produces psychic conditions, but it becomes a construction, pure form, play and speculation with tonal constellations. In the publication of the Basel Chamber Orchestra of 1928, we find a typical statement: "Music does not want to be individual expression in the Romantic sense. It recognizes nothing. The personality of the composer remains in the background. It is the play of musical elements," for example, a twelve-note scale.[22]

In 1913, August Halm states: "We have before us a drama of forces, but not a drama of persons or personifications. . . . We are caught up with the will, not, however, with that which the person Beethoven willed, desired, or suffered and endured, but with that which was willed through him."[23] And in 1920 Walther Krug writes: "The direction toward the specifically musical accordingly forms the starting point of aesthetic thinking . . . an intellectuality that denies itself every interpretation and only permits the general presentation of the working of forces."[24]

In 1883, the year of *Zarathustra,* Anton von Webern and Joseph Hauer are born. The latter, as a composer of forty-four "Tropes" from six-note scales, no doubt carried the "absolutization" of music, its autonomy and "artistic integrity," the furthest. Certainly, Nietzsche did not desire the descent to these extremes and would not have participated in completing it. For that, he was and remained too much a Romantic in his musical foundations. We may assess how long his path was from this attachment to Romanticism to a defense of a formal, autonomous art if we consider once more the convictions of his youth, as he wrote them down in August 1858:

> God has given us music so that *first* we may be led upward.
> Music unites all attributes in itself; it can uplift, it can flirt, it
> can cheer, indeed, with its gentle, plaintive sounds it is able
> to break the roughest disposition. But its chief purpose is
> that it directs our thoughts toward higher things, that it lifts
> us up, even unsettles us. This is preeminently the purpose
> of church music. . . . But then the disposition also becomes
> cheerful and drives away bleak thoughts. Over whom does a
> still, clear peace not descend when he hears the simple
> melodies of Haydn! Compositional art often speaks more
> forcefully to us in tones than poetry does in words, and it
> seizes the most secret folds of the heart. But everything that
> God gives us can only afford us blessings if we use it prop-
> erly and wisely. . . . One must consider all people who
> despise them to be spiritless, creatures similar to animals.
> May this, the most magnificent of God's gifts, ever be my
> companion on my life's path. . . . May praise be sung by us
> to God forever, who offers us this beautiful pleasure!

Four years later, in September or October 1862, Nietzsche writes:

> *On the Nature of Music:* When one hears a fugue by Fux or
> Albrechtsberger, how the notes march up at command and
> withdraw with stiff plaits and leggings, soon set on one an-
> other and stumble, soon leap, skip, then gravely strut about
> and make compliments until finally one note stands still, a
> field marshall on a stallion, who lets the others chase
> past him: if you now believe you are standing before a pup-
> pet theater and that you see the marionettes dancing on
> wires, . . . if you grin at those who were able to live in such
> a formal structure and considered it to be the peak of mu-
> sic, as the only true music: some people shake their heads
> at you and your sense also when you stand there as if
> shattered by the power of the music before the passionate
> surges of Tristan and Isolde. Both Albrechtsberger's
> counterfugues and Wagnerian love scenes are music; both
> must have something in common, the nature of music. Feel-
> ing is no standard at all for music.

The openness of the eighteen-year-old aesthetician toward the ex-
panse of the possibilities of music, from the theory of affects of the
Baroque to the "artistic integrity" of strict fugue composition, is surprising. The last sentence, bringing feelings as the judge of aesthetics
into question, suggests already in 1862 a text from Hanslick, for there
we find a very similar formulation with the same conclusion.

Did Nietzsche solve the form-content problem for music? No, for it
cannot ultimately be solved. Judgments such as "true" or "false" are
unfounded. They lead inevitably into the dogma "music is . . ." or
"music should . . ." under which music has suffered at all times, and
not only music. Every dogma in the field of human fantasy is a viola-
tion because it is a limiting and a foreshortening of the object toward
or against which it is directed.

Every epoch, in accordance with its total intellectual situation or,
most important of all, its relationship to the arts, particularly music,
possesses its own judgment in these matters, depending on what the
people of the particular epoch need and expect from music. The
"weighing" of form and content is subject to the greatest variation.
This depends in part on religious, philosophical, and economic foundations that influence the "horizon of expectations." This horizon of
expectations constitutes a chapter of its own in the history of the reception and interpretation of art.[25]

Did Nietzsche co-found and promote the transition from the Romantic to the intellectual-functional "modern" horizon of expecta-

tions, or did he merely help philosophically to consummate an intellectual-historical movement? This question of conscience for the historian must remain open here (at best, it could be answered dogmatically). In our understanding of Nietzsche, it is only certain that his lifelong dialogue with the basic problems of music was one of the strong and essential driving forces of his turbulent intellectual unrest.

■ NOTES

1. Friedrich Nietzsche, *Der Musikalische Nachlass*, ed. Curt Paul Janz (Basel: Barenreiter, 1976).

2. Søren Kierkegaard, *Either-Or*, trans. Howard and Edna Hong (Princeton: Princeton University Press, 1987). Cf. Curt Paul Janz, "Kierkegaard und das Musikalische, dargestellt an seiner Auffassung von Mozarts *Don Juan*," *Die Musikforschung* 10 (1957): 364ff.

3. Richard Oehler, *Nietzsche-Register* (Stuttgart: Kröner, 1943), and Karl Schlechta, *Nietzsche-Index zu den Werken in drei Bänden* (Munich: Hanser, 1978–79).

4. Curt Paul Janz, *Friedrich Nietzsche: Biographie*, 3 vols. (Munich: Hanser, 1978–79).

5. Georg Simmel, *Schopenhauer und Nietzsche—Ein Vortragszyklus* (Leipzig: Duncker & Humblot, 1907), 121.

6. *Ist die Musik heteronom oder autonom?* (Dissertation, Zurich, 1939), 14.

7. Hesiod, *Works and Days* 171; Pindar, *Olympian Odes* 2:71.

8. Cited in Rudolf Schaefke, *Geschichte der Musikaesthetik in Umrissen* (Berlin: Hesse, 1934), 223.

9. Friedrich Jacob, "Der Kontrabass in der Lokalmusikgeschichte Zürichs," in *Festschrift für Hans Conradin* (Bern: Haupt, 1983), 58.

10. Günther Birkener, "Luthers Verhältniss zum 'Geistlichen Gesangbuchlein' von Johann Walter und zum Erfurter Enchiridion von 1524," in *Festschrift für Hans Conradin*, 21ff.

11. Nietzsche, *Der musikalische Nachlass*, 194.

12. See Schaefke's *Geschichte der Musikaesthetik*, which is well-founded and supported with much documentary evidence.

13. Eduard Hanslick, *Vom musikalischen Schönen—Ein Beitrag zur Revision der Aesthetik der Tonkunst* (Wiesbaden: Breitkopf, 1966).

14. Schaefke, *Geschichte der Musikaesthetik*, 379.

15. Ibid., 354.

16. Hanslick, *Vom musikalischen Schönen*, 7.

17. Ibid., 50, 51.

18. Janz, *Nietzsche*, 1:696.

19. Ibid., 570ff.

20. Hanslick, *Vom musikalischen Schönen*, 59.

21. Cited in Georg Germann, "Melchior Berris Rathausentwurf für Bern

1833," in *Basler Zeitschrift für Geschichte und Altertumskunde* (Basel: Werner & Bischoff, 1969), 272.

22. *Alte und neue Musik,* vol. 2, *50 Jahre Baseler Kammerorchester* (Zürich: Atlantis, 1977).

23. August Halm, *Von Zwei Kulturen der Musik,* 2d ed. (Munich: Muller, 1920); cited in Schaefke, *Geschichte der Musikaesthetik,* 401.

24. Walther Krug, in *Die Neue Musik* (Erlenbach: Rentsch, 1920), 106ff.

25. Klaus Kropfinger, "Klassik-Rezeption in Berlin, 1800–1830," in *Studien zur Musikgeschichte Berlins im frühen 19. Jahrhundert,* ed. C. Dahlhaus (Regensburg: Bosse, 1980).

CHAPTER 5

■ Nietzsche's Musical Politics

Michael Allen Gillespie

Friedrich Nietzsche's importance for the political and intellectual life of the twentieth century is widely recognized but little agreed upon: he is exalted by some as the prophet of a new age and harbinger of a higher humanity and decried by others as a dangerous madman and spiritual father of Nazism. In part, this is the consequence of the use and abuse of his thought in the ideological struggles of our times, but it also clearly reflects something deeper. After all, he himself proclaimed, "I am dynamite!" The ideological debate has, however, made an adequate understanding of the revolutionary character of his thought difficult. Its meaning for politics has been especially obscured. One might attempt to come to terms with this question by delineating the place of Nietzsche's political philosophy in the context of his philosophy as a whole, but such a procedure is called into question by Nietzsche's claim to have gone beyond philosophy and thus beyond political philosophy. Philosophy, as Nietzsche sees it, has come to an end in the abyss nihilism. He argues that consequently we must abandon philosophy and formulate a new way of thinking that will lead us out of this abyss.

The model for such a new way of thinking Nietzsche discovers in the prephilosophic thought of the Greeks, in poetry or music. Such a music in Nietzsche's view informed the Greek world and can perhaps serve as the basis for a transformation of our own. This essay attempts to show through an examination of *Twilight of the Idols* that Nietzsche's thought is fundamentally musical and that his political teaching can best be understood not as political philosophy but as a musical politics.

My deepest thanks are due to Professor Lowell Lindgren for reviewing and correcting the musical sections of this essay.

117

TWILIGHT OF THE IDOLS

Although written in August 1888, *Twilights of the Idols* did not appear until late January 1889.[1] The work thus appeared only *after* Nietzsche's breakdown and was generally regarded as a work of madness.[2] This soon became the standard view of *Twilight* and of Nietzsche's late works in general, owing largely to his sister's distortions of his texts and manuscripts. Julius Kaften, who visited Nietzsche in August 1888, remarked that he noted no signs of insanity, but this view was exceptional, and it was not until scholars were able to examine Nietzsche's manuscripts in the 1930s that a new interpretation began to emerge.[3] Unfortunately, Nazism, the war, and the necessities of reconstruction delayed the reappraisal of Nietzsche's thought until the 1950s.[4]

Even then, severe questions were raised about Nietzsche's philosophical legitimacy. Following Jaspers, many argued that his thought was fundamentally contradictory.[5] Others argued, in part because of Nietzsche's own denigration of all systems and systematizers, that his thought was intentionally unsystematic and therefore "fragmentary" or "aphoristic."[6] Such an assertion is questionable, however, for Nietzsche is equally scornful of such a fragmentary style (VI 3, 21). Moreover, his letters and *Nachlass* indicate that he had a deep concern with the structural integrity of his thought and work.[7]

This view of Nietzsche as an unsuccessful philosopher arises out of a failure to grasp the true character of his thought. He is certainly not a systematic philosopher: systematization may produce a whole in his view but only by the "exclusion and negation of all artistically productive forms" (III 1, 162). The true basis for thinking is not systematization but art. Art alone can provide a way of thinking that is both dynamic and structurally integrated, thus authentically reflecting the essence of life itself. While Nietzsche rejects systematic philosophy, he puts in its place an artistic philosophy that is neither fragmentary nor merely aphoristic. To understand the order and character of Nietzsche's thinking adequately, it is thus necessary to understand his art.

Art for Nietzsche in the first instance always means music, as Curt Paul Janz has demonstrated.[8] "Music and composition were not only incidental occupations for Nietzsche, they were a serious concern for him, rooted in his very essence."[9] Throughout his life, Nietzsche was devoted to music. At twelve, he was an accomplished pianist and shortly thereafter taught himself composition from the textbook of Albrechtsberger, the teacher of Beethoven. He soon began composing, but his music was little appreciated. Despite this, he continued to hope for success, as his letters and repeated efforts to secure the performance of his *Hymn of Life* (1887) indicate.[10] Moreover, most of his friends were composers, musicians, or gifted musical amateurs such as Wagner, von Bülow, Fuchs, and Köselitz (Peter Gast).

That music should form a central topic of this thought is thus hardly surprising. Indeed, four of his works, *The Birth of Tragedy, Wagner in Bayreuth, The Case of Wagner,* and *Nietzsche contra Wagner* explicitly consider musical subjects. Music for Nietzsche, however, was not merely a substantive but also a stylistic concern. As Janz has pointed out, Nietzsche's sketches for works often give only the number of pages, chapters, and so on, indicating "a musical-theoretical foundation, a musical architecture."[11] In his pursuit of a nonsystematic unity, Nietzsche thus apparently turned to music. Perhaps already in *Birth,* probably in *Zarathustra,* and almost certainly in his late works, Nietzsche employs musical forms to coordinate the various aphorisms within a larger whole. In his new introduction to *Birth* in 1886, Nietzsche characterizes the work "as 'music' for those who are baptized in music" (III 1, 3). In letters to Overbeck (6 February 1884) and Wideman (31 July 1885), he calls *Zarathustra* a symphony, a claim that Janz has shown must be taken seriously.[12]

Twilight was written in the shadow of Nietzsche's projected but never completed magnum opus, *The Will to Power.* During this period, he was much concerned with musical matters. Two works of the same year, *The Case of Wagner* and *Nietzsche contra Wagner,* explicitly consider musical subjects. At the time, he was studying the musicologist Hugo Riemann's theory of phrasing, as well as Carl Fuchs's *The Future of the Musical Performance and Its Origin* (1884). He wrote to Köselitz on 15 January 1888 that "music now gives me sensations, as really never before. Life without music would simply be an error, a burden, an exile." Indeed, music cast such a powerful spell over him that he was continually distracted from his magnum opus. He wrote to Köselitz on 21 March 1888, "I recognize nothing more, I hear nothing more, I read nothing more; and in spite of all that there is nothing that really more *concerns* me than the fate of music."

His correspondence suggests that this concern with music conditioned his work. While completing *The Case of Wagner,* he wrote to Köselitz on 17 May 1888, "I lack a year of exact music studies, in order to get control of language for that." In letters of 20 July 1888, he informs Overbeck that "just now a small musical pamphlet of mine is being printed," and Köselitz that music is "the most ideal form of modern sincerity." In a letter to Brandes of 13 September 1888, he calls himself a "musician from instinct" and in another letter to

Köselitz of 18 November 1888 remarks that "The *Case of Wagner* is operetta music." This paper will attempt to show that Nietzsche employed musical forms in structuring *Twilight* and will then try to demonstrate the central importance of these musical forms and music in general for his political thought.[13]

Twilight seems to be written in classical sonata form. Nietzsche had had a preference for the classical in music since his youth, and while he was later attracted to the Romantics and especially Wagner, his own compositions vary little from the classical mode.[14] In a letter to Fuchs of 29 July 1888, Nietzsche asserts, "We are both very antidecadence musicians, i.e., antimodern musicians." Nietzsche was also well acquainted with sonata form from his previous musical studies and had read with interest Carl Spitteler's discussions of the form in his *Essays on Aesthetics.*

Sonata form is often used for single movements of sonatas or symphonies, and usually consists of three parts—an exposition, a development, and a recapitulation—generally followed by a closing statement, or coda, and often preceded by an introduction. In the exposition, the main ideas are presented, usually in two or three different themes. Various aspects of these themes are developed in a wide variety of ways in the development, usually in a dramatic and dynamic manner, and the recapitulation then repeats the exposition with, however, certain harmonic changes that are usually "prepared" for by the development. The coda is then a short phrase used to bring the movement to a clear and dramatic close. *Twilight* seems to follow this form.[15] The structure of the work might be schematized as follows:

Title	*Twilight of the Idols*
Time Signature . . .	"Forward"
Rest	Place, date, comment, and signature
Introduction	"Maxims and Arrows"
Exposition	"Socrates"-"Germans"
Theme I	"Socrates"-"Fable"
a) "Socrates"	I (1–2) II (3–10) III (11–12)
b) "Reason"	
c) "Fable"	
Theme II	"Morality"-"Improvers"
a) "Morality"	I (1–3) II (4–5) III (6)
b) "Errors"	
c) "Improvers"	
Theme III	"Germans"
a) (1–3)	I (1) II (2) III (3)

b) (4)
c) (5–7)

Development	"Skirmishes"			
Introduction	(1)			
Exposition	(2–31)			
Theme I	a (2–6)	b (7)	c (8–9)	d (10–11)
Theme II	a (12–14)	b (15–16)	c (17–18)	d (19–20)
Theme III	a (21–23)	b (24–25)	c (26–29)	d (30–31)
Development	a (32–48)			
Theme A	a (32–33)	b (34–35)	c (36)	d (37)
Theme B	a (38)	b (39–40)	c (41–42)	d (43)
Theme C	a (44)	b (45)	c (46–47)	d (48)
Recapitulation . . .	(49–59)			
Theme I*	(49)			
Theme II*	(49)			
Theme III*	(50)			
Coda	(51)			
Recapitulation	"Ancients"			
Introduction	(1)			
Theme I*	(2)			
Theme II*	(3)			
Theme III*	(4–5)			
Coda	"Hammer"			

■ TITLE

As originally conceived, the work was entitled *Idleness of a Psychologist* (VIII 3, 345).[16] In this form it ended with "Skirmishes." Köselitz wrote to Nietzsche on 20 September 1888 that the title was too unassuming, which prompted him to change it to *Twilight of the Idols; or, How One Philosophizes with a Hammer,* drawing the new title from the substance of the preface and making the minor changes necessary to harmonize the text with the new title, as Nietzsche notes in a letter to Köselitz of 27 September 1888. Shortly thereafter and certainly before the middle of November, Nietzsche decided to expand the work and added the final two sections, "Ancients" and "Hammer."

The title, according to the preface, betrays the work, as Nietzsche admits in a letter to Köselitz of 27 September 1888. *Twilight of the Idols (Götzen-Dämmerung)* is an allusion to Wagner's music drama *Twilight of the Gods (Götterdämmerung).* In *Birth,* Nietzsche had argued that a rebirth of tragedy and a new tragic age were possible because the philosophic tradition which had displaced tragedy had revealed itself as nihilistic in Kant's antinomies and because German, and in particular Wagerian, music was animated by that same spirit out of which Greek tragedy had been born. By 1888, however, Nietzsche had lost hope in Wagner and saw the specter of an untamed nihilism ready to engulf European civilization. His title is thus an implicit critique of Wagner, whom Nietzsche had come to see as a manifestation of nihilism. God, according to Zarathustra, is dead. In Nietzsche's view, however, the idols (including Wagner), the images of God, "what previously was called truth," continue to dominate human life (VI 3, 352). Belief in God, which hitherto provided the light in which a sort of truth was possible, has degenerated into idolatry. Like the hermit whom Zarathustra encounters in the forest, mankind is not aware or at least does not admit that God is dead. In the absence of God, however, the idols which men worship are enveloped in the twilight of nihilism and like the old gods of Wagner's music drama are approaching their end. In the words of Brunnhilde, "The gods' end now dawns: so I throw the torch in Valhalla's resplendent citadel."[18] Nietzsche, too, in proclaiming the end of the idols casts his torch into the citadel of Western civilization. Whether the twilight is a morning or an evening twilight and whether the death of God and the impending destruction of the idols herald the coming of conflagration and night or a new dawn of the tragic age of the overman are here left open. It is these subliminal questions, however, which underlie the entire work.

The subtitle, *How One Philosophizes with a Hammer,* further illuminates the work. The term "hammer" signifies in the first instance a tool used for building or destroying and is hence an image of power. Nietzsche uses the term in this sense in *Zarathustra* as the hammer that rages against the stone in which the image of the overman is imprisoned (VI 1, 107–8; see also VI 2, 81). In commenting upon this passage in *Ecce Homo,* Nietzsche characterizes this use of the hammer as Dionysian, as the joy even in destroying (VI 3, 347). In the preface to *Twilight,* however, the hammer is described as a tool for determining sonority. The unity of this dual image becomes clear as an allusion to Wagner's *Ring* cycle. The image of the hammer appears twice in the *Ring.* In *Rheingold,* the god Donner uses his hammer to bring a great thunderstorm to dissipate the twilight obscuring the way to Valhalla. The storm which the hammer evokes resolves into a rainbow bridge over which the gods cross into their new citadel. In *Siegfried,* the hammer appears again as the tool Siegfried uses to form the irresistible sword, *Nothung* (Necessity), with which he defeats Wotan. Nietzsche's subtitle suggests that the world characterized by nihilism, by the death of God and the twilight that this event has spread over the old idols, will be destroyed by the hammer in the hands of the philosopher which forges a new sword and a new necessity, which produces the lightning and the storm that disperse the twilight and prepare the way for the tragic age of the overman.

The philosopher, reminiscent here of the Old Testament prophets, is portrayed as calling his people back from the worship of idols to the worship of the one true god. This god, however, is not Yahweh or the Christian God but the god of tragedy, Dionysus. The hammer which reveals the hollowness of the idols is thus the god himself, whose music calls mankind to his festival and his tragic age. This is borne out by the *Nachlass,* which contains the proposed title, "The Hammer (or Dionysus)" (VII 3, 205). Whether humanity will succeed in establishing a tragic culture or even survive the attempt, however, is uncertain. *Zarathustra* was to end with the "Last speech: Here is the hammer that overcomes men/Did man turn out badly? Well, let us test to the utmost whether he can endure this hammer!" (VII 2, 73). The meaning of this enigmatic passage becomes clearer in comparison with Wagner.

The rule of the gods in Wagner's *Ring* is based upon the justice of covenant, on the strength of Wotan's fidelity to written law. In pursuit of power and glory, however, Wotan breaks his word and thus dooms himself and his pantheon to destruction. The pursuit of power, symbolized by the ring, requires the renunciation of love, which is the basis for all communal life. Power in Wagner's view drives both men and gods into the self and thus assures the collapse of the old order. The world can be redeemed only through the renunciation of power out of love. Brunnhilde fulfills this task in igniting the final conflagration in *Götterdämmerung* and returning the ring to its rightful owners. It is this idea of redemption through love, the Romantic notion that order can be established without recourse to political power, through the evocation of the communal spirit of the *Volk,* that is the determinative theme of Wagner's *Ring.*

The destruction of the old idols by the hammer of Nietzsche's musical philosophy in *Twilight* is also a redemption that subordinates the old order within the new. The old idols are "redeemed" within the eternal order of things. This redemption, however, is not the result of a renunciation of power for love but rather of the will to power that loves only the overman and its own completion in the recognition of the eternal recurrence and a new tragic age. *Twilight* is thus Nietzsche's *musical* alternative to Wagner's vision of death and renewal. He attempts to write the true music drama, the true tragedy, and thus to overcome the old idols or truths of the Western tradition, and to give birth to that which Zarathustra claims is beyond both God and the idols, to the tragic age of the overman.

■   PREFACE

The preface is divided into two sections separated by a line of Latin. There are 135 words above and 180 words below the Latin line, which constitutes an exact proportion of 3/4.[19] This division suggests that the preface is the time signature, specifying 3/4 time (triple meter). Triple meter is more or less equivalent to ancient trochaic meter, which, according to Nietzsche, is the meter of the bacchic dance, used especially by Aeschylus in his choral odes; it does not imitate speech but instead remains fundamentally musical and thus ennobles tragic poetry.[20] It is hardly surprising then that Nietzsche should employ it in a work that seeks to revive the spirit of ancient tragedy.

The preface explains this use of musical forms.[21] Music is what Nietzsche needs to avoid the "all too heavy seriousness" of the revaluation. He remarks in *Nietzsche contra Wagner,* "My melancholy wants to relax in the hiding places and abysses of perfection: for this reason I need music. But Wagner makes one sick" (VI 3, 417). For Nietzsche, Wagner's music offers no relief since it is entangled in decadence. *Twilight* is Nietzsche's convalescence, his *Idleness,* as the original title characterized it, from the burden of the magnum opus. It is not, however, mere play but, as Nietzsche asserts, a "case," that is, a polemic or war, like *The Case of Wagner.* This war, however, is "relaxation because it releases tension, because it allows the drawn bow to release its 'arrow,'" because, as Nietzsche suggests in the Latin quotation, "spirit increases and vigor grows through a wound."

This is only one side of his convalescence, as he points out in the section of the preface below the Latin line. The other is striking idols with a hammer and hearing the famous hollow sound—the sound that they are empty and worn out. This is not the destruction of the idols but the musical revelation of their emptiness, which, according to Nietzsche, can only be understood by those who have ears behind their ears. He apparently refers here to the third ear mentioned in *Beyond* for the musicality of language, for symmetry, crescendo, inflection, tone, and tempo (VI 2, 197–99; see also VI 3, 302).

This musical revelation is Nietzsche's philosophizing with a hammer. The original title, *Idleness of a Psychologist,* gives a clue to the nature of this philosophizing. Nietzsche characterizes himself in this title not as philosopher but as psychologist. Nietzsche's philosophizing with a hammer, his sounding out the idols, is fundamentally an attempt to determine whether idols such as Socrates are psychologically healthy or unhealthy, whether they represent ascending or descending life.

The final paragraph of the preface indicates how these two projects are combined. This war is a recreation or convalescence because it is a musical war in which all opposition is only the means to harmony. Philosophizing with a hammer in the twilight of a world in which God is dead is the incorporation and subordination of both contemporary and eternal idols, that is, ideals or truths, within the musical form of a new necessity. In sounding out these idols, Nietzsche reveals their emptiness. However, it is precisely this emptiness that allows them to resound. The revelation of their emptiness is thus the source of Nietzsche's music and hence of the tragic age this music is meant to engender.

This musical motif continues at the end of the preface: the place, occasion of composition, and signature are a rest inserted at the beginning of the piece—indicating that the work begins on an upbeat, which suggests, according to Nietzsche, that the piece will be lively rather than restful.[22] The date is especially significant. Nietzsche remarks in *Ecce Homo* that on this day, "On the 30th of September a great victory; seventh day; idleness of a god along the Po" (VI 3, 354).[23] Here Nietzsche marks the idleness or rest of his seventh day, after the completion of his creation of the first book of the revaluation.

■ INTRODUCTION

A sonata introduction begins in the tonic key, modulates through various keys, and then usually ends with a closing cadence leading into the exposition. The deviation from the tonic in the introduction produces a tension which is resolved by the return of the tonic in the first theme of the exposition. The introduction also often introduces in compressed form the various themes of the work although not necessarily in the same order or key. Nietzsche's introduction follows this format and achieves all these objectives.

A central difficulty for our analysis is understanding what constitutes key for Nietzsche. In this, he apparently relies upon the Greeks, who distinguished various keys or modes and named them after the political cultures or ways of life they believed represented the passions or behaviors that these modes seemed to engender, for example, the effeminate Ionian and Lydian modes, the courageous Dorian mode, and so on. Nietzsche adopts and reverses this practice—the different keys for him are the particular political ways of life. The character of each of these ways of life is represented by the idol that it worships. The idol thus reveals the true character of the political culture. Thus, Nietzsche's psychological examination and evaluation of the various idols is also an evaluation of the political cultures that worship these idols. Music thus becomes political philosophy as an evaluation of political cultures and values.

The introduction, "Maxims and Arrows," begins with three aphorisms reminiscent of the Greeks. The first, "Idleness is the beginning of all psychology," recalls Aristotle's dictum that wonder is the beginning of all philosophy. This is even clearer in an earlier version: "Idleness is the beginning of all philosophy" (VIII 1, 293; see also VI 3, 225; and V 2, 494). The second aphorism, "Even the most courageous of us only seldom has the courage for what he really *knows* . . ." recalls Socrates assertion that the unexamined life is not worth living (cf. VI 3, 67), and the third aphorism refers to Aristotle by name. Thus, Greek culture and the philosophic idol that it worships are apparently the tonic.

The introduction ends with eight aphorisms (37–44) that form a closing cadence in sharp contrast to the opening theme of the exposition ("Socrates"). Nietzsche's conclusion—"Formula of my happiness: a yes, a no, a straight line, a goal"—is opposed to the first sentence of "Socrates"—"About life the wisest of all times have judged alike: *it's not worth anything.*" This opposition between Greek philosophy, as symbolized by Socrates, and Nietzsche's musical politics is the major problem that the work itself must resolve.

The solution, however, is already implicit in the introduction. As Werner Dannhauser has pointed out, this section is implicitly an account of Nietzsche himself.[24] This is indicated perhaps by the number of aphorisms it contains (forty-four) which corresponds to the year of Nietzsche's birth (1844) and to the year of his life in which the work was written. This is more clearly indicated by the fact that much of the introduction is drawn from a collection in the *Nachlass* entitled "Maxims of a Hyperborean" (VIII 3, 271–74; see also VIII 3, 345). In *The Antichrist* (1) Nietzsche characterizes himself as a Hyperborean, a man of the north who worships Apollo, the god of poets and the god whose oracle at Delphi proclaimed Socrates the wisest of men. The resolution to the problem of the introduction and the work as a whole—the contradiction between the Greek way, personified by Socrates, and the German way, personified by Nietzsche, is thus already implicit in the introduction: the epiphany of the Greek gods among the Germans, the return of Apollo and, as we shall see, of his brother Dionysus to reconstitute out of the winter twilight of nihilism a new tragic age and culture.

■ EXPOSITION

The exposition ("Socrates"-"Germans"), which consists of forty-five aphorisms, is a sounding out of *eternal* idols. The first theme is concerned with Greek philosophic ideals, the second with Christian moral ideals, and the last with German political ideals. The Greeks thus are the tonic of the work, while the Germans are the dominant, that is, the fifth above the Greeks. The musical problem of the work is to resolve the harmonic dissonance between these two themes, to reconcile the dominant with the tonic, the Germans with the Greeks, so that they can return in the same key in the recapitulation.

Structurally, the three themes are identical. Both the first and the second contain nineteen aphorisms (perhaps pointing, for reasons we shall examine below, to the nineteenth century), while the third contains seven. The themes are also historically continuous, beginning with the Greeks, passing through Christianity, and ending with the Germans. The form of the themes, however, remains the same, which seems to indicate that the inherent problem is not solved by this development.

Theme I. The first theme is in three sections: "Socrates" (twelve aphorisms), "Reason" (six aphorisms), and "Fable" (one aphorism). It begins with an attack upon Socrates. It is not Socrates the man but Socrates the idol that Nietzsche attacks, and through his psychological examination or sounding out of Socrates he hopes to determine the health or sickness not merely of Socrates but of the philosophic tradition that idolizes Socrates.

In the first part of "Socrates" (1–2), Nietzsche opposes Socrates' view that life is no good to his own that the value of life cannot be estimated. He then attacks Socrates (3–10), arguing his virtues are symptoms of disease and a desire for revenge against life. Socrates, in his view, was only taken seriously because he seemed to offer a cure for the general Greek sickness, the chaos of the instincts, with his equation of reason, virtue, and happiness, but this was a misunderstanding, for his rationality was only a more complete manifestation of decadence and descending life (see III 1, 81, 90). Nietzsche then indicates his alternative, ascending life, in which happiness has its origin in instinct and not in reason (11), and resurrects Socrates to admit his defeat (12).

127

This section presents the fundamental problem of the work as the opposition of Socrates' and Nietzsche's political prescriptions. Socrates is the antithesis to the tragic sense of life which Nietzsche seeks to foster with his music. In *Birth,* Socrates was portrayed as the destroyer of tragedy whose optimistic dialectic drove music out of tragedy and gave birth to Hellenistic culture (III 1, 91; see also III 1, 6, and IV 1, 18–19). Nietzsche attacks Socrates to clear the way for the rebirth of tragedy, evaluating both in terms of the law of life, that is, according to whether they affirm or deny life, whether they are examples of ascending or descending life (VII 3, 60).

In "Reason," Nietzsche categorizes the basic errors of the philosophic tradition, which idolizes Socrates, as manifestations of descending life and compares them with Heracleitus and science as examples of ascending life. The continuation of the theme in the tonic is signaled by Heracleitus, who, as an integral moment of the tragic age of the Greeks, represents the real alternative to philosophic degeneracy, Nietzsche himself (see VI 3, 311). Nietzsche concludes that the actual world has falsely been characterized as the apparent world in opposition to the "real" world by philosophy as a weapon against ascending or tragic life. The distinction between "real" and "apparent" is thus only a reflection of descending life. This philosophic rejection of life is juxtaposed to Nietzsche's alternative, that is, the Dionysian artist (6), who rather than renouncing life because it is terrible affirms it for precisely this reason. The antithesis of these two positions is resolved in the final section of the theme.

"How the 'true world' finally became a fable" is a cadence leading into the second theme. This section reasserts the tonic in the person of Plato, and in a manner characteristic of sonata form sums up the first theme. Nietzsche reinterprets the entire philosophic history of the West, from the destruction of tragedy by Socratism to the rebirth of tragedy in *Zarathustra,* as the process by which the Socratic premise is overcome.

Theme II. The second theme like the first is also in three sections: "Morality" (six aphorisms), "Errors" (eight aphorisms), and "Improvers" (five aphorisms). It also begins with the confrontation of Nietzsche and his adversaries (1–3)—here Christianity (in place of Socrates) as the champion or idol of morality (in place of philosophy). Christian morality, however, is really only the generalization of the Socratic equation, as Nietzsche indicated in "Socrates" (11). The second theme is thus an extension of the first, contrasting here two ways of dealing with the passions—the Christian practice of extirpation and Nietzsche's of spiritualization. As in the first theme, Nietzsche's psychological examination reveals that Christianity rests upon a denial of life, which he argues is impossible since it assumes a position outside life (4–5). Hence, it is merely a manifestation of descending life in contrast to Nietzsche's alternative, the immoralist (6), who recognizes and affirms the fatality of everything that is.

The second section of the theme, "Errors," locates the source of this misunderstanding of life in the failure to understand that the apparent world is the actual world and the mistaken attribution of causality to the "real," noumenal world. This section ends with a further examination of Nietzsche's alternative, ascending life. Man, according to Nietzsche, is a piece of fate and cannot be disentangled from all that has been and will be—hence, he cannot judge life because it is the whole of which he is only a part. It is precisely this acceptance and love of fate, this *amor fati,* in Nietzsche's view, that characterizes the tragic artist, the Dionysian faith (of "Reason" 6) which grasps the necessity and beauty of Zarathustra and thus of tragedy. This is likewise the faith of the immoralist, the great affirmer mentioned in "Morality" (6). Indeed, an early draft of this section ("Errors") was entitled "The Immoralist" (VIII 3, 348).

In the final section of the second theme, "Improvers," Nietzsche demonstrates (as in "Fable") that all previous morality was a rejection of life as it is and hence a manifestation of descending life. He then concludes that the improvers of morals know that he is right because they always claim the right to lie, that is, to be *immoral.* Like Socrates, they themselves are thus brought forth to admit their defeat.

Theme III. The final theme of the exposition is in the dominant, that is, German political culture, and is structurally identical to the other themes, although only about one-third as long. The dominant has a special significance in sonata form, since it is the fifth above the tonic and thus forms a perfect interval with the tonic. This interval, however, does *not* constitute a harmony of the melodies of the two themes; indeed, there is an express prohibition in sonata form against parallel fifths. Thus the harmonic dissonance within each theme between Socrates' way and Nietzsche's way is identical to the harmonic problem of the exposition and hence the work as a whole, the resolution of the Greek and German difference. It is only through the development and modulation of the dominant into the tonic in the recapitulation that this contradiction can be overcome, that the dissonance of the perfect interval between Greek and German life, between philosophy and politics, between Socrates and Nietzsche, can be resolved into a thorough and perfect harmony.

In the first aphorism (as in "Socrates" 1–2 and "Morality" 1–3), Nietzsche contrasts the two opposing positions, the Germany he represents and the Germany of the *Reich,* the Germany of the mediocre. In the second aphorism (as in "Socrates" 3–10 and "Morality" 4–5), he sounds out this German spirit and argues that it is antithetical to life. In the third aphorism (as in "Socrates" 11 and "Morality" 6), he indicates that not merely the German spirit but German life itself is in decline and then calls all Europe as a witness to support his case (as in "Socrates" 12).

In the second section of the theme (as in "Reason" and "Errors"), Nietzsche points to the source of this degeneration as the failure to recognize the antagonism of *Kultur* and *Staat* (4). In *Birth,* Nietzsche had argued that German political revival and unification into a *Reich* were possible on the basis of the cultural unity fostered by Wagner's music drama. He soon became convinced of the futility of such aspirations and indeed came to recognize that such a politics was antagonistic to true "music" since it established political unity only by enervating spirituality. Nietzsche opposes nationalism and argues that one must be not a good German or Frenchman but a good European. A European, however, is not a characterless cosmopolitan man but the embodiment of the 2,500 year-old European tradition (V 2, 313). One can be such a European, however, only if one understands this tradition in terms of its unifying theme, that is, nihilism. The recognition that God is dead is thus the presupposition of tragedy and a new tragic age, of what Nietzsche calls "great politics." Zarathustra brings this truth down from the mountains, and it is with his going under that tragedy begins. The good European grasps Zarathustra's teaching and understands it as the basis for the great politics of a new tragic age.

In the third section of the theme (as in "Fable" and "Errors"), Nietzsche locates the source of contemporary decadence in the failure of the educational institutions (5) and indicates his alternative, the educator who teaches men *style.* Nietzsche here characterizes his own musical style in contrast to both Wagner and German *Bildung* as affirmative, dealing with contradiction and criticism only as a means (6).

In the *Republic,* Socrates argues that education begins with music and ends with dialectic. This relegation of music to the lowest level is in Nietzsche's view the result of Socrates' optimistic dialectic, which drives music out of tragedy and thus out of the education that informed the tragic age (III 1, 91). As he sees it, it is this dialectical optimism that characterizes Western thought. The rebirth of tragedy thus presupposes the subordination of dialectic and hence of the entire post-Socratic tradition to music. This is apparently the meaning of the conjunction of positive and negative elements in Nietzsche's thought. Nietzsche, like Plato, does not seek to annihilate his opponents but to incorporate and subordinate them, in Nietzsche's case within the harmonic structure of his music. He strives to sound out his opponents and demonstrate their necessity as harmonic moments of a musical cosmos, as necessary, even if abysmal, moments of life itself. The recognition of their necessity constitutes the essence of the tragic and is thus the affirmative musical teaching that underlies the negative or critical philosophic character of the work.

■ DEVELOPMENT

The development section of a sonata fragments and recombines the exposition themes in order to resolve their harmonic dissonance so that they can return in the recapitulation in their original order in the tonic. This means that for Nietzsche the problem of eternal idols must be resolved so they can return not as idols of a dialectical tradition but as a tragic European culture that combines philosophy, morality, and politics in a new Greek synthesis. The third section of each exposition theme indicates the way to such a reconciliation: the problems of traditional philosophy, morality, and politics culminate in the nineteenth century. The solution to the problem of eternal idols thus presupposes the solution to the problem of the "idols of the age."

The development section itself is written in a sonata form more or less equivalent to that of the work as a whole. This seems to indicate that the problem of contemporary idols in the development is formally identical to the problem of eternal idols. The title of the development, "Skirmishes of an Untimely Man," supports this thesis—it is not Nietzsche's war with eternal idols but rather his skirmishes with the lesser idols of the nineteenth century.

Development introduction. The development introduction, like that of the work as a whole, consists of a variety of compressed themes. Here Nietzsche's "Arrows," however, are directed at specific characters. With the exception of the first five, who were culture heroes of the period, all are nineteenth-century figures and the idols of the age.

Development exposition. There are three themes in the development exposition. The first is concerned with French literati, the second with Anglo-American thinkers, and the third with German and Greek philosophers.

Theme I. The first development theme consists of ten aphorisms (2–11) and, with the exception of George Eliot, is concerned exclusively with French literary culture. In the first section, Nietzsche attacks French literary decadence as a corruption of the noble taste of classical France. He points out in a letter to Köselitz of 10 November 1887 that these thinkers in many respects resemble him but that they all lack the main thing—"*la force*" (See VII 2, 254–55, and VIII 2, 253–57, 422). Nietzsche thus seeks to dissociate himself from them. As he remarks (in 7), "One must know *who* one is."

In the second section of the theme (7), Nietzsche explains that these artists failed because they believed nature conformed to some rule and attempted to copy it. Since nature is essentially chaotic, however, art must not imitate it but give it order, as Nietzsche explains in the third section of the theme (8–9). The French artists, however, lack the necessary creative frenzy and hence are a manifestation of descending rather than ascending life. In the final section of the theme (10–11), Nietzsche characterizes the three types of true artists and the sorts of frenzy that motivate them: the Apollonian (frenzy of vision), the Dionysian (frenzy of affect), and the architect (frenzy of the great will). This characterization, as we shall see, presents the three sides of Nietzsche's own art: the imagistic, aphoristic vision of the Hyperborean; the musical frenzy of the disciple of Dionysus; and the overarching fatalistic will to power of the architect.

Theme II. The second theme is a consideration of Anglo-American thought and connects French thought, the development tonic, to German thought, the development dominant. George Eliot serves as the bridge between the two themes. Carlyle, Emerson, and Darwin are close to Nietzsche but like the French lack his power (12–14) because, as Nietzsche points out in the second section of the theme (15–16), they want only little advantages over men, while the impersonal type, that is, Nietzsche himself (VI 3, 123), wants to be beyond them (15). Despite this difference, Nietzsche believes that the Germans will inevitably confuse him with them, just as they confused Schiller and Goethe, Schopenhauer and Hartmann (16).

The third section of the theme explains the differences between him and them. The most spiritual human beings do not try to escape from their contradictory passions into faith but rather honor life because of these contradictions (17). Nietzsche here develops the theme of the contradiction or opposition of philosophic reason and the Dionysian art that arose in "Reason." In the exposition, this opposition was merely presented as a dissonance; here in the development Nietzsche examines the grounds for a reconciliation or harmony by measuring both positions in terms of their responses to the passions. The greatest men in Nietzsche's view *necessarily* experience the greatest tragedies because they are motivated by the greatest passions (17). The artist understands this, as Nietzsche argues in the fourth section of the theme (as in 8–11), because he knows that man alone is beautiful or ugly, beautiful when he represents ascending, that is, passionate, life and ugly when he represents descending, that is, reasonable, life.

Theme III. The third development theme begins in the dominant, that is, with the Germans, and juxtaposes to it the tonic of work as a whole, that is, the Greeks. It thus expresses the fundamental harmonic problem of the work in its most severe form. Schopenhauer, Nietzsche argues in the first section of the theme, has treated all the greatest monuments of life and especially sexuality as monuments to nothingness. Indeed, he even understands beauty as man's *redemption* from will and sexuality. He thus directly contradicts Plato, who argued that sexuality was a prerequisite of both beauty and philosophy. Moreover, according to Nietzsche, both are in this respect irreconcilable with Spinoza. These three figures represent the three original exposition themes, and their mutual contradiction exposes the Western tradition itself as fundamentally contradictory. That Nietzsche fastens upon sexuality is hardly accidental. His standard of evaluation is life itself, and the essence of life is not self-preservation but the will to power, the will to overcome even oneself, and on the most rudimentary biological level this means sexuality. The contradiction within the Western tradition about the value of sexuality thus reveals its fundamentally contradictory and nihilistic character. With this articulation of the nihilistic essence of Western culture, Nietzsche's sonata reaches the moment of utter dissonance and greatest tension; the implicit disharmony of the exposition here becomes explicit. This is the musical and philosophical problem that Nietzsche must solve: he must subordinate the fundamental contradiction or dissonance of Western civilization concerning the basis of life within a more comprehensive harmonic unity that grasps and affirms sexuality as the essence of life itself.

The immediate source of the nihilism of the nineteenth century, which appears in Schopenhauer, is the attempt to do away with moral purposiveness in art (24). Since art, according to Nietzsche, is the source of *all* purpose, this attempt leads to nihilism. Nietzsche's alternative, the tragic artist, faces the terrible in nihilism and transforms it into man's greatest affirmation of life. Saying yes to man's most abysmal possibility, he redeems man from purposelessness.

As in the previous two themes, Nietzsche's antagonists resemble him.[25] Insofar as he resembles them, he embodies the most basic contradictions of the Western tradition. Thus, by overcoming this contradiction within himself, by saying yes to this nihilism, he believes he can give birth to a new tragic age. The contradiction of the West as a whole culminates for Nietzsche in himself, and the harmonic tension of the work is brought to a peak as the tension of Nietzsche's own soul.

The last two sections of the third theme indicate how Nietzsche lives with this tension. Just as noble hospitality is reserved for the greatest guests (25), Nietzsche's life is reserved for the greatest problems. The heavy burden they impose, however, can only be alleviated by humor. Thus Nietzsche satirizes himself as a deaf mute who did not recognize the musical potentialities of language (26) and as a literary female who believed himself filled with spirit as a classicist (27). However, he overcame the impersonality of scholarship by developing personal traits (28), and, when he became ill, the philologist (29) traveled to Italy and Bayreuth, where *"Pure foolishness restores"* (30). Finally, he concludes the theme with the assertion of the necessity of great health for the genius (31). Nietzsche here reconstitutes his life artistically to demonstrate how the most destructive passions can be affirmed and made beautiful. He sees himself as the tragic artist, the way to the future, and the solution to the problems of both the eternal idols and the idols of the age. In the development-development, this formula for the transformation of nihilism into the tragic age of the overman is made explicit.

Development-development. The development-development consists of seventeen aphorisms divided into three themes. The first is a consideration of morality, the second of freedom, and the third of genius. These three present the necessary and sufficient conditions for the rebirth of tragedy and the great politics of a tragic culture.

Theme A. In the first theme, Nietzsche contrasts the morality of the weak "ideal" man with that of the strong "real" man and asserts that the latter is more valuable since it is conducive to a higher form of life (33). The former "parasitic" morality (34–35) thus must be replaced by a morality that benefits the strong, based upon a tragic sense of life that unlike Christianity regards death as the highest moment of life (36). The greatest obstacle to such a morality in Nietzsche's view is his contemporaries' certainty of their moral superiority. This, however, is the mere consequence of their real weakness (36). It is, however, too late to return to the stronger morality of the Renaissance (37)—humanity must first pass through decadence and the most abysmal human possibilities.

Theme B. In the second theme, Nietzsche distinguishes two different types of freedom, his freedom, the freedom of the warrior, which is predicated upon inequality and danger, and liberal freedom, which seeks the safety of universal equality. The truly free man is close to both tyranny and slavery and becomes free only by disciplining his passions to avoid both tyranny and slavery. Such freedom, however, is possible only in a passionate and dangerous age, but such a possibility is lacking today because "the entire West no longer has those instincts out of which institutions grow, out of which the future grows" (39). Our instincts should not be abandoned, however, simply because they are wrong (41). Instead a new hierarchy must be established by legislators who recognize the necessity of lying (42), for without such conscious hypocrisy they will not differ from the saints and theologians of the past—the unconscious hypocrites of "Skirmishes" (18). Thus, modern European civilization must first pass through decadence if this is to be attained (43). The conservatives, according to Nietzsche, believe the opposite, but this downward movement cannot be checked; it can only be dammed up and made more sudden.

Theme C. In the two preceding themes, Nietzsche presented two parts of this program for the world of the future, a new morality and a new freedom. The third theme presents the final necessity, the great genius who exercises this freedom and imposes this morality. These three are the pillars of Nietzsche's great politics that will create a tragic European order.

Nietzsche first contrasts his conception of genius with that of the decadents considered in the development exposition (44). The great man for him is a finale, who creates a higher form of life and thus exhausts life's resources. His model here is Napoleon, the "*ens realissimum*" (49). Such geniuses, however, most often become criminals because there is no opportunity for them (45), and even those who succeed must pass through a Chandala existence.

This higher type is in fact the overman. His is a perspective beyond good and evil. "Here the view is free," Nietzsche asserts, quoting Goethe's *Faust.*[26] The genius has an unrestricted view because he is above man. Thus, like Heracleitus, he may contradict himself, he may lie, he may even sacrifice his humanity or indeed, like Christ, his divinity—not from weakness but from the height of strength and love. Genius like beauty, however, is not the product of a single individual but rather of a political community's long series of decisions about every aspect of life (47). The tragic culture of the Greeks for example was prepared by the decisions of previous generations. Socrates and Christianity were also the results of a long tradition, but of descending not ascending life.

In the final section of the theme, Nietzsche argues that Rousseau's conception of a return to nature is impossible, leading only to the depths of decadence, that is, to the doctrine of equality and the Revolution. Neither Rousseau nor the conservatives realize that God is dead and that in his absence all truths, institutions, and so on that were based upon him have become untenable. With Rousseau, however, Nietzsche returns to the development tonic, that is, to the French and thus signals the end of the development and the beginning of the recapitulation.

Development recapitulation. The recapitulation of a sonata returns to the exposition themes in their original order but harmonically modified by the development so they can all return in the tonic. According to Nietzsche, the result of the descent into decadence ushered in by Rousseau was Goethe, who represents the self-overcoming of the eighteenth century (48). Goethe, however, seems to be a return not to the development tonic, that is, to the French, but rather to the dominant, that is, to the Germans. Nietzsche resolves this problem and simultaneously indicates why Goethe is the recapitulation: "Goethe no German event, but a European one" (49). Goethe embodies all the development themes: the French, English, and German and indeed all post-Socratic European culture. This unification of the various cultural moments of the exposition is achieved through the unification of the three themes of the development-development in Goethe's own character. Goethe embodied all the strongest instincts of the eighteenth century (49), overcame them, and created himself by adopting a higher *morality,* becoming *free* through trust in fate (49), and striving for universality as the *genius* must (50).

The problem of the idols thus seems to have been solved by Goethe, but unfortunately "Goethe might have been merely an interlude, a beautiful 'in vain' not only for Germany but for the whole of Europe" (50), and the nineteenth century merely the brutalized eighteenth century. Goethe failed because he was unable to solve the problem of the eternal idols. The source of his inability becomes clearer when we consider his place in the musical structure of the work as a whole. Goethe is the recapitulation and resolution of contemporary European culture. The harmony that he represents is merely the harmony that arises from sounding out the idols of the age. Thus, the problem of eternal idols that begins with Socrates is left unresolved. Despite the universality of his genius, Goethe remains within the Socratic horizon. He is thus only the last and greatest precursor of Nietzsche himself.

Coda. The coda is the concluding section of a sonata, which succinctly and dramatically restates the principle themes of the recapitulation and the work as a whole. Nietzsche's development coda fulfills all these tasks in pointing explicitly to the solution of the problem of the idols, that is, to Nietzsche himself. Nietzsche presents himself here as a higher and more profound Goethe, as the genius, the great artist, who will complete the transformation of European culture.

As originally conceived, the work ended with this section (see Nietzsche to Köselitz, 12 September 1888). This original form apparently consisted of an introduction and exposition considering eternal idols, a development considering the idols of the age, and a recapitulation considering the necessities for the future—that culminated in Goethe and Nietzsche. Nietzsche's solution, however, was not stated in the original work. Biographical data are helpful here. Nietzsche's late works were apparently prompted in part by his publisher's request for some short works to prepare the public for the magnum opus. This apparently played some role in *Twilight.* The original ending of "Skirmishes" (51) points to the coming work. As the preface indicates, *Twilight* was finished on the day *The Antichrist,* then conceived as the first book of the magnum opus, was completed. Nietzsche, however, soon decided not to use *The Antichrist* as the first book of the magnum opus. It seems likely that the decision to expand *Twilight* arose in conjunction with this decision to abandon or modify the *Will to Power.* If this is the case, then the expansion may be the result of Nietzsche's desire to make it a self-sufficient work that articulated both the fundamental problems of Western civilization *and* their solution.

■   RECAPITULATION

In the recapitulation, Nietzsche returns to the tonic, the Greeks. The recapitulation, however, is also a return to Nietzsche himself. The title of the section, "What I Owe to the Ancients," emphasizes both elements. The *Nachlass* also contains an early draft of *Ecce Homo*, four sections of which form the core of "Ancients" (VIII 3, 435–41). This draft is dated October-November 1888, that is, *after* Nietzsche had already completed the original draft of *Twilight* and decided on the new title. Thus, this addition points to Nietzsche himself.

The recapitulation consists of an introduction (1), a consideration of Greek philosophy (2), Greek morality (3), and Greek political life (4), and a conclusion which unites these three in Greek art (5). The recapitulation thus repeats the themes of the exposition in their original order, although now they are all in the tonic.

Introduction. The introduction is a discussion of the classical style which Nietzsche himself has adopted. *Twilight,* according to Nietzsche, is neither a yes nor a no to everything it considers; in fact it says nothing at all; it does not judge (1). *Twilight* is rather a new approach to the ancient world that goes beyond *Birth* and Wagner to Nietzsche's own fusion of image, emotion, and form, a fusion of the Apollonian, the Dionysian, and the architectonic. According to Nietzsche, his style is Roman—a mosaic of words, "where each word streams out its strength as sound, as place, as concept, to the right and left and over the entirety" (1). Each word is thus music (sound), architecture (place), and philosophy (concept). This stylistic unity is the key to understanding Nietzsche's "return" to the Greeks, to the tonic—it is a return through the art of the *"imperium Romanum,* until today no one ever built or dreamed of building on the same scale!" (VI 3, 243). It is this Roman architectural element, that is, the frenzy of the will of power, that was lacking in Nietzsche's account of the Greeks in *Birth* as an independent element to unite the Apollonian and the Dionysian. There, it was only one aspect of the Apollonian. With this element as the basis of a unified style, Nietzsche is able to return to the Greeks and overcome Socrates, philosophy, morality, and nationalism by subordinating them as dissonant elements within the architectonic structure of the work as a whole.

Like Goethe, Nietzsche uses his art to create himself and a new aesthetic doctrine with which to overcome not merely the idols of the age but the eternal idols as well. This was made possible by the development. Through his "Skirmishes" with nineteenth-century writers,

Nietzsche developed a notion of art based upon life. Thus, he is able to return to the eternal idols of the original exposition in the recapitulation and subordinate them within his musical form.

Theme I*. In the recapitulation of the first theme Nietzsche overcomes the contradiction between his way and that of Socrates by exposing Plato's style and hence the Platonic Socrates as decadent. Such a judgment is possible because of the identification of beauty with ascending life and ugliness with descending life in the development, which allows Nietzsche here to discover a decadent Plato in an ugly Platonic style. Circumventing the Socratic barrier, he can return to an earlier writer, Thucydides, as an example of good style and ascending life. This return to the pre-Socratic or at least to the pre-Platonic tradition is in fact a return to the world of tragedy, made possible because Thucydides and Nietzsche are heirs of an older tradition, that of the Sophists, just as Napoleon was the "heir of a stronger, longer, older civilization" (VI 3, 139).

Theme II*. The second theme also returns in the tonic with its tension resolved. The dissonance of Christian morality finds its resolution and harmony in the original, moral instinct of the Greeks, the will to power. It is not through philosophy, morality, or politics, however, that the rebirth of tragic culture is possible, but through an art that comprehends and portrays the psychological essence of life. This is the basis for Nietzsche's return to the pre-Socratics and for his reinstitution of the tragic world.

Theme III*. The third exposition theme returns in the tonic as the consideration not of German but of Greek political life and its misinterpretation by the Germans. This way of life, according to Nietzsche, bears the name Dionysus and is characteristic "of the older, still richer and self-overflowing Hellenic instinct" (4). It is the instinct and way of life that Nietzsche seeks to foster.

The third exposition theme considered contemporary Germany and particularly the antagonism of *Kultur* and *Staat*. Nietzsche finds the resolution of this dissonance in the pre-Socratic polis. Hitherto, the Germans and even Goethe failed to understand this phenomenon because they did not understand Dionysus, the antithesis to Christ and Christianity (4). Goethe still lived within the horizon of Socrates and Christianity and did not realize the fundamental truth that God is dead. Hence, he was unable truly to return to the political-religious life of the Greeks symbolized in Dionysus.

Dionysus for Nietzsche represents "*eternal* life, the eternal recurrence of life; . . . *true* life as the over-all continuation of life through procreation, through the mysteries of sexuality" (4). As such, however, Dionysus also means suffering, for the pain of the woman giving birth is a necessary aspect of the sexual essence of life. The orgiastic Dionysian faith that Nietzsche claims to have discovered in the Greeks is thus the fundamental characteristic of ascending life. It is, however, also fundamentally tragic because it necessarily entails suffering. To deny the necessity of this pain is a sign of descending life, which seeks to escape from suffering by denying the orgiastic. Thus, Nietzsche can argue that Christianity "made something impure out of sexuality; it threw *dung* on the beginning, on the presupposition of life" (4). As such, it is the most abysmal example of descending life.

The last section of "Ancients" is a recapitulation of the last section of the third development theme and indicates the synthesis within which these themes reside. In the last part of "Germans," Nietzsche explained why educators were necessary for genuine political life and concluded that his German contemporaries did not satisfy this need. This problem is resolved in the recapitulation: the tragic poet is the true educator and thus the alternative to the Socratic notion of education that culminates in German *Bildung*. The poet-philosopher can establish the basis for a new politics because he does not seek to extirpate the creative passions by means of dialectic and philosophy but harmonizes and glorifies them in his music. He thus makes it possible for humanity to bear the suffering of a new tragic age (5). The tragic poet can bear the contradiction of the passions because he is able to subordinate them as dissonances within a higher musical harmony. The poet must speak and transmit his solution, informing the public and teaching it how to live with and thrive upon the contradictions that are an integral part of life. This was the original Greek way, and it is the basis of Nietzsche's political prescription for the future.

The last section of the final aphorism substantiates this; Nietzsche returns to *Birth,* to his concern with the birth of tragedy out of music and to the rebirth of tragedy in his own time, to both Aeschylus and Wagner. In *Birth,* Aeschylus was the poet-musician whose art expressed the basic Hellenic instinct and informed Greek political culture; Wagner with his music drama was to recreate a tragic political culture in Germany. In *Twilight,* it is not Wagner but Nietzsche himself who plays this role. As this educator and founder of a new tragic age, Nietzsche characterizes himself as the last disciple of the philosopher Dionysus (5).

His reference to "the philosopher Dionysus" is surprising in light of his assertion in *Birth* that philosophy destroyed Dionysian culture and tragedy. This apparent paradox, however, points to the solution, to the mutual necessity and mutual incompatibility of Dionysian poetry or music and Apollonian philosophy that Nietzsche discovered in *Birth*. There, he suggested the rebirth of tragedy would require a Dionysian philosophy or a musical Socrates but did not explain how such a synthesis was possible. He claims, however, that he himself is the first tragic philosopher, the first to convert Dionysian into philosophic pathos (VI 3, 310). Nietzsche discloses the ground for this synthesis in *Twilight* as the architectural unity of his art.

The recognition of the independence of this architectural element, still considered part of the Apollonian in *Birth,* allows Nietzsche to reconcile music and philosophy. The *Nachlass* gives us an indication of the character of Nietzsche's architectonic art and its relationship to the "philosopher Dionysus." Nietzsche lists a title for a proposed work as *"Dionysos philosophos. A Satura Menippea"* (VIII 1, 228). The reference here is to Menippean satire, a combination of poetry and philosophy, invented by the Cynic Menippus of Gadara, continued by his Roman follower Varro, and completed by Petronious in his *Satyricon,* as Nietzsche notes.[27] Apparently, the philosopher Dionysus is a cynic and satirist like Petronious who, according to Nietzsche, "more than any great musician hitherto, was the master of presto in inventions, notions, words" (VI 2, 43). It is this "grand style" that his disciple Nietzsche similarly employs to combine music and philosophy within an overarching architectonic unity.

Such a grand style has hitherto been lacking in music, according to Nietzsche (VIII 3, 38–39). *Twilight* and Nietzsche's work in general are his solution to this problem: "I was the first to discover the art of the *great* rhythm, the *great style* of the periodicity of the expression of a monstrous up and down of sublime, superhuman passion" (VI 3, 302–3). This is the character of Nietzsche's music—music in the grand style that combines image and tone within the architecture of the classical sonata form. It is in this sense that Nietzsche is the last disciple of Dionysus the philosopher and, as he characterizes himself in the last sentence of "Ancients," the teacher of the eternal recurrence.

The rebirth of tragedy and the tragic age, which Nietzsche seeks to engender, rests ultimately upon the recognition and acceptance of the doctrine of the eternal recurrence. The beauty and meaning of the tragic view of life depends upon the recognition of necessary and irreconcilable contradictions within the cosmos as a whole. In establishing the necessity and completeness of the cosmos, the doctrine of the eternal recurrence constitutes the central thesis of Nietzsche's thought and teaching. It is thus surprising that he does not discuss the eternal recurrence in *Twilight* or for that matter in any of the published works except *Zarathustra,* where it appears only in dreams, in songs, and from the mouths of animals—in short, only mythologically. Are we then to conclude that Nietzsche does *not* teach what he himself claims is his fundamental teaching?

Nietzsche gives us some indication of how to solve this perplexity. In an outline for his proposed magnum opus, he specifies the subject of one section as "the teaching of the eternal recurrence as *hammer* in the hand of the most powerful man."[28] The eternal recurrence is the hammer with which Nietzsche philosophizes, that is, with which he sounds out idols and demonstrates that they are hollow. It is thus the standard against which he measures them. Evaluation, however, is not rejection—the idols are not destroyed. Rather, Nietzsche demonstrates that each is a necessary moment of the structure of life as a whole, that is, of the eternal recurrence. The eternal recurrence is thus the standard insofar as it establishes the musical structure of the whole within which the idols have their tragic meaning.

We saw in our consideration of the title how the hammer for Nietzsche formed a new sword and a new necessity, how it produced the lightning and the storm to dissolve the twilight and reveal the new tragic age. Here, we see explicitly how this is to be achieved. The doctrine of the eternal recurrence is the great tool with which the overman and the tragic age he embodies are to be liberated from the stone within which they are imprisoned and the musical instrument which gives a tragic meaning to the contradictions or dissonances of the Western tradition. Nietzsche thus intended to have Zarathustra proclaim immediately after the recognition of the eternal recurrence, "*I have the hammer!*" (VI 1, 516) and later, in proclaiming the advent of the overman, "Man is that which must be overcome. *Here I hold the hammer* that overcomes him" (VII 1, 637; see also VIII 1, 130). The hammer of the recurrence with which Nietzsche teaches and seeks to foster the overman and tragedy is the musical form, the grand style, of his work as a whole. Nietzsche's fundamental teaching is thus never explicitly articulated but is imparted only formally, only in and as the musical form of the work as a whole. It is in this sense that the disciple of Dionysus the philosopher is also the teacher of the eternal recurrence. It is the architectonic combination of music and philosophy that is the proper vehicle for the transmission of the doctrine of the eternal recurrence. The coda of the work as a whole, entitled "The Hammer Speaks," makes this clear.

■ CODA

"Hammer" was added to the work after the body of the work was completed, perhaps at the same time as "Ancients." It is a slightly altered version of the untitled section 29 of the third part of *Zarathustra,* entitled "On the Old and New Tablets." Nietzsche apparently first intended to use it at the end of *Ecce Homo* but sometime shortly after 4 November 1888, when *Ecce Homo* was completed, attached it to the end of *Twilight of the Idols.*

The section in *Zarathustra* is the penultimate section before Zarathustra's recognition of his most abysmal thought, that is, the eternal recurrence, in "The Convalescent." Nietzsche perhaps means to draw attention to this section from *Zarathustra* when he characterizes *Twilight* in the preface as a convalescence. As the culmination and summation of *Twilight,* "The Hammer Speaks" thus seems to present itself and the work as a whole as the penultimate moment in mankind's developing recognition of the eternal recurrence and hence as the penultimate moment in the development of tragedy and a tragic culture. This is also suggested by the fact that Nietzsche decided to use the last section of "On the Old and New Tablets" as the conclusion to the work following *Twilight,* that is, *The Antichrist,* after he decided it would not be the first book of the magnum opus. The series of works was thus apparently meant to lead mankind over the last two steps of the path to the revelation of the eternal recurrence and the birth of the tragic age.

Nietzsche may have given us a subtle indication that this is indeed the case. Zarathustra argued that man was a rope stretched between beast and overman and that he would reach his great noon, the time of decision, the moment of the recognition of the eternal recurrence, when he stood precisely at the *middle* of his way. Is *Twilight* this middle? The first and last words of the text proper seem to indicate as much: "In the middle . . . of the eternal recurrence." If this is the case, then the last words of the coda may articulate the necessity that Nietzsche discerns for the present: "Become hard!"

■ MUSIC AND PHILOSOPHY

The goal of Nietzsche's project is nothing less than the transformation of the West, a renewal of European political culture and of humanity itself. In the words of Zarathustra, "God died: now *we* want the overman to live" (VI 1, 353). The overman, who lives beyond God and all idols, is the basis of this new tragic age. He grasps the doctrine

143

of the eternal recurrence and hence understands the *necessity* of the highest and the most abysmal human possibilities, or, in the terminology of *Twilight,* of both ascending and descending life. The death of God is thus the necessary presupposition of the overman and hence of tragedy and the great politics of the tragic age, but it is not in itself sufficient to engender them. Nihilism merely prepares the way for the musical transformation of Western civilization.

As we have seen, Nietzsche's music is fundamentally bound up with philosophy in his architectonic synthesis. He suggests this in a letter of 20 October 1887 to Hermann Levi: "Perhaps there was never a philosopher who was a musician to the degree that I am." With this synthesis Nietzsche returns, however, not merely to the ancient tragedians but also to the pre-Socratic philosophers. Of first importance are the Pythagoreans.

The Pythogoreans in Nietzsche's view provided the basis for the reconciliation of philosophy and music, of Apollo the god of measure and Dionysus the god of ecstasy, by demonstrating the mathematical basis of tonality and the musical basis of mathematics. They were thus able to transform all qualitative differences, that is, all contradictions or dissonances, into quantitative differences and consequently could conceive of the world with all its contradictions and dissonances as a fundamentally rational and harmonious musical-mathematical composition. In their view, "The entire essence of the world whose image was music, although played on only one string, might be expressed purely in numbers."[29] However, this does not dispose of the contradictions. On the contrary—it is precisely the maintenance of the contradictions that is necessary to harmony. The world harmony is thus "the unity of the manifold and the harmony of conflicting dispositions. If contradiction is an element in everything, then harmony is in everything too."[30] As Nietzsche himself points out, however, this is nothing other than the doctrine of Heracleitus.[31]

Heracleitus, who saw the "eternal crash of waves and rhythm of things," understood nature as becoming, "which he comprehended in the form of polarity, as the separation of a force into two qualitatively different, antithetical activities that strive toward reunification" (III 2, 316, 319).[32] This world of contradiction and becoming seems to ordinary human beings to dissolve into meaninglessness, but, for those who have ears to hear, "all opposition runs together into a harmony" (III 2, 324). This is the essence of the tragic that the harmony and beauty of the world are impossible without contradiction, that is, without suffering. The meaning of music as the Dionysian art that expresses this world harmony thus resides in "the wonderful meaning of *musical dissonance.* . . . The Dionysian, with its original joy even in pain, is the common womb of music and tragic myth" (III 1, 148; see also III 1, 40). This is truly comprehended and given form only by the aesthetic man, who has learned from the artist and the genesis of an artwork how the conflict of multiplicity can bear in itself law and right, how the artist stands contemplatively above and efficaciously within the art work, how necessity and play, opposition and harmony, must couple themselves in the procreation of art (III 2, 325). Only through art and the artist can one grasp the character of the world harmony and hence of tragedy.

For Nietzsche, this conception of music as world harmony is the basis for the transformation of nihilism, which recognizes contradiction only as meaninglessness, into a tragic culture, which understands contradiction as characteristic of a harmonious cosmos. This harmonizing of contradictions, which Nietzsche attributes to music, is also called the will to power.

The will to power presupposes opposition but subordinates it within itself. This in Nietzsche's view is the essence of all that is, and it is this essence that music represents (III 1, 46–47, 101–4; see also IV 1, 43).[33] Music is thus the most fundamental art and consequently the source of all other human arts, including speech (III 1, 46).[34] Since man becomes the rational animal through speech, "man as a whole is a phenomenon of music."[35] Music as the representation of the will to power thus expresses the essential truth of man and the cosmos, of life itself in the most comprehensive sense.

The harmony of opposites that the will to power assumes and music represents, however, is insufficient and can sustain itself as a coherent account of the whole only if this harmony is itself a moment of a complete and sufficiently grounded melody. If each harmony is only in itself and not *fundamentally* related to every other harmony, it is merely contingent and accidental and hence unstable and ephemeral. If music represents the essence of what is, then it must encompass all existence. Every harmony, whether dissonant or perfect, must reside within the melody that this music constitutes. Sonata form for Nietzsche represents such a complete and comprehensive melody.

If the essence of man and the cosmos, the will to power, finds its best expression in music, then its existence, the eternal recurrence, finds its best representation in sonata form. On a cosmological level, the eternal recurrence of the same ensures the wholeness of the whole and hence the sufficient reason or ground of every event and therefore of every opposition in and through the circularity of the causal series. Sonata form is the representation of this circularity, of the eternal recurrence of the same, and as such is the appropriate form for Nietzsche's work. Nietzsche thus musically bridges the fundamental metaphysical disjunction of essence and existence: both are elements of an encompassing musical whole.

Nietzsche's doctrine of the eternal recurrence is perhaps the most perplexing of the many enigmatic aspects of his thought. In fact, there are apparently two different teachings of the eternal recurrence, a metaphysical or scientific teaching that presents the eternal recurrence as a cosmological process and an existential teaching that presents it as the experience of the abyss, of the *necessity* of the most horrible human possibilities. The recognition of the musical structure of Nietzsche's work offers a clue to the resolution of this ambiguity. If Nietzsche's teaching of the doctrine is essentially formal, as I have tried to show, and if the manner of the teaching corresponds to its substance, then the teaching of the eternal recurrence is neither a metaphysical nor an existential but rather an aesthetic doctrine that demonstrates the fundamental unity of the will to power and the eternal recurrence. As the synthesis of progression or development and circularity or repetition, sonata form is the most appropriate representation of the will to power as the eternal recurrence. The exposition themes recur in the recapitulation and hence constitute a circular *melodic* structure. The entire form, however, is a *harmonic* progression which aims at the resolution of the original harmonic tension or opposition between the exposition themes through a development of these themes. This development is the subordination of harmony to melody, that is, the transformation of the harmony to correspond to the original and recapitulated melody. In sonata form, as in the music of Greek tragedy, "*melody* is thus the first and most general" (III 1, 44). This melody, however, is not the Wagnerian infinite melody but an architectonic concatenation of melodic phrases into a rational and balanced circular whole.

The musical expression of the will to power thus finds its completion in the representation of the eternal recurrence in sonata form. The metaphysical teaching is reflected in the architectonic *circularity* of the form as a whole, and the existential teaching in the recognition that the abysmal last man is as necessary as the exalted overman. This is made bearable by the recognition of the *progression* from dissonance to perfect harmony, from the tension in the exposition of descending and ascending life, of Socrates and Nietzsche, of Christianity and tragedy to the harmony of the highest and lowest moments of life in the tragic age portrayed in the recapitulation.

The distinction between the philosophical and the musical in *Twi-*

light is thus resolved. Hence, Nietzsche completes in his own way a task which the twentieth century has considered peculiarly its own—the resolution of the dichotomy of philosophic and poetic thinking. In different ways, this problem lies at the basis of analytic philosophy, existentialism, and hermeneutics. Of course, it has long been recognized that Nietzsche sought such a resolution, but most scholars have doubted that he actually attained it. Nietzsche recognized, however, more clearly than many of his successors the greatest obstacle to the attainment of this goal—the thought of Socrates-Plato. Plato expresses the problem succinctly and dramatically in book 10 of the *Republic* when Socrates tells Glaucon of an old quarrel between philosophy and poetry and admits that, while he feels poetry must be banned from the city they have constructed in speech, he hopes that it can find an argument for its readmission since he is so charmed by its beauty. Nietzsche produces such a argument. It is an argument, however, not for the admission of poetry to Plato's philosophical republic but for the unity of philosophy and poetry in a Nietzschean republic that harks back to the tragic character of Greek political actuality and yet looks forward beyond the twilight of the present nihilistic age and its idols, indeed beyond the West itself, to the tragic culture and great politics of the overman. Whether his argument would have convinced Socrates remains questionable.

∎ NOTES

1. Curt Paul Janz, *Friederich Nietzsche: Biographie,* 3 vols. (Munich: Hanser, 1978–79), 2:265.

2. See for example the initial review in the *Allgemeiner Schweizer Zeitung* (Basel), 9 February 1889.

3. Julius Kaften, "Aus der Werkstatt des Übermenschen," *Deutsche Rundschau* 31 (1905): 253ff; Janz, *Nietzsche,* 2:620.

4. Martin Heidegger's seminal Nietzsche lectures of the 1930s were, for example, not published until 1961. *Nietzsche,* 2 vols. (Pfullingen: Neske, 1961), 1:486.

5. Karl Jaspers, *Nietzsche: Einführung in das Verständnis seines Philosophierens,* 4th ed. (Berlin: de Gruyter, 1974), 17—21.

6. Jacques Derrida for example doubts there is any totality in Nietzsche's text. *Spurs: Nietzsche's Styles/Éperons: Les Styles de Nietzsche* (Chicago: University of Chicago Press, 1979), 134.

7. In a letter of 14 September 1888, he recommends to Paul Deussen that he "read this piece once from the standpoint of taste and style: no one writes like this in Germany today"; to Malwilda von Meysenbug, he remarks in a letter of 4 October 1888 that "in the end I myself am now the single refined

Germany stylist"; and to his sister in a letter of October 1888 that "in this golden fall I write the most beautiful things I ever experienced."

8. Janz has considered Nietzsche's substantive concern with music in his Nietzsche biography cited above, his edition of Nietzsche's *Der Musikalische Nachlass* (Basel: Barenreiter, 1976), and his "Die Kompositionen Friederich Nietzsches," *Nietzsche-Studien* 1 (1972): 172–84. See also his essay in this volume.

9. Janz, "Kompositionen," 185.

10. Nietzsche to Köselitz, 17 May 1888; Janz, *Musikalische Nachlass,* 341–43.

11. Janz, *Nietzsche,* 2:215.

12. Ibid., 211–21; Janz, "Kompositionen," 175.

13. Werner Dannhauser notes the almost musical cohesion of the work. *Nietzsche's View of Socrates* (Ithaca: Cornell University Press, 1974), 203. Janz suggests that in *Twilight,* "the 'music' becomes dissonant" (*Nietzsche,* 2:220).

14. Friedrich Nietzsche, *Werke in Drei Bänden,* 3 vols., ed. K. Schlecta (Munich: Hanser, 1954–56), 3:27.

15. The structure of the other four works of 1888 also seems to be based upon musical forms. *Ecce Homo,* like *Twilight,* seems to be written in sonata form. Its structure might be schematized as follows:

Introduction	"Forward"
Exposition	
Theme I	"Why I Am So Wise"
Theme II	"Why I Am So Clever"
Theme III	"Why I Write Such Good Books"
Development	"Birth of Tragedy"—"The Case of Wagner"
Recapitulation	"Why I Am Destiny"

Here the structure is made clear even in the chapter titles. Both the *Case of Wagner* and *The Antichrist* are apparently in ternary form (ABA). They might be schematized as follows: *The Case of Wagner* A (1–4), B (5–7), A (8–11), Coda (12); *The Antichrist* A (1–23), B (23–43), A (44–61), Coda (62). Such a division of course would require a thorough explanation that cannot be given here. The fourth work, *Nietzsche contra Wagner* is apparently written as a theme and variations. Each variation begins with a "w" word, i.e., *Wo, Wo, Wagner, Eine Musik, Wir, Wohin, Wagner, Wie, Der Psycholog.* The themes are thus separated by an intermezzo and a music of the future, both of which point to the musical character of the work. The end of the work is apparently the statement of the psychologist about this music.

16. On the development of *Twilight* as a manuscript, see Mazzino Montinari's "Nietzsche Lesen: Die Götzen-Dämmerung," *Nietzsche-Studien* 13 (1984): 69–79.

18. Richard Wagner, *Götterdämmerung,* act 3, scene 2, lines 189–92.

19. While this might seem far-fetched, Nietzsche was concerned with such numerology in his classical scholarship. See Christopher Middleton, "Nietzsche on Music and Meter," *Arion* 6 (1967): 58–65.

20. Friedrich Nietzsche, *Gesammelte Werke, Musarionausgabe,* 23 vols. (Munich:Musarion,1920–29),2:245–47;5:121–25.(Hereafter cited as *MusA.*) While in Basel, Nietzsche often taught courses on both Greek meter and Greek rhythm.

21. For the original preface to *Idleness,* see VIII 3, 345–47.

22. *MusA,* 2:289.

23. Cf. also Nietzsche's proposed conclusion to *The Antichrist:* "*Law against Christianity.* Given on the day of convalescence, on the first day of the year one (—on 30th of September 1888 of the false chronology)" (VI 3, 252).

24. Dannhauser, *Nietzsche's View of Socrates,* 207.

25. Nietzsche recognizes Spinoza as his precursor in a letter to Overbeck of 30 July 1881. He refers to Schopenhauer in a similar vein at VII 3, 254.

26. Goethe, *Faust,* line 11,989 (VIII 3, 324).

27. Erich Podach, *Friedrich Nietzsches Werke des Zusammenbruchs* (Heidelberg: Kampmann, 1961), 236.

28. Friedrich Nietzsche, *Werke: Grossoktavausgabe,* 15 vols. (Leipzig: Naumann, 1894–1904), 14:414.

29. Friedrich Nietzsche, "Die Pythagoreer," in *Werke: Grossoktav Ausgabe,* 2d ed., 19 vols. (Leipzig: Kroner, 1901–13), 10:118.

30. Ibid., 119.

31. Ibid.

32. In a note in the *Nachlass,* Nietzsche tries to express his own experience of this world harmony: "Five, six seconds and no more: there you suddenly feel the presence of the eternal harmony. . . . In these five seconds I live an entire human existence, for them I would give my entire life and I would not have paid too much" (VIII 2, 388).

33. See also *MusA,* 3:344.

34. Ibid., 342, 376.

35. Ibid., 376.

PART III

Visions of the Blessed Isles: Nietzsche's New World

CHAPTER 6

■ Nietzsche's Political Aesthetics

Tracy B. Strong

The painter and the political man shape others much more than
they follow after them; the public at whom they aim is not given,
but is rather only the public that their work will bring into being.
— Merleau-Ponty, *La prose du monde*

To say it briefly (for a long time people will still keep silent about
it): What will not (henceforth) be built any more, *cannot* be built
any more, is—a society, in the old sense of that word; to build
that, everything is lacking, above all the material. *All of us are no
longer material for a society;* this is a truth for which the time
has come.
— Nietzsche, *The Gay Science,* # 356 (V 2, 279)

At the end of his life in sanity, Nietzsche writes to a number of corre-
spondents as if he were becoming the political opposition to the
dominant regimes in Europe. He advises Overbeck late in December
1888 that he is "working up a memorandum for the courts of Europe
with an anti-German league in view." He suggests that Peter Gast may
write him in the Palazzo del Quirinale and announces to Strindberg
that he is having the young emperor shot. In the preface to *Nietzsche
contra Wagner,* written on Christmas Day, 1888, in Turin, he chides
the Italian prime minister for going too far in the Triple Alliance:
"With the Reich an intelligent people can only enter into a *mésalli-
ance*" (VI 3, 413). But for one line, the last words he ever wrote are to
his old friend and Basel colleague, Burckhardt: "Wilhelm[,] Bismarck
and all anti-Semites shot."[1] His stance, severely burdened by madness, is of a politics that sets him in opposition to all that is dominant
in Europe. He is "ready to rule the world" (VIII 3, 460).

These letters and the notes that accompany them in the *Nach-*

lass—indeed, his entire last notebook[2]—stand importantly distinct from the writings that Nietzsche had prepared for publication. In those, the text predominated; each book gives us a different authorial Nietzsche. The writer of the *Genealogy of Morals* is what a moralist would be in our time; he is a prophet in *Zarathustra;* in *Ecce Homo,* he is Nietzsche. And in each book, the author also calls himself into question such that we both are given a perspective and denied its finality at the same time. However, in these last letters and notes (and even to some necessary degree in *Ecce Homo*), Nietzsche no longer appears to care how we take him—he is ready to assume command.

In part, of course, this is the insanity that comes from taking oneself seriously. Yet one senses an impatience in these lines and a refusal to take satisfaction with being his texts.[3] He wants to act.

What leads Nietzsche, at the end of his life, to fall into the position of a political opponent of the regime, to think that a political act is a necessary prerequisite for any transfiguration of European society? At the beginning of his public life, he had argued in *The Birth of Tragedy* that an aesthetic moment was necessary for the reconstruction of European culture. According to that book, an aesthetic renewal could make possible a vibrant self-reproducing political life. At the end of Nietzsche's life, however, politics has become the master trope; the appreciation of the relation of the present has changed. How did this happen?

To answer this, one must understand what the components of his original aesthetic vision were. One approaches this problem best by looking back to the beginning of Nietzsche's career: in whom did he find himself as he left Leipzig for a career as an academic at Basel in the late 1860s?

Influences are as much the result of an active choice as they are a natural force. I have no intention of claiming that Nietzsche's work is simply an amalgam of his environments. But it is quite clear that among those to which he chose to respond were the musical criticism of Schopenhauer, the ambitions of Richard Wagner, the example of Jacob Burckhardt, the full manifestation of Bismarck's vision of the state in the Schleswig-Holstein crisis and the Franco-Prussian war.

Nietzsche's appreciation of Schopenhauer is, of course, well known. It is, however, still not without difficulty. There is a standard interpretation of Schopenhauer, often attributed to Nietzsche, according to which Schopenhauer would have argued that music is distinguished among all human activities by virtue of being a "copy" of the will.[4] It *is* quite true that this judgment seems to rest quite easily on a number of passages in Schopenhauer, such as those in which he declares that music gives an account of the "secret history" of the will and expresses its most "intimate essence."

The problem with this interpretation is that it runs up against specific declarations by Schopenhauer himself. He asserts that music has only an indirect relation to the will and that it never expresses what is "of" or "in" the will, only the "essence" of the will. In fact, he also declares that one might see the world as an incarnation in music. There is not, therefore, for Schopenhauer, any real indication that the will stands somehow "behind" the world; rather one has to say that for him the world (as we experience it) and the will are contemporaneous.

Music, for Schopenhauer, is, or can thus be understood as, revelatory of the world *before* the will, since the will can only be reproductive of the world with which it is coterminous. Therefore music, as art, is not concerned with what the will reproduces but with the possibilities of reproduction by the will, with what underlies the will and makes it possible.

The point here is that Schopenhauer does not argue that the will is the most basic manifestation of our being in the world but rather that it is made possible by something else. It is to this aspect of Schopenhauer, I believe, that Nietzsche pays most of his attention. That which "underlies" the will is what Nietzsche calls "life" (or occasionally in the *Birth,* the *Ureine*) and which he designates as the existence of a living form that has a will. The major difference between Nietzsche and Schopenhauer, as Nietzsche himself recognizes even in the *Birth,*[5] is that Nietzsche thinks that the underlying actuality—"life"—can itself assume different forms and that one should pay attention to the particular form of life. Thus Nietzsche will write a "genealogy of morals" that distinguishes among various forms of life. Schopenhauer, for whom all life is the same, remains a pessimist; Nietzsche has at least the possibility of change.[6]

Second, Nietzsche's relations with Wagner are manifold. Contrary to what is usually asserted, it is doubtful that the major portion of their mutual attraction came because of their shared high opinion of Schopenhauer; there was in fact much more in Wagner's persona in the late 1860s for Nietzsche to take note of than in his rather poorly digested version of Schopenhauer.[7] Wagner was best known as the man who was trying to bring art and politics together. In relation to the events of 1848, at which time he had been a socialist, Wagner had written that it was for art, and art above all else, to teach [the] social impulse its noblest meaning, and guide it towards its true direction. Only on the shoulders of this great social movement can true art lift itself from its present state of civilized barbarism, and take its post of honor. Each has a common goal, and the twain can reach it only when they recognize it jointly. This goal is the strong fair man, to whom revolution shall give his strength and art his beauty.[8]

Shortly before Nietzsche made his acquaintance, Wagner published "German Art and German Politics," in which he argued that the "German spirit's aptitudes" for art made possible an ennobling of the "public spiritual life" of the Germans because it gave the requisite energies to those in whom "repose the political fortunes of the German peoples."[9] Nietzsche calls Gersdorff's attention to this essay in a letter of 4 August 1869 and reminds him of it again the next March. It is clear that one of the things about Wagner that appealed to Nietzsche was the political role he saw for art: that is what he points his friends toward in the correspondence of the period.

From Schopenhauer, Nietzsche retained the idea that the quality of one's being in the world is a mediated reproduction of that which underlies such a presentation of self. With Wagner, he saw that this mediation is both aesthetic and political in nature. In addition to that of Schopenhauer and Wagner, at Basel Nietzsche put himself under the influence of the great historian, Jakob Burckhardt. The attraction was one of the first after Nietzsche arrived at Basel. He saw "a great deal" of him and attended his weekly seminar on the study of history, a "lovely but rare refrain" in the "spirit of Schopenhauer."[10] Burckhardt had recently (1860) published *The Civilization of the Renaissance in Italy.*[11] The three parts of the first volume were "The State as a Work of Art," "The Development of the Individual," and "The Revival of Antiquity." Burckhardt argued that the artistic qualities that the state sometimes assumed in the Renaissance were a "new fact" and permitted the overcoming of, or compensation for, "the modern political spirit of Europe, surrendered freely to its own instincts, often displaying the worst features of an unbridled egoism. . . ."[12] In other words, the achievements of the Italian Renaissance were due to a victory won by the human spirit over the unbridled aggressive instincts that had become characteristic of the world in modernity and could once again become a problem. Nietzsche was to take a version of this understanding and, as Burckhardt was also to later, read the Greeks in the same manner.[13]

If Burckhardt taught Nietzsche to see in society the same forces that were at work in the individual, the fourth dominant factor to which Nietzsche responded at the beginning of his public and professional life was sociopolitical: the full development and practice of Bismarck's *Machtpolitik*. Nietzsche had originally had a burst of nationalist enthusiasm for the new Prussian politics but found himself rapidly dismayed by Bismarck's politics.[14] The instrumentalism of Bismarck's *Kleindeutschpolitik* served only, it seemed to Nietzsche, to leave one disenchanted with the state so totally that no one would have any reason for being a member of it.[15] The nationalism fostered by Bismarck's policies is, writes Nietzsche, "a *névrose nationale* . . . [which has] deprived Europe of its reasons—driven it into a dead-end street" (VI 3, 358).

What is the appeal of art in relation to political questions? Why would this lead Nietzsche to reject Bismarck? If he rejects Bismarck's politics, in the vision of what kind of politics does he establish himself as an oppositional figure at the end of his life? One more element needs to be added.

It is clear from the above sketch of the influences of Schopenhauer, Wagner, and Burckhardt that many of the ideas that became part of Nietzsche's early work were in the intellectual air which was his natural environment. Yet, in his earlier work, he also goes much deeper than did ever Wagner or Burckhardt. How, can be seen in the manner in which Nietzsche adds to the intention of his first writings a concept that is probably the source of his attraction to Emerson.[16]

We know that Nietzsche had read Emerson at least as early as 1862, when he was eighteen years old. He mentions him favorably throughout his life. It is also clear from the beginning of the 7 April 1866 letter to Gersdorff that he had been particularly struck by the "Divinity School Address." Nietzsche writes: "Sometimes there come those quiet meditative moments *in which one stands above one's life* with mixed feelings of joy and sadness, like those lovely summer days which spread themselves expansively and comfortably across the hills, as Emerson so excellently describes them. *Then nature becomes perfect,* as he says, *and we ourselves too; then we are set free from the spell of the ever watchful eye.* . . . "[17] The passages I have italicized are indicative of the attraction that Nietzsche felt. They quote or paraphrase Emerson's text and describe a state of being both of and above the world, a moment of lived perfection, such as that which Nietzsche recovers for himself in 1888 in the epigraph to *Ecce Homo:* "On this perfect day, when everything is ripening and not only the grape turns brown, the eye of the sun just fell upon my life: I looked back, I looked forward, and never saw so many and such good things at once" (VI 3, 261). In the letter to Gersdorff, Nietzsche goes on to lament Bismarck's development of the Schleswig-Holstein crisis and opposes it to the perfected world of which he has spoken. For shorthand, I shall call this this instance of transparency, when our intentions and our abilities are unified in a perfected praxis, the "Emersonian moment."

What is the nature of this moment? Alexander Nehamas is clearly partially correct to identify it as the creation of an artwork out of one-self,[18] but, just as is an artwork, it is much more. It is also a source of this-worldly authority. The major theme of the "Divinity School Address" is what Emerson calls "intuition." Speaking of the sentiment by which men are able to make sense of the world and by which society is itself founded, Emerson writes that it is guarded by "one stern condition; . . . it is an intuition. It cannot be received at second-hand. Truly speaking, it is not instruction, but provocation, that I can receive from another soul. What he announces, I must find true in me, or reject."[19] The presumption in Emerson is that the perfect melding of the knowing self and the world is attainable only when that which guides a person to it can also be found in oneself. We mean by "authority" that which stands as valid for a person simply by virtue of the person who asserts it. Emerson is clearly speaking about what we would call authority and arguing that at this level authority can only be legitimate if it be also found inside oneself. This paradoxical combination of aristocracy and democracy is, as we shall see, repeated in Nietzsche's analysis of the Greeks. It is important to note here that the "intuitive" basis of authority necessarily gives to it an ambiguous state, in that I must always find in myself that which is from another. In this sense, the form of "intuition" is like my appreciation of a judgment about art: I am being asked to find in myself a judgment that appears to be the subjective conclusion of another. If I do find it, the two of us will form a community of judgment. "That's a good painting" is a what Emerson calls a "provocation"—a calling forth—which enables me to find myself with you, or to refuse that recognition. It is, however, also a political matter when the question "Who am I?" can only be answered in the context of an answer to the question "Who are we?"

The *Birth of Tragedy* is premised on the same themes. It opens with the possibilities of attaining certainty of understanding. Nietzsche suggests that the intention of this book is to show how one may attain "unmediated certainty of vision." I take this to mean that Nietzsche seeks to understand how Greek tragedy produced the authoritative understanding of what it meant to be Greek and produced it so deeply that it could not be called into question.

For something not to be able to be called into question means that it stands so basic—so authoritatively—to our life and actions that we would literally be another being were we able to question it.[20] Any form of life must be so grounded; without such a grounding, that life can have neither pose nor definition.

In the *Birth*, Nietzsche thinks that the aesthetic mode provides the only finally possible human approach to the problem of attaining final satisfaction of the collective (and individual) understanding. He does so for the following three reasons.

First, he thinks that the human world is built on the metaphors in terms of which human beings make sense. In the essay "On Truth and Lie in the Extra-Moral Sense," written around the time of the *Birth*, he notes in a Schopenhauerian mode that the "formation of metaphors" is the "fundamental drive" of humankind (III 2, 281). What makes the world a world is that human beings take the metaphors and build: "All that distinguishes man from animal depends on the faculty of rendering [*erflüchtigen*] transparent [*anschaulichen*] metaphors into a framework." It is these frameworks that make possible a life that was not possible with the simple metaphors. Now humans can have "the building of a pyramidal structure on the basis of caste and degree, the creation of a new world of laws, privilege, subordinations, delimitations . . ." (III 2, 375). The elaboration of metaphors into a framework—a working of art—gives us a world together, a world of differences and thus of language and politics.

Second, both the necessity of the metaphoric basis of the understanding and the elaboration of metaphors into a schema are traced to the realm of *human* art. As Nietzsche later makes clear, art itself rests on nothing but human action. In the notes preparatory for *Human, All-Too-Human*, Nietzsche writes in a section entitled "Art Does Not Belong to Nature, But Only to Human Beings."

> In nature there are no sounds, she is dumb; no colors. Also no form, for this is the result of the reflection [*Spiegelung*] of surfaces in the eyes, but in itself there is no up or down, no in nor out. . . . A nature from which one removed our subject would be something very indifferent, uninteresting, not a mysterious original source, not the unveiled riddle of the world. . . . The more we take humans out of the world, the more the world becomes meaningless and empty for us. . . . Art does not seize the nature of things, . . . for in the

159

final analysis there is no 'thing,' nothing that endures. (IV 2, 554–55)

Third, in this perspective, the presence of the world to a person—its availability—is coterminous with its meaning. This is what I have called the Emersonian moment. The *realization* of this—its acknowledgment—would be a world in which human experience was transparent to its own ontology. (This is, incidentally, one of the reasons that Nietzsche and Emerson both inveigh against idolatry.) It is clear that there can be such a world only if it has reference solely to human beings and not to any thing or being that might transcend the human world. Anything that transcends the human world cannot be transparently lived and thus will always surpass the human world. The aesthetic mode thus provides Nietzsche with a world which is thoroughly human and which does not seek to move beyond itself.

In one version of classical thought, a purely human world could be found in the political life. Aristotle, as we know, taught that it was the glory of politics to be a human activity, in that the political life was both self-sufficient and autotelic. Thus, when Aristotle undertook an examination of the world of art (in the *Poetics*), he found that artistic actions were imitations of other actions and thus necessarily pointed beyond themselves. As purely human activities, they were thus inferior to politics, although this was not a reason to reject them outright, as had Plato.[21]

By the time one reaches the later part of the nineteenth century, for reasons that cannot detain us here, politics is no longer seen as the realm of self-sufficient human activity that it had been for Aristotle. It has rather become more or less instrumental, the means to obtaining or protecting other goals not themselves part of the political realm. The use of politics to protect that which is not political is the source of Nietzsche's disappointment with Bismarck. Nietzsche had hoped that Bismarck might be the source of a recentralization of the political but found that in fact Bismarck was exacerbating the tendencies already well entrenched in modern life.[22]

When the devaluation of politics is coupled with a devaluation of the availability of a transcendental realm—this is what Nietzsche means by the "death of God"[23]—few realms remain in which the activity of human beings can be thought of as fully human. One in which it could was a transformed aesthetics that no longer conceived of art as the imitation or representation of that which is not art but now as an activity that built the very world to which it had reference.

The elements of this new vision of art develop in the early eighteenth century. Karsten Harries has the following to say about the work of Kant's teacher, A. G. Baumgarten, the man who developed the claim that a work of art could be thought of as perfect unto itself without reference to a transcendental realm:

> The metaphysician's descriptions [of the world] are inherently inadequate in that he has to content himself with abstract ideas, with a mirror that cannot capture the richness of God's creation. For the sake of clarity and distinctness he sacrifices the concrete and sensuous. The poet does not make that sacrifice. His work is not a pale representation of the world but a second world that addresses itself to sense and spirit. Fusing matter and form into a perfect whole, the poet sacrifices our demand for both completeness and concreteness, as even God's creation cannot, for its order, although perfect, is infinitely complex and thus incommensurable with our finite faculties.[24]

In this vision, art plays the same role in human affairs that politics had for Aristotle. It is an activity that is particularly and only human. This activity does not point beyond itself, either in actuality or in necessity.[25]

It is important to realize immediately that the central question that this vision of aesthetics raises, as had politics, is the question of collective judgment. Both aesthetics and politics seek to ground the significance of the action of an individual in its collective acceptance, but without reference to any entity that might create a community by transcending that act. This was inherent in the thought of Baumgarten and was given its significant modern form in Kant's third critique. There, as Paul Guyer has written, Kant tried to show that it was possible "to ground publicly valid assessment of objects on particularly private feelings and responses."[26] Aesthetics and politics are the realms in which one must determine an authoritative relationship between the private and the public, between individual response and collective validity.

With this in mind, we may return again to the *Birth of Tragedy* with a new understanding of what it meant for Nietzsche to claim that "existence and the world appear as justified only as an aesthetic phenomenon" (III 1, 148; see also III 1, 43). What attracts Nietzsche to Greek drama is his conviction that it is through this form of art that an entire people could discover and recover for itself its certainty of who it was. The problem to which tragedy is the means of a solution for Nietzsche is what we would recognize as a political problem: the

task of a creative renewal of a collective identity. In Nietzsche, however, aesthetics has taken pride of place from politics as the basic
human activity. It lays the groundwork for the creative renewal of a
social identity. Nietzsche speaks of the fact that while the Greeks were
"placed between India and Rome, and pushed toward a seductive
choice, . . . [they] succeeded in *achieving the invention* [*hinzuzuerfin-
den*] of a third form" (III 1, 12). Whereas for Aristotle the point of tragedy had been to produce self-recognition (*anagnorisis*), for Nietzsche
the point was "transformation" (*Verwandlung*). Hence, at the high
point of a performance, the following happens for Nietzsche: "The
proceeding of the tragic chorus is the dramatic proto-phenomenon:
to see oneself [as embodied in the chorus] transformed before one's
very eyes [as spectator] and to begin to act as if one had actually entered into another body, another character . . . . And this phenomenon is encountered epidemically: a whole throng experiences this
magic transformation" (III 1, 57).[27]

What is being attacked in the *Birth* is thus the notion that self-
knowledge is a sufficient or appropriate ground on which to found a
culture and a polity. The problem for Nietzsche is not that of selves
meeting each other and seeking forms of mutual acknowledgment.
Let us call this Hegelian or liberal politics. For Nietzsche, the problem
lies deeper: it is the having of selves at all that is first in question,
then, second, and necessarily coterminous, the kind of self that is attained. Only then do Hegelian problems of mutual recognition come
into play.

We might remember here that politics was for Aristotle the definition and manifestation of what it meant to be a (human) person, as
opposed to a beast or god. Nietzsche is proposing to understand in
aesthetic terms the basis of the activity that would result in the definition of a self. One might phrase the situation like this: the (Hegelian)
politics of recognition and the search for mutuality suffice as long as
selfhood is possible. When, however, we have become strangers to
ourselves and to each other, then *Verklärung,* the Emersonian moment of transfiguration, is the necessary preliminary step that makes
possible a self where there was none.

The turn toward aesthetics as the basis for the political realm thus
corresponds to Nietzsche's attention to a principle of authority that
might meet the problem of modernity. Against modern (liberal/
Hegelian) thought, Nietzsche asserts that the selves that would be capable of relations with others have systematically undermined their
capacities for such relations. In the end, his accusation against Socrates (and, indeed, that against Christianity) is one of privatization,

of a progressive solipsism such that nothing that is said, even to one-self, can stand. If the problem of authority is the problem of being able to recognize in oneself the validity of another's judgment, modernity has made that progressively more and more difficult. This is the actuality of nihilism.

Nietzsche was not the first to have recognized this as a central problem of modernity, but he is one of the first to have generalized it beyond the religious sphere. Whereas Kierkegaard had addressed explicitly the problem of *religious* authority in an age of unbelief,[28] Nietzsche extends the problem to all spheres of existence. Like Kierkegaard, he sees the problem of authority in aesthetic terms: the only source of authority comes from its assertion in the world. A preacher speaks—for whom? A painting requires attention—from whom? How does it happen when we find these assertions in ourselves, when we are, in Emerson's words, "provoked." The problem of authority is a problem of the capacity to acknowledge an other.

Here, Nietzsche runs into a problem. The above claims that, for authority to be possible, there can be no terms by which to understand a claim to it except those that it provides. One might be tempted here to advance a kind of Kantian criticism to the extent that, even if an entity can be self-referential in this manner, it is nonetheless about something.[29] Nietzsche can only counter this by speaking as if a person or a work of art can be experienced as if it had no origin and no past, that is, has no relation other than to itself.

It is clear that there are good arguments for finding this characteristic (perhaps not *only* this one) in works of art. As Stanley Cavell has asked, "What is a text that it has the power of overcoming the person of the author?"[30] Jacques Derrida has seized on this apparent quality of Nietzsche's texts and argued that a text is whatever is made of it.[31] Derrida has taken seriously the place of music in Nietzsche's thought and argued that his writings exist in relation to their audience(s) in the manner that Schopenhauer thought music did. Music could have, Nietzsche writes in *Ecce Homo,* a "world-transfiguring, Yes-saying character" (VI 3, 355). To the degree that one sees Nietzsche's writings as Nietzsche saw the possibilities of music, those writings are a kind of *langue sans parole,* or, what is ironically the same thing, *paroles sans langue.*[32]

In this reading, the role of tragedy is to mediate between music and speech—to make possible the attainment of selfhood both individually and collectively. Nietzsche's interest is in tragedy as a medium; one might almost say as making (Greek) politics possible. Tragedy is not "about" nature, human or otherwise, for no nature is intelligible or even translatable. Tragedy *establishes* the authority of a human sense before the audience in a manner that this sense can be experienced both as something external and found in oneself. (This was the point of the analysis of the proceeding of the tragic chorus, above.) Thus the intention of the *Birth* is "at the same time to have to see and longing to be beyond seeing" (III 1, 146).[33] Authority is made for oneself; that is, one is compelled (not against one's will) to recognize one's experience with others as authoritative.

However, not any text, not any claim, will automatically have the quality of standing for and in itself. Nietzsche makes it quite clear in the *Birth* that authority is not inevitable or guaranteed. Socrates, for instance, by his (and Euripides') inability to be a member of an audience and by his insistence that authority be grounded in a manner transcendent to human activity, ends up by destroying authority. To counter this, Nietzsche intends the book of the *Birth* to provide a kind of test by which the reader will be able to see if she or he is able to receive authority. Nietzsche writes here:

> Whoever wishes to test himself completely accurately as to how closely related he is to the true aesthetic member of an audience or whether he belongs to the community of Socratic-critical persons, has only to examine honestly the feeling with which he receives the wonderous spectacle present to him on stage: does he feel offended in his historical sense, relying as it does on strict psychological causality; does he benevolently concede that it is intelligible to the childish, but alien to him; or does he feel something else? (III 1, 141)

"Something else" is a weak ending to Nietzsche's rhetorical question, as if he knew already in the early 1870s that an alternative would be difficult to achieve. Nietzsche is asking who, in our times, can let him- or herself be provoked to find an other in him- or herself. This appears to be possible insofar as the persons who do this experience each other as works of art, without pasts. They must also, of course, experience themselves in this manner, as an eternal return of the present. Yet the question arises, and arose to Nietzsche, of whether or not it was possible for anyone ever to so experience himself.

Nietzsche's appreciation of the difficulty of achieving a state without, as it were, a past as a necessary preliminary for aesthetic transfiguration had become quite complex by the time he wrote *Thus Spoke Zarathustra*. The reason, he had come to see, had to do with the persistence of the past in the present, Emerson's "corpse of memory," that nightmare from which both Joyce and Marx had sought to escape.[34]

The major published analysis of this problem comes perhaps in the chapter "On Redemption" in *Zarathustra*.[35] The chapter opens with a temptation scene: having crossed over a "great bridge" Zarathustra is surrounded by cripples and beggars who beg him to heal them. Healing is not the solution, however, and Zarathustra replies with a bit of folk wisdom to the effect that if "one takes away the hump from the hunchback, one takes away his spirit." Worse than these men, Zarathustra continues, are those men he had previously encountered, who had so developed one part of their personalities that everything else had fallen away. These "inverse cripples"—Nietzsche is stealing directly from Emerson's "The American Scholar"[36]—are the products of the tyrannical division of labor of a misbegetting society.

This strange and surreal introduction marks two things. First, Nietzsche does not think that these people are ill in the sense that removal of their illnesses will make them whole. Indeed, their illnesses are who they are. Second, to reach a state other than the one that makes these people who they are, the "now and the past" will have to be changed.

We are thus launched headlong into the problems of dealing with the past and with one's genealogy. If we are to be redeemed from who we are, we will have to be redeemed from our pasts. If humans are to be more than time's fools, they must do more than simply acknowledge that they have pasts (which Hegel had done brilliantly), they must aim "higher than reconciliation." Redemption might thus *appear* as "recreating all 'it was' into 'thus I willed it.'"

This possibility, however, is immediately rejected as too easy. "The will itself is still a prisoner . . . ; it cannot will backwards, it cannot break time and the covetousness of time." As I read this, it indicates that Nietzsche does not think that willing can break the world of the past, for it is fatally tied to the movement of time. Any will—this much he had learned from Schopenhauer—is part of a configuration that has a past. It cannot break that past without destroying itself. Thus, since implicit in it are elements of the past by which it came to be—that makes it what it is—it can never break the past, that is, "will backwards."[37]

Indeed, to drive his point home and to distance himself from his previous approach to this problem, Nietzsche now proceeds to give five summaries of previous attempts to deal with the problem of the past. The arguments are not mentioned by name but are not hard to identify. These summaries are capsules of what Nietzsche develops elsewhere. First come Hegel and Anaximander, who, he suggests, attempt to solve the problem of transitoriness precisely by locating value in the phenomenon of change and thus in the whole. But, if the whole is, as Nietzsche argues, itself the problem, this is no solution.

Nietzsche then turns to the "as if" fatalism of Kant and Anaxagoras, who posit an unknowable and unchanging world which is nevertheless fraught precisely with the characteristics of that which is valued. Here, the solution is too pat, and Nietzsche moves next to the cosmic fatalism of Schopenhauer, where not having a will becomes an answer. Indeed it is, replies Nietzsche, but what would that be?

As he had in life, Nietzsche moves from Schopenhauer to Wagner. In Wagner, "the will at last redeems itself and becomes nonwill." This is in fact the central thrust of all Wagner's operas, from *The Flying Dutchman* to *Parsifal.*[38] For Nietzsche, this is, in the end, simply sociologically unacceptable. That the solution to the problems of the world should depend on the sudden appearance of a man who has remained totally outside the world was impossible. Nietzsche later, in *The Case of Wagner,* suggests caustically that what the world needs is "redemption from the redeemer."

Nietzsche thus suggests that we must move away from redemption, insofar as that concept implies that existence and the past are crimes which must be expiated, from which one must be rescued. He turns to a fifth attempt, his own, in the *Birth:* "I led you away from all these fables when I taught you 'the will is a creator.' All 'it was' is a fragment, a riddle, a dreadful accident—until the creative will says to it 'But thus I willed it.' . . . But has the will spoken thus? And when will that happen?" The *Birth of Tragedy* points in the right direction but does not provide the right answer. The will can only "speak thus" when there is "reconciliation with time," and "something higher than reconciliation [i.e., not just expiation], only when the will is taught to will backwards."

What does this mean in practice? Nietzsche has Zarathustra break off the exchange here; for a long time he will speak with no one. Nietzsche seems to be saying that the standard notion of redemption attained through an act of will which comes to terms with, or simply eliminates, the past is unsatisfactory. Previous attempts are all deficient in that they either permit an attempt to ignore the weight of the past or simply assert the possibility of escaping from it. For Nietzsche, these older conceptions of will are all mistaken; they "do not exist at all," for, "instead of grasping the formulation of a single willing into many forms, [in them] one eliminates the character of willing by subtracting from the will its content, its 'Whither?'"

With this in mind, let us return to Nietzsche's casting of himself as the political opposition to the European state system during the months before his insanity. As noted above, it should be apparent that these passages constitute a break with the mode of the writing during the intervening years. It is not just that they have not been finished for publication—there is nothing else like them in the *Nachlass*. The years that have intervened between the writing of the *Birth* and *Ecce Homo* were in part occupied with "idols," what one might call the criticism of ideology.[39] Yet the general mode of all of them, even, and perhaps in special desperation, of *Ecce Homo,* is not simply to expose but to set a stage for a reader. This means that Nietzsche does not think that his attacks on the various idols he finds all around him will, in themselves, suffice. Instead, he is most concerned with whether or not he will be read.[40]

The unity of the early and the late writings comes precisely in Nietzsche's assurance—ambivalent at first in the *Birth,* clear-cut by the time of *Zarathustra* and *Beyond Good and Evil*—that his texts are what they are because of their readers. He wants us to encounter these texts as we would encounter another person, with the assurance of his presence. As with other people, we can never start or end by claiming to know what they mean—we do not mean the statement "I know John" to be equivalent to "I know what John means." We do not, therefore, if Nietzsche be correct, learn from them by determining what they mean, as if they were a container for his "message."[41] We learn from them by finding ourselves in them—precisely the source of authority that Nietzsche had found too easily in the experience of Greek drama and that his subsequent writings all try to make possible in different realms of human existence. Thus, in the *Genealogy,* Nietzsche explores morality; in *Beyond Good and Evil,* he explores various aspects of knowledge, what is called *Wissenschaft;*[42] in *Zarathustra,* the various aspects of social organization as concretized in the historicity of human practice; in *Twilight of the Idols,* authority itself.

It is in *Ecce Homo* that Nietzsche explores what it means for an author to explore these topics. *Ecce Homo,* that is, is about writing itself and is thus, in this mode, an autobiography. And here, necessarily, he must allow others to find themselves in him. He must warn them away from finding a message. That is why he separates himself from his writings at the beginning of the section "Why I Write Such

Good Books" and why he suggests that he will be born posthumously, that is, in his readers: "Ultimately, nobody can get more out of things, including books, than he already knows. For what one lacks access to from experience one will have no ear" (VI 3, 296).[43]

The passage is often read as the bold assertion of the power of philosophy. Such a reading, true though it may be, fails to deal with its own idealism. What if we do not have the experience because we do not know it? Or, if we do not know the experience because we do not have it? The two are part of a circle of praxis, and we must ask what anxiety is expressed in this passage.

A considerable evolution has occurred since the first writings. At the end of the *Birth,* he had tried to justify the mixture of academic (argumentative) and intuitional modes that intertwine through the book. He suggests there that scholarship can help us recover the sense of what it means to encounter a myth as myth. He is quite clear that ordinary philological arguments *are* possible for his position in relation to the Greeks. For instance, on 16 July 1871, he sends a long letter to Rohde suggesting a number of scholarly citations in support of the article that his friend is drawing up in reply to Wilamowitz's attack on the *Birth.* But it is also equally clear that he does not think that this *approach* is the most important thrust of his book. That he manifestly failed in his scholarly hopes, especially with those philologists whom he greatly admired, such as Friedrich Ritschl and Hermann Usener,[44] was the source of great distress. Nietzsche had thought that his scholarship could prepare the way such that aesthetics could lead to a recovery of a legitimate common authority.

By the time he left the university, however, the hopes for scholarship were gone, and his sense of the steel box of modernity was overwhelming. Both the academic and intuitional modes fail because of the hold that our pasts have on ourselves. It is important to realize that *Ecce Homo* is not Nietzsche's *Rêveries d'un promeneur solitaire.* Nietzsche did not think, as Rousseau did in *his* madder moments, that the lack of attention paid to him was due to a conscious social conspiracy. The danger is that each person will see only himself in Nietzsche and find himself confirmed in himself. Such a picture of individual isolation—"Whoever thought he had understood something of me, had made up something out of me after his own image" (VI 3, 296)—can only be overcome by a breaking of the will that continues to reproduce the solipsistic world.

Nietzsche has thus moved from scholarship to aesthetics, and now he comes in desperation to politics. On the epistemological level, this is required, for Nietzsche sees himself as having risked the full challenge of solipsism, of the loss of the possibility of authority. In the 1886 preface to the second volume of *Human, All-Too-Human,* he writes of an earlier time when he acquired "that form of solitary speech understood only by the most silent and the most suffering. I spoke without witnesses, or rather, indifferent to the presence of witnesses." Yet, in the end, he found himself rewarded in that he became himself: "At last we receive life's great gifts. . . . We regain *our task* (IV 3, 8 – 9).[45] And in the preface to the first volume of *Human,* after asking, "Who knows today what loneliness is?" Nietzsche goes through the steps a self traverses as it "slowly, stubbornly, distrustingly" draws near "life." Eventually, the self is beside itself, no longer alone; then a person will be able to "generalize" his case and recognize a common problem (IV 2, 11 – 16). All this development has the following sources:

> When I could not find what I *needed,* I had to gain it by force artificially, to counterfeit it, or create it poetically. (And what have poets ever done otherwise? And why else do we have art in the world?) What I always needed most to cure and to restore myself, however, was the belief that I was *not* the only one to be thus, to *see* thus—I needed the enchanting intuition of kinship and equality in the eye and in desire, repose in the trust of friendship; I needed a shared blindness [*eine Blindheit zu Zweien*], with no suspicions or question marks. . . . (IV 2, 5)

Whereas in the *Birth* and the earlier writings, Nietzsche had seen an aesthetic experience as making the recognition of self and other and thus politics possible, at the end of his life he thinks that a political act is necessary to make the aesthetic experience possible. Thus, in *Ecce Homo,* Nietzsche also announces *Geisterkrieger,* ideological warfare, "the like of which has never yet been seen." He explicitly differentiates this position from that which he had adopted at the end of the *Birth,* which, he suggests, was problematic in its lack of concern with politics. There, he notes, he had spoken with "tremendous hope." Had it been successful, then "the highest art in saying Yes to life, tragedy, [would have been] reborn when humanity [had] weathered the consciousness of the hardest but most necessary wars *without suffering from it*" (VI 3, 311).

In the coming century, Nietzsche argues, the nature of war will change. Men will no longer fight over what there is to divide up but instead over the very definition of what is worth having. When he announces that "the *Reich* is a lie," he means that it cannot possibly address itself to the demands of the day. The coming conflict will be, he thinks, for the "domination of the earth," which I take to mean that people will struggle over who will say what is of significance to human beings. The democratization of the modern world makes it possible, Nietzsche thinks, for there to be conditions such that new values could be impressed on a whole people. By 1888, Nietzsche had begun to fear not only that the world did not contain a redeeming dialectic—about which he had always been clear—but had also made impossible the aesthetic experience that had been at the core of the claims advanced in the *Birth of Tragedy.*

The danger to authority is then the danger of skepticism become solipsism, where we cannot find an other nor our selves. Part of what Nietzsche's genealogical investigations have taught him—perhaps too well—is the strength and depth of the hold of the "idols" on not just perception but on the determination of what it means to be a person. Hence, breaking that hold will be the primary task. How then should he present himself to the world?

The anxiety in his autobiography which becomes apparent in his last notebook is, I think, an anxiety about letting himself into the world as a text, rather than as a person. If Nietzsche could be his writing, if we found ourselves and him in *Ecce Homo,* then he will have accomplished his task. It is, I think, Nietzsche's fear that he had arrived at the limits of what he could do through aesthetics that leads him to the explicitly political reflections on domination with which I started this essay and which form the entirety of his last notebook.

And, even in his discussions there, Nietzsche manifests an ambivalent attitude, almost as if he were afraid to set loose what his thought had led him to. He thinks that war has in the past been the consequence of the rule of "the dynasties and the priests" (i.e., of the state structure and religion), but that people have become "habituated to the insane notion [*Wahnsinn*] that it is necessary to have armies in order to have war." This is, he concludes, "an absurdity." On the other hand, the prevalence of war and the social leveling found in the army are the best ways "to educate a whole people to the virtue of obedience and command, to proportion [*Takt*], . . . to the freedom of the spirit." War can be an education in freedom, apparently, providing that it is not used, as for the dynasties and the priests, for "service, duty, . . . and obedience." It is "madness," he concludes, to send "a selection of strength and youth and power before the cannons" (VIII 3, 458–59).[46]

Gilles Deleuze has claimed that for Nietzsche "all justification is *ressentiment.*"[47] Such a conclusion is too easy. If the problem for modernity is that we have lost the capacity to find the judgments of another in ourselves and to find ourselves in another, it is because of this that we have also lost the capacity of accepting justification. This means that nothing stands authoritatively for us. It is to recover this possibility that Nietzsche, on the edge of madness, proposes "great politics." But then the question becomes how one could manage such wars. They would come, he was sure, for they are the consequence of the beings we have become. Hence, fascism, communism, bureaucratic states, are not for Nietzsche radically different political forms. These are all the politics of domination, understood as the inability to live in authority. Nietzsche, as I have tried to read him, is not a thinker of domination. But ironically, at the end, he can only try to prevent a politics of domination by proposing one of his own. Politics is never the cure for solipsism. Life is always more than art can make of it, which is why we need art—to make a life possible.[48]

■   NOTES

1. All these letters may be found in translation in Christopher Middleton, ed., *Selected Letters of Friedrich Nietzsche* (Chicago: University of Chicago Press, 1969) and in the original in vol. III 6 of the *Nietzsche Briefwechsel: Kritische Gesamtausgabe* (Gruyter, 1984). Letters will ordinarily be cited by addressee and date; any not found in the Middleton edition will be given specific reference in the *Briefwechsel.*

2. The notebook may be found in VIII 3.

3. See the epigraph to *Ecce Homo:* "How could I fail to be grateful to my whole life?" (VI 3, 261). See the brilliant analysis in Alexander Nehamas, *Nietzsche: Life as Literature* (Cambridge: Harvard University Press, 1985), last chapter. Nehamas reads the epigraph as uncompromisingly positive; I detect a note of doubt, as if Nietzsche could fail. See below.

4. Schopenhauer's discussion of music occurs in the thirty-ninth chapter in the third book of *Die Welt als Wille und Vorstellung* (Berlin: Tillger, 1924), 424–36.

5. See the discussion in III 1, 129, where he asserts that the Greeks found a new form between Rome and the Orient.

6. I am conscious here of the influence of Clement Rosset, *L'Esthetique de Schopenhauer* (Paris: Presses universitaires de France, 1969), 91–117.

7. See the excellent analysis of Wagner's understanding of Schopenhauer in Jack Stein, *Richard Wagner and the Synthesis of the Arts* (Detroit: Wayne State University Press, 1960).

8. Richard Wagner, "Art and Revolution," in *On Music and Drama,* ed. Albert Goldman and Evert Sprinchorn (New York: Dutton, 1964), 67.

9. Wagner, "German Art and Politics," in *On Music and Drama,* 443.

10. See the letter to Elizabeth, 29 May 1869; to Rohde, 23 November 1870.

11. See the important article by Peter Heller, "The Virtue of the Historian:

Nietzsche in His Relation to Burckhardt," in his *Studies in Nietzsche* (Bonn, 1980), 89–117. Heller gives a capsule summary of the other major work on the relation between Nietzsche and Burckhardt in his n. 8.

12. Jacob Burckhardt, *The Civilization of the Renaissance in Italy* (New York: Harper and Row, 1965), 22.

13. Burckhardt's *The History of Greek Civilization* shares with Nietzsche the appreciation of the agonistic and cruel qualities of Greek civilization. It postdates the *Birth* and existed only in lecture manuscript form by the time that Nietzsche was writing *Human, All-Too-Human.* See the reference in the letter to Rohde, 23 May 1876, where incidentally he notes that both Rohde and Burckhardt avoid the topic of pederasty in the Greeks.

14. See Theodor Schieder, *Nietzsche und Bismarck* (Krepeld: Scherpe, 1963). For Nietzsche's comments on Bismarck, see IV 2, 304; VI 2, 206–8. Nietzsche attacks the parliamentarism used by Bismarck as the means by which the "herd-animal makes himself into the master." See the collection of passages assembled in *Die Unschuld des Werdens,* ed. Alfred Bäumler (Stuttgart: Kröner, 1956), 2:426–27. For a more sympathetic view of the relation between Nietzsche and Bismarck, colored, one suspects by the context of its publication, see H. Fischer, *Nietzsche apostata, oder die Philosophie des Aergernisses* (Erfurt: Stenger, 1931). See the discussion in my *Friedrich Nietzsche and the Politics of Transfiguration* (Berkeley: University of California Press, 1975), 210–12.

15. For a similar but much more detailed analysis, see Max Weber, "Parliament und Regierung," in *Gesammelte Politische Schriften* (Tübingen: Mohr, 1978).

16. See the excellent discussion by Walter Kaufmann in his introduction to his edition of *The Gay Science* (New York: Random House, 1974), 7–13.

17. Cf. R. W. Emerson, "Divinity School Address," in *The Portable Emerson* (New York: Viking, 1975), 49ff. There is an extended comparison of Emerson and Nietzsche in E. Baumgarten, *Das Vorbild Emersons im Werk und Leben Nietzsches* (Heidelberg, 1957).

18. See Nehamas, *Nietzsche: Life as Literature,* 8 and *passim.*

19. Emerson, "Divinity School Address," 52.

20. See my discussion in *Politics of Transfiguration,* 24.

21. This is not to say that there was only politics for Aristotle; obviously not. I say only that he had such a conception of the political life.

22. Thus Nietzsche could write, before his disappointment, to Gersdorff on 16 February 1868 that "Politics is now the organ of collective thinking [*Gesamtdenkens*]. . . . Bismarck makes me immeasurably happy; I read his speeches like strong wine."

23. See Strong, *Politics of Transfiguration,* 250–53; see Martin Heidegger, "The Word of Nietzsche: 'God is dead,'" in *The Question Concerning Technology and Other Essays,* trans. W. Lovitt (New York: Harper and Row, 1977).

24. Karsten Harries, "Metaphor and Transcendence," in *On Metaphor* (Chicago: University of Chicago Press, 1979), 74. I have tried to describe the

personae of this world in "Texts and Pretexts: Reflections on Perspectivism in Nietzsche," *Political Theory* 13 (May 1985): 164–82 and in an unpublished essay, "Drama, Politics and the Recognition of Persons." See the brilliant discussion of these themes in the later eighteenth century in Michael Fried, *Absorption and Theatricality: Painting and Beholder in the Age of Diderot* (Berkeley and Los Angeles: University of California Press, 1980), esp. 80, 147, 158.

25. This is a point worth examining at greater length. Leo Strauss spent his life and writing denying that either art or politics could avoid pointing beyond itself—this was the role of "nature" in his thought. Machiavelli and Augustine argued that at least politics did not have to point beyond itself; the most extensive exploration of this theme is to be found in J. G. A. Pocock, *The Machiavellian Moment* (Princeton: University Press, 1973). It is not surprising that Pocock and the followers of Leo Strauss disagree so strongly. This seems to me the substantive source of their disagreement. Hannah Arendt agreed, I think, with Machiavelli, although she did not deny the validity perhaps of the primacy of a philosophical realm that was neither one of politics nor of art. George Kateb, in *Hannah Arendt* (Totowa, N.J.: Rowan and Allenheld, 1984) has examined the costs of trying to maintain Arendt's position. I suspect that one of the sources of Plato's anxiety about poets, and I know that Rousseau's anxiety, has to do with the fact that if the aesthetic realm has not limits other than those of human action there will in fact be no limits to the worlds that can be played. All the agora is then a stage.

26. Paul Guyer, *Kant and the Judgment of Taste* (Cambridge: Harvard University Press, 1976), 1, 4.

27. See the discussion in Strong, *Politics of Transfiguration,* 162–66.

28. See Søren Kierkegaard, *On Authority and Revelation* (New York: Harper, 1966), esp. 116–17. See my "The Deconstruction of the Tradition: The Greeks and Nietzsche," in *Nietzsche and Nihilism;* ed. Thomas Darby et al. (Toronto: University of Toronto Press, forthcoming) for a discussion.

29. See Alexander Nehamas, "How One Becomes What One Is," *The Philosophical Review* 92 (July 1983): 385–417. Bernd Magnus has suggested that for Nietzsche the world is a kind of pentimento of interpretations. In his "Immanent and Transcendent Perspectivism in Nietzsche," *Nietzsche Studien* 12 (1983): 473–90, Nehamas argues against this on the grounds that, even if a text had been lost and survived only as its interpretations, there still was an original text. See my comments in "Text and Pretext," 176–77.

30. Stanley Cavell, "The Politics of Meaning," in *On Metaphor.*

31. See my discussion of Derrida in "The Deconstruction of the Tradition."

32. See comments that anticipate Derrida and my interpretation of him in Bernard Pautrat, *Versions du soleil* (Paris: Editions du Seuil, 1971), 42.

33. See Strong, *Politics of Transfiguration,* 160–62.

34. Cf. Marx's line in the beginning of *The Eighteenth Brumaire of Louis Napoleon* ("The weight of the past lies on the brain of the living like a nightmare") to that of James Joyce in the second chapter of *Ulysses* ("The past is a

nightmare from which I am trying to awake"). See Emerson, "Self-Reliance," *The Portable Emerson,* 138–64.

35. Some of the material that follows appears in a more detailed fashion in my *Politics of Transfiguration,* 221ff. All unfootnoted citations are from *Thus Spoke Zarathustra,* "On Redemption," until further notice.

36. R. W. Emerson, "The American Scholar," *The Portable Emerson,* 24.

37. The attempt to do so produces what Nietzsche calls "the spirit of revenge" and *ressentiment.* See here Martin Heidegger, "Who Is Nietzsche's Zarathustra?" *Review of Metaphysics* 20 (March 1967): 422.

38. See Nietzsche's desperately funny comments in VI 3, 10–13.

39. See Monika Funke, *Ideologie und Ideologiekritik bei Nietzsche* (Stuttgart: Fromann, 1974).

40. I am conscious here of the fact that I have for many years found part of myself in the works of my friend Alexander Nehamas. See his *Nietzsche: Life as Literature* (Cambridge: Harvard University Press, 1985).

41. See here the seminal work of Stanley Fish, the appendix to *Self-Consuming Artifacts* (Berkeley and Los Angeles: University of California Press, 1974).

42. No one has made this analysis as convincingly as has Robert Eden, *Nihilism and Leadership* (Gainesville: University of South Florida Press, 1980).

43. It is worth reflecting on the relation of this idea to that in Plato's *Meno* of knowledge as recollection.

44. See the unsympathetic discussion and the references in William Musgrave Calder III, "The Nietzsche-Wilamowitz Struggle: New Documents and a Reappraisal," *Nietzsche-Studien* 12 (1983): 214–54 as well as the more general claim in Wilhelm Wurzer, "Nietzsche's Return to an Aesthetic Beginning," *Man and World* 11, no. 1/2 (1978): 63.

45. See the passages in *Ecce Homo* ("Why I Write Such Good Books") on the "thoughts out of season," where he claims that the essays on Wagner and Schopenhauer were cases also of his coming to himself. On solitariness, see my article "Psychoanalysis as a Vocation: Freud, Politics and the Heroic," *Political Theory* 12 (February 1984): 67–68.

46. Bernd Magnus has recently convincingly argued that the material known as the *Nachlass* consists mostly of material that Nietzsche discarded. I agree with his argument but would not apply it to this very late material, which Nietzsche never had a chance to revise and retain or discard. In any case, the themes he was addressing in the last months are the ones described here.

47. Gilles Deleuze, *Nietzsche et la philosophie* (Paris: Presses universitaires de France, 1965), 18.

48. Martin Heidegger reads Nietzsche as a thinker of absolute technology and brutalized energy. By starting with what Nietzsche has to say about art and the Greeks and politics, I have come to a different understanding.

CHAPTER 7

Baubô: Theological Perversion and Fetishism

Sarah Kofman

Translated by Tracy B. Strong

As my father I am already dead, while as my mother I live on and grow older.

—*Ecce Homo*

AN OLD WOMAN

In a frequently cited passage from *Twilight of the Idols,* Nietzsche uses the term *fetishist* to describe a primitive psychology found at the origins of language, reason, and metaphysics (VI 3, 71). In these cases, humans think of the self as a substance and as the cause of their actions. The will is seen also as a cause, and when one projects this conception onto the world, one believes the world to be made up of things, substances, beings, and will. These beliefs constitute fetishism.

Is Nietzsche here the inheritor of August Comte, for whom "fetishism" was the first stage of the "theological" era and a kind of childhood period in which the human spirit was least developed and in which people were incapable of explaining natural phenomena to themselves except by projecting fictions onto the world?[1]

It is true that Nietzsche does think that language activates a genetic psychology; nevertheless, fetishism is not for him, as it was for

Translated by permission of Editions Galilée from Sarah Kofman, *Nietzsche et la scène philosophique* (Paris: Union Générale d'Editions, 1979; Editions Galilée, 1986). This essay was written at the invitation of Jean Gillibert of the Institute of Psychoanalysis on rue Saint-Jacques, Paris, in May 1973 and was published in its first version in *Nuova Corrente* 69–69 (1975–76). The postscript was written for the American edition.

I should like to express my gratitude to Sarah Kofman for her persistent help with this translation.—Trans.

Comte,[2] a necessary and spontaneous solution discovered early by the human spirit as a result of the torment over the need to explain phenomena. Contrary to Comte, Nietzsche does not derive the notion of causality from a speculative need, but from a feeling of *fear:* "The causal instinct is thus conditional upon, and excited by, the feeling of fear" (VI 3, 87). Humans do not invent "the idea of causality" out of a need for causality: they do not invent *causality* per se, but a *particular kind* of cause, "a cause that is comforting, liberating, and relieving . . . [that] searches . . . for a particularly selected and preferred kind of explanation. . . . One kind of positing of causes predominates more and more, is concentrated into a system, and finally emerges as *dominant,* that is, simply precluding other causes and explanations" (VI 3, 87). For Nietzsche, "causality" is thus not strictly a simple error, another "one of the four great errors," but rather an illusion or yet again a lie. "By lie I mean wishing *not* to see something that one does see; wishing not to see something *as* one does see it. . . . The most common lie is that with which one lies to oneself. . . . Now this wishing *not*-to-see what one does see, this wishing-not-to-see *as* one sees, is almost a first condition for those who are of a *party* in any sense" (VI 3, 236).

If fetishism should not be considered as an error necessary and particular to certain periods of human development and thus destined to disappear over time, but corresponds instead to a *refusal* to see, then one can ask oneself if Nietzsche's notion of fetishism is not close to that of Freud. For Freud, abnegation is the particular process of fetishism whereby castration is at once recognized and denied, and where the absence of a penis in women, more particularly in the mother, is both grasped and disregarded.[3]

Castration? Penis? Nietzsche does use Comte's expression of "coarse fetishism," but he seems very far from thinking of Freud's referents. It is, of course, true that Freud notes that a feeling of fear is attached to these concepts; nevertheless, nothing here allows us to say that Nietzsche is afraid of women, still less of his mother. And yet. . . .

And yet: woman, a woman, an old woman, accomplice to the belief in the existence of God, continuously haunts Nietzsche's text.

And yet: Nietzsche designates as *perverse* that system of theological judgments that ends up by dominating to the point of excluding anything that is not itself.

And yet: well before Freud, many passages in Nietzsche do invoke the notion of castration.

With what stitches might one knit a cloth from castration and the perversion of the ascetic priests, from women, and from the concept of causality? Should we distinguish young women from old? Does Nietzsche not himself repeat the ancient theological misogyny that woman is the locus and source of all evil? (IV 3, 224–25). Or should this famous misogyny not itself be rethought and reevaluated from a standpoint that would differentiate it into types?

■ PERVERSION

"Fetishism" occurs rarely in Nietzsche, whereas "perversion" plays a major and varied role. Perversion appears with multiple connotations and referents and is associated with the inversion or the transposition of values. Perversion is the diagnosis by the philosopher-physician of the reversal or the transposition of values. It is decoded as a symptom of sickness and as a state of degeneration. As a corruption of nature or life, perversion consists in preferring those values that are in opposition to natural "finality," to the affirmation of life, to the will to increasing power, to aggression. Perversion denies the immanent finality to life understood as will to power.

Thus, perversion is the "choice" of values other than those that affirm life. It is a will to death, to nothingness. It is a typical disease of the ascetic priest, but also of all those who are animated by the theological instinct. There are thus as many forms of perversion as there are forces that make use of and take form as (*s'emparent*) the ascetic ideal, which, by itself, has no definition (cf. VI 2, 357). All that which wills (*veut*) death may be called perverse. The term is even more accurately applied to that which *cannot* will anything other than death and which therefore always takes the side of that which is feeble, low, misbegotten, the side of all that is opposed to a life of strength and to that which permits a life to grow. Perverse values are nihilistic values hiding themselves under sacred names. It was the work of the priest to falsify the meaning of names and nouns; this was the condition of survival and of the triumph of the weakest.

> I call an animal, a species, or an individual corrupt when it loses its instincts, when it chooses and prefers that which is disadvantageous for it. . . . Life itself is for me the instinct for growth, for durability, for an accumulation of forces, for *power.* . . . All the supreme values of mankind *lack* this will. The values symptomatic of decline, *nihilistic* values, are lording it under the holiest names. (VI 3, 170)
>
> The Christian conception of God—God as God of the sick, God as a spider, God as spirit—is one of the most corrupt conceptions. . . . God degenerated into the *contradiction* of

life instead of being its transfiguration and eternal "Yes."
(VI 3, 183)

The history of Israel is invaluable as the typical history of all
denaturing [*Entnatürlichung*] of natural values. (VI 3, 191)

A parasitical type of man, thriving only at the expense
of all healthy forms of life, the priest . . . at all natural oc-
currences in life, at birth, marriage, sickness, death, . . .
meals—the holy parasite appears in order to denature
them—in his language, to "consecrate." (VI 3, 194)

Everything that contains its value *in itself* is made altogether
valueless, *anti*valuable by the parasitism of the priest. . . .
The priest devalues, *desecrates* nature: this is the price of
his existence. (VI 3, 193–94)

I call Christianity the one great curse, the one great inner-
most corruption [*Verdorbenheit*]. (VI 3, 251)

Perversion is thus antinature. Drives change goals, turn back
against themselves, become denatured and in turn denature all that is
living. This is a reflexive movement, no longer a direct discharge. It
correlates with the invention of a fictitious, abstract world that one
has placed beyond nature, made *super*natural, and set down as the
origin of the world here below. Such a world inverts the relations of
cause and effect, perverts reasons, and is a symptom of the corruption of nature (VI 3, 82).

How should one understand the ideas of "denaturing," of "antinature," and of perversion? There is not an obvious answer. Many
passages in Nietzsche denounce the idea of a nature in itself, as they
do that of a finality, indeed of the whole idea of nature. Like most of
the other "old words," "nature" (as well as denaturation and thus also
perversion) needs to be revalued, read as if crossed-out. This is because the abstract, "denatured," "antinatural" world is still a "natural" world: it too is the expression of a certain form of life. In this
sense, all "culture" is natural. These forms of life are, however, "denatured," in that their will to power has "degenerated," which means
they are not strong enough to rejoice in (*jouir*) and affirm themselves
in the very activity of their strength. Their affirmation and rejoicing is
rather shadowy, oblique, cunning. A "denatured" world is nonetheless "natural" as it is still a means—the only means—by which the
weak can affirm their power and win out over the strong. That which
is perverse and against nature is the will to impose one's own nature
on another, the will to impose the perspective of illness on all, the will
to project the "evil eye" on everything, the will to corrupt that which

is healthy. It is to designate as "supernatural" the fictitious world and not to will to recognize its natural, too natural character. It is, in short, the refusal to acknowledge perspective as such. Denaturation resides in the transformation of names, in the counterfeiting that sanctifies. The changing of a name creates the belief that nature has changed and imposes on life the ideal of a higher, supernatural, origin.

> When through reward and punishment, one has done away
> with natural causality, an *antinatural* causality is re-
> quired. . . . *Morality*—no longer the expression of the con-
> ditions for the life and growth of a people, no longer its
> most basic instinct of life, but become abstract, become the
> antithesis of life—morality as the systematic degeneration
> [*Verschlechterung*] of the imagination, as the "evil eye" for
> everything. What is . . . Christian morality? Chance done out
> of its innocence, misfortune besmirched with the concept of
> "sin"; well-being as a danger, a "temptation." It is a physio-
> logical disposition poisoned by the worm of conscience.
> (VI 3, 192)

How has this counterfeiting succeeded? How have the weak man-
aged to win out over the strong and thus generalize decadence? The triumph of the weak is so "antinature" that it may be understood only as the result of a magical enchantment and a cunning seduction. The general process of denaturalization works by blocking the way (*le dé-tournement*) of the strong, a detour that leads to death along a path embellished with the tawdry tinsel of morality and religion. What is important here is that the weak act like *women:* they try to seduce, they charm, by misrepresenting and disguising nihilistic values under gilded trim.

First of all, then, woman is a picture of weakness and magical seduction: she is the figure of the magical Circe who knew how to se-
duce Ulysses' companions in order to transform them into pigs. Circe? She is a scorpion, a Medusa, or yet again a she-devil.

> [Morality], often with no more than single glance, succeeds
> in paralyzing the critical will and even enticing it over to its
> own side; there are even cases in which morality has been
> able to turn the critical will against itself, so that like a scor-
> pion it drives the sting into its own body. It [*sie*] is expert in
> every diabolical nuance of the art of persuasion. . . . For as
> long as there has been speech and persuasion on earth,
> morality has shown itself to be the greatest of all mistresses

179

of seduction [*Verführung*] . . . the actual *Circe of philosophers*. . . . All philosophers were building under the seduction [*Verführung*] of morality, . . . they were apparently
aiming at certainty, at "truth," but in reality at "*majestic
moral structures*" (V 1, 5)

So: Circe is the appearance of woman, known for and knowing dis-
guise and adornment, with reason to pervert reason, with reason to
have nothingness taken for being, with reasons not to show herself
naked. Does not Nietzsche take up here the old theological motif of
the female seduction? It would seem that, on the one hand, he "deconstructs" metaphysics and theology and denounces the ascetic
ideal, but, on the other, remains caught in the net of the theologians.

Yet: Is Circe "woman"? Or simply a *certain* woman? Is there for
Nietzsche *woman* in herself? Does only woman escape differentiation
and typology? Even more, is it really true that the art of seduction
is thus scorned by Nietzsche? Is it not, rather, the special art of
Dionysus?

Let us not then rush headlong to "decide" this question and pro-
nounce Nietzsche "misogynist." Rather, we must weave a cloth from
both theological perversion and the veils whose reality one cannot or
will not see, a reality which one has a reason to hide. Freud, himself,
taught that women invented cloth, by which this dissimulation operates. And Freud, again, called attention to the importance of clothes
for fetishism, especially the undergarments of a beloved woman.

■ THE REVERSAL

A counterfeit is a perverse invention of a fictional metaphysical realm;
its goal is to pass off the "real" world as a world of "appearances."
Nature is devalued and held, as it were, in suspension in order to establish a supernatural world which alone would be true, consistent,
and eternal. Nevertheless, the value of perverse judgments appears
only in opposition to natural judgments; they are thus secondary to
the judgments of the strong. An instinct of hatred tends to devalue all
that is natural and affirmative; new values are not shaped by a positive
instinct of preservation. *Ressentiment* toward life and its affirmative
force is the basis of the construction of a perverse and phantasma-
goric neoreality. It is a need to struggle against pain and to malign
life, not a desire for satisfaction by using one's ability (*pouvoir*). The
ascetic ideal is negative and destructive; perversion is always also *inversion* and *reversion (renversement)*. The fictional perverse world is

defined purely negatively. It is distinguished from that of dreams in that dreams are positive accomplishments of desire and reflect the real world; it is especially different from the worlds of play and art— of true art—in which appearance is willed and the world repeated not in order to devalue it but to enhance the creative capacity (*pouvoir*) of life. Thus art wills for life yet again its eternal return in difference, a dionysian mimetic power at one with creation and affirmation. Dreams and art are the doubles of reality: they imply positive relations. Fictions born from *ressentiment* are inverted and evanescent shadows, able only to depreciate it.

> So that it could say No to everything on earth that represents the ascending tendency of life, to that which has turned out well, to power, to beauty, to self-affirmation, the instinct of *ressentiment,* which had here become genius, had to invent *another* world from whose point of view this affirmation of life appeared as evil, as the reprehensible as such. . . . [The Jewish people] have a life interest in making mankind *sick* and in so twisting [*umzudrehen*] the concepts of good and evil, true and false, as to imperil life and slander the world. (VI 3, 190–91)

> I have dug up the theologians' instinct everywhere: it is the most widespread, really *subterranean,* form of falsehood found on earth. Whatever a theologian feels to be true *must* be false: this is almost a criterion of truth. His most basic instinct of self-preservation forbids him to respect reality at any point or even to let it get a word in. Wherever the theologians' instinct extends, *value judgments* have been stood on their heads and the concepts of "true" and "false" are of necessity reversed [*umgekehrt*]: whatever is most harmful to life is called "true,"; whatever elevates it, enhances, affirms, justifies it, and makes it triumphant, is called "false." (VI 3, 173–74)

> This *world of pure fiction* is vastly inferior to the world of dreams insofar as the latter *mirrors* [*widerspiegelt*] reality, whereas the former falsifies, devalues, and negates reality . . . : This whole world of fiction is rooted in *hatred* of the natural (of reality!); it is the expression of a profound vexation at the sight of reality. *But this explains everything.* Who alone has good reason to lie his way out of reality? He who suffers from it. But to suffer from reality is to be a piece of reality that has come to grief. The preponderance of feelings of displeasure over feelings of pleasure is the cause of this fictitious morality and religion; but such a preponderance provides the very formula for decadence. (VI 3, 179–80).

If the phantasmagorical world is born out of *ressentiment* and the reversal of noble values, how can it deny its origins and cut itself off from its living roots so as to appear as an autonomous world and a reality in *itself*? How can the world of "appearances" and that of "reality" seem to be in opposition to each other when the latter derives all its "reality" from the realm of "appearance"? If the fictitious world is born out of a simple reversal of the natural world, it loses all autonomy: from whence then the illusion of autonomy? How is the rift [*coupure*] between it and the real world possible? The aim of the weak is to struggle against pain; to do this, they invent a ruse whose aim is *not* to grasp the real—it would be difficult to imagine such a general and generalized negative hallucination—but no longer to be *affected* by it. Reality is, properly speaking, not denied but held in suspension by the disqualification which afflicts it. Thereafter, all that touches us belongs to the other world, the divine world, the internal, immaterial world with which contact is never a wound:

> *The instinctive hatred of reality:* a consequence of an extreme capacity for suffering and excitement which no longer wants any contact at all because it feels every contact too deeply. . . .
>
> The fear of pain, even of infinitely minute pain—that can end in no other way than in a *religion of love.* (VI 3, 198–99).
>
> We know a state in which the *sense of touch* is pathologically excitable and shrinks from any contact, from grasping a solid object. One should translate such a physiological *habitus* into its ultimate consequence—an instinctive hatred of every reality, a flight into "what cannot be grasped," "the incomprehensible," an aversion to every formula, to every concept of time and space, to all that is solid, custom, institution, church; a being at home in a world which is no longer in contact with any kind of reality, a merely "inner" world, a "true" world, an "eternal" world. . . . (VI 3, 198)

If weakness thus "spontaneously" cuts itself off from the real world (*le réel*) and becomes the means of avoiding all sensuous contact with the world (*tout contact solide*), religion is the only means of elaborating this into a system and of radicalizing the rift between the two worlds. Only religion permits the movement from the reversal of values to the edification of an autonomous and absolute metaphysical world. Religion operates by interiorization, isolation, and symbolization. Concepts are progressively purified and spiritualized; they become increasingly bloodless, ghastly, and fleshless as they are reduced to the state of a symbol.

Here the priest plays the central role. As a noble in whom the *pathos of distance* works to pathological excess, he is responsible for the chasm that has been dug between "reality" and "appearance." Because of the priest, purity—in the symbolic sense—becomes the fundamental value. The ideal is to have a pure heart, to reach a world of pure ideas. (VI 2, 261ff). Thus "reality testing" in the fictitious world cannot be a matter of being "in touch" (*se faire par le toucher*): the ideal is pure unadulterated being, disqualified, neither touching nor touched by the lower world, nor by the higher one. At most, the intelligible heavens may be contemplated, a privilege perversely awarded by the eye, that most speculative organ at the top of the face.

The reversal of values effected by the priests always goes in one direction, from low to high. Here one has to take into account the fact that the metaphor of reveral is spatial as well as perverse, even though Nietzsche's reversal is not in fact spatial. Nietzsche's "deconstruction" implies that one passes through a phase of reversal of hierarchy where that which traditionally has been depreciated and placed in the lowest rank is placed at the top and generalized. Spatial reversal is the metaphor of the hierarchical reversal. For, if Nietzsche places "at the top" that which metaphysics judged to be low and vile, he retains "the top" as the metaphor for true value. Affirmative, noble evaluations are those that go from "top to bottom." Their point of view is that of the heights, of the summit, of mountains. Evaluations of the slaves are rather from "bottom to top," the point of view of the quagmire, the mud, of the swamp in which frogs delight. A gulf separates these perspectives and points of view; no communication is possible between them. The weak, however, understand this radical difference to be one of opposition, and, in fact, the spatial metaphor seems to make such a misunderstanding inevitable. Why then does Nietzsche keep this old metaphor with its opposition of high and low? Why does he keep the companion metaphor of "perspective"? Is it his usual practice of keeping an "old" noun in order to reevaluate it? Or is it rather that difference cannot be described other than as distance, a metaphor necessarily of spatial opposition? Difference is always described by Nietzsche as between points of view: that of health and sickness; of the aristocrat and the plebian; the esoteric point of view of the few which has no need of ratification and the exoteric and vulgar one that wants to generalize its perspective.

> Our highest insights must—and should—sound like follies
> and sometimes like crimes when they are heard without
> permission by those who are not predisposed and predes-
> tined for them. The difference between the exoteric and the

esoteric, formerly known to philosophers—among the In-
dians as among the Greeks, Persians, and Muslims, in short,
wherever one believed in an order of rank and *not* in equality and equal rights—does not so much consist in this, that
the exoteric approach comes from the outside and sees,
estimates, measures, and judges from the outside, not the
inside: what is much more essential is that the exoteric approaches sees things from below, the esoteric looks *down
from above.* There are heights of the soul from which even
tragedy ceases to look tragic. . . . . There are books that have
opposite values for soul and health, depending on whether
the lower soul, the lower vitality, or the higher and more vig-
orous ones turn to them: in the former case, these books are
dangerous and lead to crumbling and disintegration; in the
latter, they are heralds' cries that call the bravest to *their*
courage. Books for all the world are always foul-smelling
books: the smell of small people clings to them. Where the
people eat and drink, even where they venerate, it usually
stinks. One should not go to church if one wants to breathe
pure air. (VI 2, 44–45).

The first draft of this passage added: "But there are few men who are
entitled to pure air and who would not die were they to breathe pure
air. This by way of answer to those who suspect me of wanting to invite free thinkers into my garden."

Does not the necessity of retaining the metaphor of high and low
and the ongoing valuation of high over low derive from the necessity
of marking the difference as hierarchical, does it not come from the
belief in hierarchy, that is, in a situation where "top" has always
served to describe the first rank of society? If, however, "noble" and
"aristocratic" are for Nietzsche metaphors for the point of view of
health, for affirmation, then the determination of health is inseparable
from a sociopolitical connotation, at least to the degree that it implies
relations of mastery and subordination or power relations between
different drives [*pulsions*—French for Freud's *Triebe,* "instincts"—
TRANS.]: The *problem of hierarchy* is Nietzsche's problem; difference
is difference in the will to power; and the spatial metaphor is necessary to give expression to difference even though it risks confusing
difference with opposition (cf. IV 2, 15–16).

More important, even if Nietzsche keeps the old metaphor and the
privilege of "top" over the bottom, he still achieves a hierarchical reversal by generalizing the most devalued term. In one sense, there is
for Nietzsche nothing except that which the tradition called the

"base": drives and the will to power. By holding on to the ancient metaphor, even while he reevaluates it, Nietzsche is able to take hold of it and effectuate a reversal of the reversal. The perverse, theological point of view denies perspective by its reference to God and to the world above us; it finds itself entitled to look down from the heights to the world here below. Nietzsche reverses these terms: the so-called absolute world "above" us is only the result of an evaluation from a lower perspective, one which goes from the bottom to the top. The theological point of view finds its roots in the will to power, in the very instinctive nature that the priests see as base and vile. To borrow the language of morality: since all evaluations are instinctive, they have a "low" origin. From this common origin, one can distinguish those evaluations that go from "bottom to top" and those that go from "top to bottom."

> I have found the theologians' instinctive arrogance . . . wherever a right is assumed, on the basis of some higher origin, to look at reality from a superior and foreign vantage point. . . . As long as the priest is considered a *higher* type of man—this *professional* negator, slanderer, and poisoner of life—there is no answer to the question, What *is* truth? For truth has been stood on its head when the conscious advocate of nothingness and negation is accepted as the representative of "truth." (VI 3, 172–73)

Precisely that which priests and metaphysicians refuse is to admit a common origin for the base and the sublime, to good and evil; they refuse to admit that the sublime, the "high," could have had a beginning.

> They place that which comes at the end . . . namely, the "highest concepts," which means the most general, the emptiest concepts, the last smoke of evaporating reality, in the beginning, *as* the beginning. . . . The higher *may not* grow out of the lower, may not have grown at all. Moral: whatever is of the first rank must be *causa sui*. . . . Thus they arrive at their stupendous concept, "God." That which is last, thinnest, and emptiest is put first, as *the* cause, as *ens realissimum.* (VI 3, 70)

The reevaluation of the metaphor of height and baseness thus permits a denunciation of the metaphysicians' fundamental prejudice for the autonomy and the opposition of values. As the sublimation of "low," height is the provisional point of view of a certain form of life—a "perspective from a certain angle, from low to high, a 'frog perspective' to use an expression proper to painters" (VI 2, 10).

In "frog perspective," images are flattened and persons appear foreshortened and crushed. The world is flattened, devalued, and made ugly; the weak are unable to start action from a noble and "elevated" point of view. Everything is seen by an evil eye. Thus the English psychologists, who start by ignoring hierarchy and distance, give to moral sentiments a perverse, inverted genealogy: "But I am told that they are simply old, cold, and tedious frogs, creeping around men and into men as if in their own proper element, that is, in a *swamp*" (VI 2, 272).

Nietzsche persists in privileging the "high," but he associates "high" with the earth and not with "heaven," even if he still prefers the pure air of heights and the summit of mountains to the swamp and the confined air of churches. He does not hesitate to sink his gaze into the abyss, even at the risk of being thrown there, even at the risk of death.

> [We others], we daredevils of the spirit who have climbed the highest and most dangerous peak of present thought and looked around from up there—we who have looked *down* from there. (VI 2, 20)

> Those who can breathe the air of my writings know that it is an air of heights, a *strong* air. One must be made for it. Otherwise there is no small danger that one may catch cold in it. . . . How freely one breathes! How much one feels *beneath* oneself! (VI 3, 256)

Whether the perspective be that of the frog or of the eagle, no perspective—by definition—can be true, but only that of a particular form of life, a certain species. As there is no absolute "high" or "low," Nietzsche's reversal is not a simple reversal of Platonism. What is called truth is the result of an evaluation that proceeds from bottom to top, which stands "truth" on its head by seeing it as absolute and denying the plurality of perspectives. Considered as perspectives of a certain form or life, truth is irrefutable. The mistake is the will to impose truth on other points of view, to think of truth as "the" truth. If a perspective corresponds to determinate dynamic (*pulsionnelles*) conditions, then it cannot be changed at will. But how then is it possible to do what Nietzsche has done and transmute values? Nietzsche thought himself particularly well qualified for this enterprise in that he had a double set of judgments that allowed him to remain neutral and easily to change perspectives. Having inherited from his father and mother opposing evaluations—he is always his own double—he always has a second gaze for everything, and, perhaps, even a third:

> This dual descent, as it were, both from the highest and the lowest rung on the ladder of life, at the same time a *deca-dent* and a *beginning*—this, if anything explains that neutrality, that freedom from all partiality in relation to the problem of life, that perhaps distinguishes me. (VI 3, 262)

> Looking down from the perspective of the sick toward *healthier* concepts and values and, conversely, looking again from the fullness and self-assurance of a *rich* life down into the secret work of the instinct of decadence—in this I have the longest training, my truest experience; if in anything I am master it is in *this*. Now I know how, have the know-how, to *reverse perspectives:* the first reason why a "revaluation of values" is perhaps possible for me alone. (VI 3, 264)

The ease with which one moves from high to low and back again is a lightness and absence of weight, a dance, or rather *flight*. The privilege of being able to transmute values is linked to the privilege and happiness of *flight*. It corresponds to a frequently repeated oneiric experience.

> Suppose someone has flown often in his dreams, and finally, as soon as he dreams, he is conscious of his power and art of flight as if it were his privilege, also his characteristic and enduring happiness. He believes himself capable of realizing every kind of arc and angle simply with the lightest impulse: he knows the feeling of a certain divine frivolity, an "up-ward" without tension and constraints, a "downward" without condescension and humiliation—without *gravity!* How could a human being who had had such dream experiences and dream habits fail to find that the word "happiness" had a different color and definition in his waking life, too? How could he fail to desire happiness differently? "Rising" as described by poets must seem to him, as compared with this "flying," too earthbound, muscle-bound, forced, too "grave." (VI 2, 116–17)

To what desires does such a dream correspond? In relation to the father? To the mother? According to Freud, such a dream is *typical* and is a symbolic representation of coitus.[4] Such a general explanation, however, does not take account of the particular shadings in this dream, nor of the impression of lightness. Nor, as Bachelard remarks, does it take into acount its aesthetic character, unless it be by the invocation of the general need for camouflage to avoid censorship.[5] Bachelard, like Nietzsche, insists on the deep mark that such oneiric experiences leave on waking life and their importance for the development of the psyche. They are even more important than love itself.[6]

Such a dream must thus be understood in relation to the dynamism of the body, with what Bachelard calls an "ascensional psychology" rather than with psychoanalysis. One sees then that the spatial metaphor of the hierarchical transmutation of values is more than a simple metaphor, for affirmative values are precisely those that make one "light," whereas nihilistic values are those that weigh one down psychologically speaking and are choking and oppressive. The spatial metaphor is more than a simple metaphor because, in the last analysis, the body evaluates and thus serves as the guiding thread.[7] The values of height and depth are anchored in the body. The dream of flight indicates that the Nietzschean "reversal" refers us to a fundamental oneiric experience; this experience is in turn tied to the body's sense of itself as light or heavy. The dream of flight is, however, also a forbidden experience. If, in Nietzsche, the double system of evaluations takes us back to the double heritage from father and mother, one can ask if such a dream might not effect an equilibrium between these double tendencies. It would permit the simultaneous seduction of the father and the mother, without *touching* either. It would allow one to "journey" freely and "fly" from one to the other without assistance. Such a being would be in contrast to Faust's son, Euphorion (one knows what importance he had for Nietzsche), who had only the right to jump wildly about (*bondir*), and all of whose strength came from the earth-mother.

> Naked, a genius without wings, faunlike but without bestiality,
> He springs on the solid ground; but the ground, counter-
>   acting,
> Hurries him to the airy heights, with the second, third spring
> He rests on the vault of heaven.
> Anxiously, the mother cries: "Spring again and at your
>   pleasure,
> But guard yourself against flying. Free flight is denied you."
> And the faithful father warns you: "In the earth lies the
>   elastic force
> That propels you upward. If you touch earth only with
>   your toe,

Straightaway like the son of earth, Antaeus, your strength is
renewed.[8]

■ CAMERA OBSCURA

Nietzsche's concept of reversal cannot be completely understood except by placing it in relation to the metaphor of the camera obscura,
Nietzsche's image (*figure*) for universal perspectivism.[9] The camera
obscura was invented in order to give the most perfect imitation possible of nature. There is, however, no imitation without selection,
without the work of filtering reality. The imitation of nature consists
in selecting as model not *natura naturata* but *natura naturans:* it is a
repetition of its creative power. Art repeats nature by idealizing it, by
placing certain forms in relief, by hiding others, and closing up gaps.
In herself, nature is not beautiful but the play of chance: "She exag-
gerates, deforms, leaves gaps." The affirmative artist corrects nature,
not in order to devalue it but to make beautiful the "necessity of
things" and to permit *amor fati.* The artist prefers appearance to reality, but "appearance means reality repeated *once again,* as selection,
redoubling, correction."

The camera obscura of painters is immanent in the eye of each
viewer and does not give a preexisting reality. Rather, it constitutes
for each his or her own "reality" which is in fact one with "appearance." The claim to see reality "as it is" is the symptom of an "anti-
artistic spirit," a bad sign of fatalism and weakness (VI 3, 109–10). We
are thus all artists, whether we would be or not. However, the "artist"
is characterized by the fact that he wills himself to be one, just as he
wills appearance, whereas the scientist, for example, refuses to admit
that he works in an artistic mode and believes that the world is up-
right (*droit*) and real. In fact, he sees it reversed like the rest of us.

> World of phantoms in which we live! Inverted, upside-down,
> empty world, yet dreamed of as *full* and *upright!* (V 1, 109)
>
> For us important relationships are those that are reflected
> in the mirror, not the true ones. . . . No matter how precise
> our relationships may be, they are descriptions of men, not
> of the world: these are the laws of that supreme perspective
> beyond which it is impossible for us to go. . . . It is not an
> appearance or an illusion but a coded writing where an un-
> known thing is expressed for us very readably, as if made
> for us: it is our human position in relation to things. It is
> thus that things are hidden from us. (V 1, 638; cf. V 1, 635)[10]

A camera obscura, all-too-human, encloses humanity in an unsurpassable perspective and imprisons it as if in a spider's net: nature has thrown away the key.

> My eyes, however strong or weak they may be, can see only
> a certain distance, and it is within the space encompassed
> by this distance that I live and move, the line of this horizon
> constitutes my immediate fate, in great things and small,
> from which I cannot escape. Around every being there is
> described a similar concentric circle, which has a center
> and which is particular to him. . . . Now it is by these hori-
> zons, within which each of us encloses his sense as if be-
> hind prison walls, that we *measure* the world. . . . There is
> absolutely no escape, no backway, no by-path that leads to
> the real world. We sit within our net, we spiders, and, what-
> ever we may catch in it, we can catch nothing at all except
> precisely that which allows itself to be caught precisely in
> *our* net. (V 1, 108)

This general reversal derives from the ineluctable "error" that characterizes humanity. This is not, however, to say that every camera obscura is equal. *Particular* errors, illusions, or lies are inscribed on the general background of error inside this unsurpassable dream— unsurpassable even to him who knows he dreams. Each camera obscura is distant and different from the other; those of the perverse, alone, give us, in a more restrained sense, the world inverted from bottom to top. Theirs is an indecent and dangerous perspective because the "perspective" pretends to emerge from the dark prison and to see the world as it is; it claims, that is, to deny the perspective that is part of the vital condition of all that lives. This perspective is dangerous because it is that of a living being that *wills* death. It seeks to look indecently through a keyhole and see all without discrimination, to see nature unveiled, like a woman. It is dangerous to lift the veil of nature, for she is fierce like a woman, like a tiger. Those who claim to look outside the dark room of consciousness (*la conscience*) forget that "Man rests in the indifference of his ignorance on that which is pitiless, voracious and murderous; he is attached to dreams as if to the back of a tiger." [11]

The tiger and the panther, all felines and animals of Dionysus, [12] are related to woman, the most feline and natural animal of all. [13] She is beautiful, graceful, and fierce. To will to look through the keyhole is to outrage feminine modesty.

■   OF WOMEN

By the indecent glance that he directs towards "truth," the perverted individual shows not only that he treats truth like a woman but also that he does not know how to approach women. He misunderstands both "truth" and woman and sees them with their "head to the ground" (VI 3, 140–42; IV 2, 139–40). He misapprehends truth as the absence of truth, as an abyss without a bottom, and fails to understand that life is feline, fierce, lying, and protean. He does not see that the most characteristic virtue of woman is modesty (*pudeur*) and that for women the loss of modesty is the symbol of degeneration.[14] The will to strip woman naked is a sign of a lack of virility and of instincts insufficiently strong and insufficiently beautiful to love appearance and the veil. Such a will misunderstands that behind the veil is another veil and behind the cave is another cave.[15] Who but a fetishist thus seeks the perverse from bottom to top?[16] "Among women: 'Truth? Oh! you don't know truth! Is it not an attempt to assassinate all our *pudeurs*?'" (VI 3, 55).

Woman is a surface that mimes depth (VI 3, 57). She is mistress of the veil and of the simulacrum, both artifices by which she makes men believe that she is "deep," both ruses through which she holds immense influence over them. The example of Napoleon's mother bears witness to this point. Modesty appears as a beguilement that permits the male to desire a woman without being petrified (*médusé*); it is a veil which avoids male homosexuality, a spontaneous defense against the horrific sight of female genitalia, and the opportunity for life to perpetuate itself.

Nevertheless, certain women also seek "truth" and show themselves as immodest as the theologians. These "degenerate" women, who seek knowledge and assert equality of rights, engage in politics, or write books. Instead of bearing children, they seek to gain a penis. These women believe themselves to be "castrated," and, thus delegitimized, conclude that "woman as woman" is castrated. This is *ressentiment* of sterile women against life, and it is symptomatic of a degeneration of femininity: "woman" is neither castrated nor not castrated, any more than man retains control (*détient*) over the penis. The whole idea of castration and its opposite is part of the syndrome of weakness and keeps one from speaking of a truly living and affirmative life, be this masculine or feminine. The immodest woman is the accomplice of the theologians and of their conception of woman. By dropping her veils and exhibiting a fawning baseness, she makes man fall into pessimism and nihilism. He becomes a disappointed (*déçu*) dogmatist and a skeptic. The belief in castration is the other side of fetishism. Sterile women and old women thus join the perverse theological point of view. Such women are the worst enemies of women, for their *ressentiment* annihilates the fertility that is one with life and with its power of creative affirmation.

> Woman wants to become self-reliant—and for that reason she is beginning to enlighten men about "woman as such": *this* is one of the worst developments of the general *uglification* of Europe. For what must these clumsy attempts of women at scientific self-exposure bring to light! Woman has so much reason for shame. . . . Woe when . . . woman . . . begins to unlearn thoroughly and on principle her prudence and her art—of grace, of play, of chasing away worries, of lightening burdens and taking things lightly. . . . Is it not in the worst taste when woman sets about becoming scientific that way. Before, luckily, explanation of this sort was man's affair. . . . Whatever women write about "woman" we may in the end reserve a healthy suspicion whether woman really *wants* enlightenment about herself—whether she *can* want it. . . . Unless woman seeks a new adornment [*Putz*] for herself that way—I do think adorning herself is part of the eternal feminine?—she surely wants to inspire fear of herself—perhaps she seeks mastery. But she does not *will* truth: what does truth have to do with woman! From the beginning nothing has been more alien, repugnant, and hostile to woman than truth—her great art is the lie, her highest concern is appearance and beauty. Let us men confess it: we honor and love precisely *this* art and *this* instinct in women. . . . We men wish that woman would not go on compromising herself through explaining herself, just as it was man's thoughtfulness and consideration for women that found expression in the church decree: *mulier taceat in ecclesia!* It was for woman's use that Napoleon gave the all-too-eloquent Madame de Staël to understand that *mulier taceat in politicis.* And I think that it is a real friend of women [*une authentique féministe*] that counsels women today: *mulier taceat de muliere!* (VI 2, 176–78)

In the first draft of this passage, Nietzsche wrote, "Is not the desire to 'explain' woman a denial of the feminine instinct, a degeneration? Is it not the will to disillusion men?" (cf. VI 2, 88, 95, 181–84, 98).

Is this another case of Nietzsche's well-known misogyny? It seems that woman herself does not like woman: this seems at least so for the botched and sterile women, who have the will to emancipate themselves and hate the affirmative well-shaped (*bien conformée*) woman. Such a woman differs not at all from the man of *ressentiment* and like him erects her perspective as an absolute. "The abortive woman . . . wants to lower the level of the general rank of woman. . . . At bottom, the emancipated are anarchists in the world of the 'eternally feminine,' the underprivileged whose most fundamental instinct is revenge" (VI 3, 304).[17]

Even though Nietzsche takes up the notion of the "eternal feminine" again here, he still distinguishes different types of women, just as he distinguishes different types of men. From a genealogical point of view, an affirmative woman is closer to an affirmative man than a degenerate woman. And some women are more affirmative than are some men.

Is it correct then to refer that which Nietzsche says of women to truth, when a certain woman is the image (*figure*) of truth? Can one legitimately speak of castration and noncastration? In *whose* picture is truth a woman (Qui *se figure la vérité comme une femme*)?

To speak of truth as a woman derives from a theological perspective and is an image that appears at a precise moment in the long story of error that is the history of truth. "*How the true world became a fable:* The true world—unattainable for now, but promised for the sage, the pious, the virtuous man ('for the sinner who repents'). . . . (Progress of the idea: it becomes more subtle, insidious, incomprehensible—*it becomes female;* it becomes Christian)" (VI 3, 74).

The idea of truth presented here as an unveiling leads to a self-castration. *Aletheia,* placed in a comprehensible firmament, is barely perceivable, and woman/truth remains inaccessible even to those who subject themselves to the most severe tests. Skepticism is both the necessary consequence and the reverse side of dogmatism. "As an outline: the last philosopher—modified position of philosophy since Kant. Metaphysics has become impossible—Self-castration. Tragic resignation. The end of philosophy. Only art can save us."[18]

One may ask if placing truth/woman in an inaccessible location is not a way to protect oneself against her. It would be as if it were better not to be able to see that there is nothing to see, and better not to dive into the abysses of truth as an absence of truth. Self-castration appears to be a preventative defense against the castration provoked by the "sight" of the "truth." Oedipus, "the most daring and the most unhappy of men," dared to cast his glance on the abyss and blinded himself. "'And if thine eye offend thee, pluck it out: it is better for thee to enter into the kingdom of God with one eye, than having two eyes to be cast into hell fire: Where their worm dieth not, and the fire is not quenched' (Mark 9:47f). It is not exactly the eye which is meant" (VI 3, 219; cf. VI 3, 209–11).[19]

Truth cannot be unveiled without provoking horror. Were she to show herself naked, the metaphysicians would create a scandal and quickly run away. Rendering truth inaccessible first makes the fetish that suspends the real world and nature/woman; then it disqualifies both as vain apperances. The theologians are seduced by the tawdry brilliance of Circe, by emptiness and by nothingness understood as the fullness of being. They refuse to recognize women and life as fecundity and disclaim the eternal return that is beyond suffering and death.

Life is neither appearance nor reality, neither surface nor depth, neither castrated nor not. Its charter cannot be expressed metaphysically, for castration and fetishism are the perverse invention of instincts that are not virile enough to "penetrate" woman.

> Supposing that truth is a woman. . . . Would there not then be grounds for the suspicion that all philosophers, insofar as they were dogmatists, have been very inexpert about women? That gruesome seriousness, that clumsy obstrusiveness with which they have usually approached truth so far have been very awkward and improper attempts at winning a woman's heart? What is certain is that she has not allowed herself to be won. (VI 2, 3)

> We no longer believe that truth remains truth when the veils are withdrawn; we have lived too much to believe this. Today we consider it a matter of decency not to wish to see everything naked, or to be present at everything and "know" everything. "Is it true that God is present everywhere?" a little girl asked her mother: "I think that's indecent"—a hint for philosophers! One should have more respect for the bashfulness with which nature has hidden behind riddles and iridiscent uncertainties. Perhaps truth is a woman who has reasons for not letting us see her reasons? Perhaps her name is, to speak Greek, *Baubo?* Ah, these Greeks! They knew how to live! What is demanded is to stop courageously at the surface, at the fold, the skin, to adore appearance, to believe in forms, tones, words in the whole Olympus of appearance. These Greeks were superficial—*out of profundity.* (V 2, 20; cf. V 2, 248–49)

To respect female modesty is thus to be able to hold oneself to appearance, to interrogate oneself indefinitely on the infinite riddles of nature/Sphinx, without seeking—perhaps it is only prudence—to "unveil" truth (cf. VI 1, 193–94). "Who has the courage to see these 'truths' without veils? Perhaps there is a legitimate modesty in the face of these problems and postulates, perhaps we are mistaken on their value, perhaps we too are obedient to their will?" (VI 2, 10).

Nietzsche worked this passage over particularly carefully. In the second draft, he wrote: "But who needs to preoccupy himself with such maybes? It is against good taste, especially against virtue, for truth to become so scandalous and deny all modesty: some caution is needed before this lady." Then a third draft: "When truth becomes to this point scandalous, when the woman without scruples strips herself at this point of her veils and renounces all modesty: Back! back! may this seductress go away and follow hereafter her own path. One can never be prudent enough with a woman like this. It would be better, you tell me with a wink of the eye, to commit oneself with a modest and chaste mistake, a small gentle lie."

The attitude of metaphysicians is ambivalent. They wish to see and strip away all veils, but they also fear to see. What is the case with the person of a true philosophical disposition? Does he look truth in the face and risk blindness or death? Does he remain with appearance, with lies and art? Oedipus is the last of the philosophers and the greatest of the unhappy; he is a tragic philosopher, a man petrified by nature who still dares to confront truth but requires forgetfulness and transfiguration by tragic art. "Formidable solitude of the last philosopher, nature petrifies him [umstarrt], vultures plane about him. And he cries to nature: give us forgetfulness! to forget! It is not that he supports suffering as did Titan, until a pardon is granted him in the supreme tragic art."[20]

Ebb and flow are necessary for the philosopher. One must love "truth" enough to dare to die, love life enough to forget, adore appearance as such, as art. With the movement of coming and going, from understanding to life and from life to understanding, the voyager, after having seen the depths of the abyss, calls for still one more mask: "Wanderer, who are you? I see you walking on your way without scorn, without love, with unfathomable eyes; moist and sad like a sounding lead that has returned to the light, impatient for new depths—what did it seek down there—with a breast that does not sigh, with a lip that conceals its disgust, with a hand that now reaches only slowly: Who are you? What have you done?" [And the voyager answers] "Another mask! a second mask!" (VI 2, 239).

On the third draft, Nietzsche adds: "Who are you? I don't know—perhaps Oedipus, perhaps the Sphinx?"

When the name of Oedipus comes up, Hamlet is never far away: "What must a man have suffered to have a need of being such a buffoon? Is Hamlet *understood?* Not doubt, *certainty* is what drives one insane. But one must be profound . . . to feel that way. . . . We are all *afraid* of truth" (VI 3, 285; cf. III 1, 44–48).

So as not to become blind like Oedipus or mad like Hamlet, one must know how to keep oneself on the surface. One must know how to love life like a woman who has deceived you but remains beautiful, to know how to bless life while leaving it, as Ulysses bade farewell to Nausicaa.[21] The true philosopher is a tragic philosopher, for he must will illusion as illusion, knowing that woman has a reason to hide her reasons. Mastery means to know how to keep oneself at a distance, to know how to close doors and windows and keep the shutters closed. To hold oneself in the camera obscura, not to refuse appearance but to affirm it and to laugh, for if life is ferocious and cruel, she is also fecundity and eternal return: her name is *Baubô.*

The name of a woman: What is her link with the more insistent figure of Dionysus in Nietzsche?

■ BAUBÔ

Baubô appears in the mysteries of Eleusis consecrated to Demeter. Under the pain of the loss from the disappearance of Persephone, Demeter, goddess of fecundity, had been comporting herself like a sterile woman. For nine days and nine nights, she did not drink, eat, bathe, or adorn herself. Baubô made her laugh.

She made her laugh by pulling up her skirts and showing her belly on which a figure had been drawn (it is thought to be that of Iaachos, the child of Demeter, an obscure deity sometimes identified with Dionysus). This episode is known from six lines of a much-censured orphic verse that the church fathers designated as obscure. Reinach interprets it as a magic scene whose aim is to restore to earth the fecundity that it had lost during the sorrow of Demeter.[22] Comparison with Greek legends such as those of Bellerophon, and with Irish and Japanese ones, allows us to assert that wherever a woman raises her skirts, she provokes laughter or flight, such that this gesture can be used as an apotropaic means.[23] The belly of the woman plays the role of the head of Medusa.[24] By lifting her skirts, was not Baubô suggesting that she go and frighten Hades, or that which comes to the same, recall fecundity to herself? By displaying the figure of Dionysus on her belly, she recalls the eternal return of life: "Demeter recovers joy in the thought that Dionysus will be reborn. This joy, which announces the birth of the genius, is Greek serenity." [25]

The figure of Baubô indicates that a simple logic could never understand that life is neither depth nor surface, that behind the veil, there is another veil, behind a layer of paint, another layer. It signifies also that appearance should cause us neither pessimism nor skepticism, but rather the affirming laugh of a living being who knows that despite death life can come back indefinitely and that "the individual is nothing and the species all."

By calling life "Baubô," one identifies it not only with woman but also with her reproductive organs: *Baubô* is the equivalent of *koilia,* another of the "improper" words used in Greek to designate the female sex.[26] Baubôn, the symbol of the male sex, derives from Baubô. Through the intermediary of Baubôn, the story of Baubô crosses that of Dionysus. On the one hand, Dionysus is born in Nysa, at the spot where Hades carried off Persephone; on the other, when Dionysus was looking for the road to Hades, he encountered Proshymnos with whom he had unspeakable relationships.[27] After Proshymnos's death, Dionysus replaced him with a figwood phallus as a sort of consolation: such an instrument seems to have been called *baubôn.*[28] Baubôn and Baubô, as personifications of the two sexes, appeared under this aspect in the Eleusian rites where Baubô is an animated *koilia.* In the Eleusian mysteries, the female sexual organ is exalted as the symbol of fertility and a guarantee of the regeneration and eternal return of all things.

From this, Baubô can appear as a female double of Dionysus—in fact Otto and Jeanmaire insist on the feminine character of Dionysus himself, or at least on his equivocal sexuality. One can say that like life he is beyond the "metaphysical" distinctions of male and female. There is also a tie between Dionysus and the myths of death and rebirth: according to Nietzsche the Dionysiac cult ensured eternal life, a triumphant affirmation of life beyond death and change.

> I know no higher symbolism that this *Greek* symbolism of the Dionysian festivals. Here the most profound instinct of life, that directed toward the future of life, the eternity of life, is experienced religiously—and the way to life, procreation, as the *holy* way. It was Christianity, with its *ressentiment* against life at the bottom of its heart, which first made something unclean of sexuality: . . . Saying Yes to life even in its strangest and hardest problems, the will to life rejoicing over its own inexhaustibility even in the very sacri-

fice of its highest types—*that* is what I called Dionysian, . . .
the eternal joy of becoming, beyond all terror and pity—
that joy which included even joy in destroying.

And herewith I again touch that point from which I once
went forth: *The Birth of Tragedy* was my first revaluation of
all values. Herewith I again stand on the soil out of which
my intention, my *ability,* grows—I, the last disciple of the
philosopher Dionysus—I, the teacher of the eternal recurrence. (VI 3, 153–54)

Baubô and Dionysus would thus be both multiple names for protean
life. Contrary to Baubô, however, Dionysus is naked. His nakedness
does not signify the revelation of a truth but the unveiled affirmation
of appearance: it is the nakedness of the strong who is beautiful
enough, virile enough, not to need to veil himself. On the other hand,
Dionysus is the god of masks; as with woman, "to know how to appear
is part of his mastery." "He says nothing, nor risks a glance behind
which there is not the thought of seduction." Dionysus, a Greek god
anterior to the system of theological oppositions, crosses himself out
(*se rature*) of the distinction between the veiled and unveiled, masculine and feminine, fetishism and castration.

Does it still make sense, then, to speak of misogyny in Nietzsche?

One might rather ask oneself: What is it in Nietzsche that leads him
to judge woman as he does? What instinct speaks out and or interprets here? For Nietzsche does not pretend to speak the "truth" about
"woman in herself," but rather gives an understanding derived from a
constraining perspective that limits such a pretense. More than anything else, judgments on "woman" are symptoms.

> Whenever a cardinal problem is at stake, there speaks an
> unchangeable "This I am." About man and woman, for ex-
> ample, a thinker cannot relearn but only finish learning—
> only discover ultimately that which is settled [*gesteht*] in
> him on this matter. . . . After this abundant civility that I
> have just assumed in relation to myself, I shall perhaps be
> permitted more readily to state a few truths about "woman
> as such," given that from here on one knows how very much
> these are only—*my* truths. (IV 2, 176)

That which is "arrested" in him about women is arrested most particularly on the image of his mother that he carries in him. "Every
man carries within him an image of woman that he gets from his
mother; that determines whether he will honor women in general, or
despise them, or be generally indifferent to them" (IV 2, 273).

If one is to believe Nietzsche's many heterogenous texts on woman, one may conclude that this image must have been at least ambivalent. It is an ambivalence that is transposed, in and by its desire, its fear of "looking into the abyss," into the depths of nature. And it requires, after one has dared so to gaze, the cure from luminous images of which the *Birth of Tragedy* speaks. The camera obscura is perhaps *a* mechanism that can ward off evil (*une machine à valeur apotropaïque*). This ambivalence is displaced from the mother to his sister Elizabeth, his lama, the only being except Wagner he says he ever loved.

> I am not always able to be "just." Malwida once wrote me that there were two people to whom I was unjust: Wagner, and you, my sister. Why so? Perhaps because I have loved you two the most and am not able to still the resentment that you abandoned me. Read then in my unhappy thoughts and in the severity of my language the sorrow of having lost you and of seeing your name linked with a party [anti-Semitism] with which you have no common thought and with which you have nothing to do. (Letter to Elizabeth, 26 December 1887).

The maxims and arrows Nietzsche directs toward women: Is not their very severity the mark of this ambivalence? Are they not symptomatic of a deep love for women, all of whom had abandoned him, when they might have served him as a lightning rod . . . or even an umbrella? (IV 2, 289).[29]

In the letter of 23 March 1887, he gives five conditions which he indicates might make life livable; none, he indicates, seems realizable.

> I would need (1) someone to oversee my stomach; (2) someone gay to laugh with me; (3) someone proud of my company who would hold the others in front of me at a respectful distance; (4) someone who might read to me without making it dull and stupid. There is a fifth but I do not even want to mention it.
>
> To marry now would be asinine and would lead to the loss of the independence that I have won at a bloody price. . . . Besides, parenthetically, I have not yet found a woman whose company agrees with my character, who didn't bore and bother me. The lama was a good companion, I can't find a replacement for her, but she really wanted to sacrifice herself and to unleash all her energy. And for whom? For a pitiful humanity completely strange to her, and not for me. Yet I would have been such a thankful beast, always ready to laugh joyfully. Are you still able to laugh?[30]

POSTSCRIPT

One should recall here the joke by Christian Ehrenfels, analyzed by Freud in *Jokes and Their Relation to the Unconscious* (New York: Norton, 1960, 110–11): "A woman is like an umbrella: sooner or later one takes a cab." For a commentary, see S. Kofman, *Pourquoi rit-on?* (Paris: Galilée, 1986). In addition, it seems very important to refer to Nietzsche's letter to his grandparents (2 November 1857), where we learn that Nietzsche received an umbrella from his mother for his birthday. In another letter (*Kritische Gesammmelte Briefe* I 1, 321–23), his mother reminds him especially not to forget his umbrella when it rains. . . .

NOTES

1. For Comte, "coarse fetishism" is the necessary starting point for all intelligence, human as well as animal. "Its fundamental principle consists in transporting the human type everywhere. We always come back to thinking the beings that concern us to be alive, in that we explain what properly pertains to them in terms of corresponding phenomena." Auguste Comte, *Cours de philosophie positive,* bk. 3 (Paris: Ballière, 1864).

2. The matter is not so simple, even for Comte; there, even the theoretical impulse required a "practical impulse," even if it was not derived from it.

3. Cf. "Fetishism" in Sigmund Freud, *Collected Papers* (London: Hogarth, 1950), 5:198–204.

4. Sigmund Freud, *The Interpretation of Dreams* (New York: Avon, 1968), 428–31.

5. Gaston Bachelard, *L'Air et les songes* (Paris: Corti, 1943), 28.

6. Bachelard: "The dynamic trace of lightness or heaviness is much more profound. It marks being more deeply that a passing desire, . . . Oneiric levitation is a deeper, more essential, simpler psychic reality than love itself."

7. Cf. Sarah Kofman, *Nietzsche et la métaphore* (Paris: Payot, 1983; Galilée, 1986).

8. Goethe, *Faust,* II, lines 9603–11.

9. Cf. Sarah Kofman, *Camera obscura de l'idéologie* (Paris: Galilée 1973).

10. Friedrich Nietzsche, *Le Livre du philosophe* III 114, 475.

11. *Le Livre du philosophe* III, 175.

12. The panther and the tiger are generally the animals attached to Dionysus's chariot. In the notes for *Zarathustra,* we read: "Dionysus on a tiger, the skull of a goat—a panther: the dreaming Ariadne abandoned by the hero, dream of the overman."

13. Cf. VI 2, 32–33. In "On Narcissism: An Introduction," *Collected Papers* 4:30–59 at 46, Freud, probably by the intermediary of Lou Salomé, seems to have drawn upon this conception of the woman-panther. It permits him to

introduce a differential typology, to admit that there is another kind of woman than the penis-envy woman. This is a new type, the narcissistic woman, affirmative, envied by men and feared for her enigmatic character. Any comparison between Nietzsche and Freud must go through this essential text. Cf. S. Kofman, *L'Enigme de la femme* (Paris: Galilée, 1980); English translation by Cathy Porter, *The Enigma of Woman* (Ithaca: Cornell University Press, 1985).

14. Nietzsche's text stands joined here to those of Hume and Rousseau.

15. Cf. VI 2, 243–44. In a recent particularly Nietzschean film by Roman Polanski, *What!* the heroine is progressively stripped of her "veils" but is never completely naked: a coat of blue paint covers one of her legs when at last one might think her completely undressed.

16. "Thus the foot or the shoe owes its attraction as a fetish, or part of it, to the circumstance that the inquisitive boy used to peer up the women's legs toward her genitals" (Sigmund Freud, "Fetishism," *Collected Papers* 5:201).

17. Freud, who in general sees "penis envy" as the bedrock of the female structure and not as the product of *ressentiment*, also links literary aspirations in women with hostility toward men and penis envy: "Behind this penis envy there comes to light the woman's hostile bitterness against the man, which never completely disappears in the relations between the sexes, and which is clearly indicated in the strivings and in the literary productions of 'emancipated women'" (Sigmund Freud, "The Taboo of Virginity," *Standard Edition* [London: Hogarth, 1975], 2:205).

18. *Le Livre du philosophe.*

19. From a completely different approach and in a completely different style, Jacques Derrida, in *Eperons/Spurs* (Chicago: University of Chicago Press, 1979) has decisively shown what is going on for Nietzsche with women and castration. More particularly, he shows that one cannot find any theses that are for castration or against it. He tries to formalize the different points of view which castration gives us into a code which cannot be exhaustive. The "drawing of the hymen" (*le graphique de l'hymen*), a logic of the space between and the threshold, substitutes itself for the opposition of castration and fetishism in order to inscribe that which might well be the nature of life or of Dionysus, neither veiled nor unveiled, neither masculine nor feminine. As to the "misogyny" of Nietzsche, Derrida shows that there is an enigmatic but necessary congruence between "feminist" and "antifeminist" claims.

20. *Le Livre du philosophe,* p. 85.

21. Refer again here to Roman Polanski's film *What!* in which the old father blesses life as he dies between the legs of the heroine.

22. Salomon Reinach, *Cultes, mythes, religion,* vol. 4 (Paris: Leroux, 1912). Freud, in his "A Mythological Parallel to a Visual Obsession," also links this episode with the fantasy of one of his patients, who represented his father "as the naked lower part of a body, provided with arms and legs, but without the head or upper part. The genitals were not indicated, and the facial features were drawn on the abdomen." The terra-cottas of Priene "represent Baubô

[and] show the body of a woman without a head or chest, with a face drawn on the abdomen: the lifted dress frames this like a crown of hair" (*Standard Edition* 14:337–38).

23. *Apotropaïque* is a neologism from the Greek *apo-tropos:* to displace in space.—TRANS.

24. One of the figures drawn on the belly of the statuettes of Priene is considered by Picard to be the analog of the Gorgon.

25. *Fragments posthumes,* 9:261, 269.

26. This relationship is already found in Empedocles.

27. Sexual initiation and opening to the beyond go hand in hand. Proshymnos is to be related to the lyrical muse Polymnie, who Plato says in the *Symposium* represents certain turpitudes of fleshly love.

28. In several of his plays, Aristophanes describes substitute phalluses (*Baubôn*), which women used while their men were away at war.

29. In a letter to his sister, he says that Madame Wagner was a lighting rod for her husband. See also IV 2, 289, where he says that certain women are useful to their husbands (who are egoistic enough to accept it) as "lighting rod, storm-protector [*paratonnerre*] and voluntary umbrella." Wagner, it seems, was the inventor of an umbrella with two handles, apparently on exhibit at Bayreuth. We are grafting all these remarks about the "umbrella" onto the aphorism "I have forgotten my umbrella," which has been brilliantly "commented" upon by Derrida in *Eperons/Spurs*. He shows that there is no reading that can take away from this aphorism its undecidability; it is a paradigm for any text. This is even the case for an analytic reading, which nevertheless must be undertaken but could never be decisive. Derrida's umbrella thus protects us from all dogmatism.

30. Friedrich Nietzsche, *Briefe an Mutter und Schwester*, ed. E. F. Nietzsche (Leipsig: Insel, 1926), 457.

CHAPTER 8

Nietzsche's New Experience of the World

Eugen Fink

Translated by Michael A. Gillespie

■   I

With all his contradictions, his masks and metamorphoses, there may not be another thinker who is as open to so many possible interpretations as Nietzsche. "I am the most concealed of all the concealed,"[1] a note in the *Nachlass* reads, and "all that is deep, loves masks" (VI 2, 53).

Every Nietzsche interpretation is thus a hazardous enterprise and at best only a perspective. Nietzsche has been styled a heroic legend and his "psychological achievements" lauded, while he himself is revealed by means of this same psychology as a man who suffered deeply and dreamed of a strong and healthy life of abundance. He has been denounced as the precursor of Fascism, as the prophet of incipient nihilism and the like. All these interpretations are facilitated by Nietzsche's supreme command of language. He makes use of insights drawn from experience, formulated in the colors of passion, and expressed with an unprecedented brilliance that persuades our hearts as it convinces our minds.

Nietzsche's many faces are also the result of his distrust of concepts strictly understood, of their exactitude and power to petrify, and of his unwillingness to sacrifice the concrete with its half shadows and in-between colors to the universality of logic. But perhaps most important in this regard is his dedication to suggestive images, visionary configurations, and strange metaphors. His style in this respect is fragmentary, aphoristic, dictatorial, seductive, and provocative.

Is Nietzsche's person, his empirical existence, however, the right point of departure for understanding his thought, or should we begin with what he says about the essence of man?

The fascination with Nietzsche's literary work, which since the

Translated from the German by permission of the Fink estate and the publisher from *Nietzsche aujourd'hui,* 2 vols. (Paris: Union Générale d'Editions, 1973).

turn of the century has captivated intellects of the highest order and young people open to enthusiasm, has faded away. His dual struggle against the Western tradition and "modern ideas" disturbed the spirit of the times but did not fundamentally alter it. The reality of technocracy, the world-encompassing spirit of rational planning, and the ever greater efficacy of the principle of equality set in motion by the French Revolution are the uncontestable reality in both hemispheres of our globe, in opposition to Nietzsche's dream of the mastery of the earth by the overmen. For us today the pathos of his language is occasionally unbearable, even if we must admit that he astonishingly enriched the possibilities of expression in German by loosening its rhythms as well as by increasing its sensibility for sublime spiritual moods and for intermediate stations between thought and feeling. The sober man of our times, yoked to the mechanism of a rational-technical civilization, reads his works with a mixture of astonishment and uneasiness. They describe the position and problem of man with concepts drawn predominately from the Romantic conception of nature; they employ the illusion-shattering method of thought developed by the Enlightenment; they dare to speak the deepest secrets in prophetic style and do not shy away from hieratic ornamentation, opposing Christianity while imitating the Bible. Nietzsche's strongly stylized consciousness of mission alienates and annoys us, as does his inclination to deafen, to overpower, and to play roles. He is a virtuoso of the artistic medium of suggestion, who can describe postures and fundamental stances toward the world and things, as well as existential attitudes and images of man with the sharpness of a silhouette while giving them the illumination of an icon.

What Nietzsche thought about human beings is fixed in a series of suggestive images. He does not describe a phenomenal state with the cool objectivity of positivistic science but takes a position, engages himself passionately, and adds the excited and vital speech of self-assertion and the calumny of his opponents to his image of man. His sketches are polemical; each project is coupled with negation. None of Nietzsche's images of man rests in itself, none is at peace in itself. Where he comes close to the idyll, it is the "heroic idyll" which shines forth out of the pictures of Claude Lorrain. Where he brings forward essential human possibilities, he also always attacks. Where he builds, he hoists the flag of war.

In an intellect so rich in contradictions as Nietzsche's, it is to be expected that his vision of man will be splintered into a multiplicity of "images." In his work we do, in fact, encounter the most contradictory forms, and the human essence is frequently broken up into many facets. In the course of this work, Nietzsche presents us with a series of stylized figures in which he objectifies the stations of his own path of thought. With some caution, one can distinguish roughly painted figures and more refined, more sublime forms in this series. Probably the roughest of these forms is the image of man as a "predator." Man in this light is characterized as a crafty and deceitful beast of prey who mercilessly uses his weapon, the intellect, against all other creatures and even dismembers, represses, loots, and enslaves other members of his own species. In crass naturalistic phrases, Nietzsche seeks to expose the true man, who is even now only half-hidden by a mendacious and superficial cultural veneer, to reveal the "blond beast" as the reality of human being. One plainly hears the provocative undertone of such descriptions, which the not so distant past throws in our face. Nietzsche's cynicism is revealing, for he is no naive zoologist who considers man one of the animals. Whenever Nietzsche asserts the bestiality of man, he is struggling against the metaphysical view of man as a "rational animal" and the theological view of him as the "image of God." He takes a diabolical joy in declaring war against the whole "idealistic swindle" and in destroying man's self-deception. In this way, concepts that otherwise describe biological conditions acquire a higher meaning—medical points of view take on philosophical relevance: "health" and "sickness," "strength" and "weakness" become measures of value. Vitalistic categories govern the evaluation of all human things. Nietzsche extols the life that is instinctively certain, strong, powerful, and healthy. He first sees it embodied in the type of the warrior and master, but then suddenly abandons this way of looking at things when he rethinks the nature of "health" in conjunction with the notion of nobility. In this light, he sees the warrior as the knight or believes that he sees his image in the aristocratic society of ancient Greece. These biological value concepts spring out of an unsystematic metaphysics of life that Nietzsche deploys more emotionally than rationally.

For him it is not the cherry-faced health of everyday human beings, not their normality and not their healthy common sense, that is the valid measure of man's being. Man's essence resides in the "productive man," in the man who creates. With this expression, Nietzsche does not refer to the "worker" in industrial society nor to the producers of our modern technical world, but rather to the artists, the thinkers and poets, the lawgivers and heroic founders of states. Nietzsche's image of man as a "predator," which was formulated in defiance of Christianity and all philanthropic "humanism," soon becomes an aesthetically defined naturalness.

It must be added that, despite all his encomiums to the wild and strong life, Nietzsche also had a sharp psychologist's eye for the creative possibilities that can lie in suffering, sickness, and extreme weakness. *"Morbidezza"* can lead to a more intensive consciousness of human existence, but also to a desire for revenge on life. With great penetration, Nietzsche demonstrated the uncanny and equivocal creative power of sickness and weakness in his analysis of decadence, *ressentiment,* and slave morality. The creative is ambivalent. On the one hand, Nietzsche sketches an image of man drawn from an aesthetic interpretation of nature. He sets it up as a model in opposition to the traditional European image of man and proclaims "the creator" the measure of health and viability. On the other hand, he admits that sickness, suffering, and declining life have a creative potency. Thus, the standard against which he wants to measure man is confused. Even if man is not the locus of reason or the image of God, he is not simply an animal.

The critique of Nietzsche often begins by attacking this weak point in his argument, that is, the naturalism and biologism that underlie his image of man. However, such a critique does not see that this naturalism is hyperbole, and intentionally coarse hyperbole at that. In no sense does Nietzsche put man back into nature or give him over to the natural scientists. He does not yield the floor to either the theologian or the zoologist. On the contrary, Nietzsche forcibly attempts to bend back the transcendental relation by means of which Western man for the past 3,000 years has directed himself toward that which stands over him, whether it be reason or the divine. To accomplish this, Nietzsche must first locate and explore the place of man on earth; he must demarcate the natural creature who in his own way is a creator. In Nietzsche's writings, this double character of man's being, which we traditionally understand as the dualism of nature and freedom, reveals itself in many forms. It is crucial for Nietzsche, however, that the human essence not be divided into an earthly part and a part that belongs to a Platonic or Christian heaven. Nietzsche claims man fully and wholly for the "earth." This is the deepest meaning of his often crass and provocatively formulated "naturalism."

This meaning is also clear in Nietzsche's other representative images of man. The first period of his thought, for example, is ruled by the figure of the "genius." The realm of man, as Nietzsche sees it, is sundered by the antithesis between the "many, all-too-many" and the men of greatness, who stand in a creative relationship to the world. In the genius, the primordial and actual are given voice and appear in the work of art. For Nietzsche's first period, the period of his art metaphysics, the genius is the man who has been struck by lightning and becomes the oracle of a superhuman power. However, this conception of man soon is transformed by man's recognition of himself in that power which he hitherto set over himself.

He becomes conscious of his self-alienating projection and recognizes how he previously fell prey to his own creation. Thus, the motive arises for scientific and critical analysis of man's productive powers, which Nietzsche had generally forgotten. Man is liberated and able to redeem himself from the delusion that put him on his knees before the works of his own unconscious, creative power. This leads to the recognition that the ostensibly "superhuman" is in fact only the "human, all-too-human." Nietzsche gives poetic form to this critical impulse toward freedom in the figure of the enlightened, free-spirited man, who ultimately takes the form of the "free spirit" and "Prince Vogelfrei." The pathos of the faith in science that had governed *Human, All-Too-Human* gives way to a bold cheerfulness of spirit in Nietzsche's later work. There, Nietzsche employs a psychology that unmasks human illusions, namely, the illusions of metaphysics, religion, and morality. Yet Nietzsche's problem here remains tied to the problem of human "greatness." The philosopher, the saint, the artist, and the genius are puzzles for him. His critique grapples with life itself, destroying its apparent certainty and the illusions that serve to blind man.

The figure of the free spirit has wonderful features for Nietzsche—it is far removed from the sobriety of the age of the Enlightenment and far from the deadly earnest belief in reason. Above all, the free spirit is distant from himself and moves with an intrepidness that shrinks back from nothing. In this sense, he is a precursor of the halcyon cheerfulness of Zarathustra. The experimental is his element, and he experiments with all things, including himself. He sets his question mark over everything and does not spare even that which humanity most highly admires. He mistrusts as perhaps no one has ever mistrusted, he employs a psychology with a double bottom, and pulls up more than the well-concealed background into the harsh light of day. He has a sixth sense for the secret and underhanded ways of the "ideal" and is far ahead of the others on all voyages.

The free spirit, however, is a transition figure. At first glance, he seems to be one who brings enlightenment, who shatters ideals, and who tears humanity loose from its thousand-year anchorage with a serpent's cunning. However, what one does not see at first glance is that he himself is drunk, that the wisdom of the free spirit is a "bird's wisdom" that flies away over everything determinate, over all boundaries and frontiers. One also does not immediately see that his mistrust and coolness are only the No that opens up the space for a future Yes. Nietzsche's enlightenment is enlightened about itself and does not share the common belief in reason, progress, and science. Rather, it uses science as a means to put religion, metaphysics, art, and morality in question. When Nietzsche's free spirit sings the high song of science, he has not forgotten that science itself is still a problem from the perspective that takes human existence as a bold enterprise and experiment. The free spirit is not "free" because he lives according to scientific insight. Rather, he is free insofar as he does as he likes *with* science and uses it as a means to break humanity's servitude to "transcendent" ideals. As long as man lives under the dominion of ideals and moral statutes, he is alienated from himself; he has put a crushing weight upon his existence by bowing down before the "superhuman." He lives in the "terror of the lord" and does not know that he himself has created his lords and tyrants. In Nietzsche's opinion, the superhuman is actually only a tenacious and murky illusion, a fata morgana in which the producer encounters the product as if it were a superior and alien power. This disclosure of the concealed all-too-human foundation of the supposedly superhuman shatters all illusions and leads to the collapse of the religious, metaphysical, and moral firmament which man had erected over his existence. This brings about still another decisive revolution in the human condition, a metamorphosis of human existence. Henceforth, man seeks the goals of his highest hopes not outside himself but within himself. Life loses its character as something encountered. It is no longer bound by binding norms, no longer directed by God's will, no longer steered by the idol of absolute morality, no longer conditioned by a metaphysical hinterland beyond appearance. Man has become free. He establishes himself and his goals. The free spirit in this sense is the precursor of Zarathustra.

This said, it still surprises everyone who seeks to follow the path of Nietzsche's thought that the figure of Zarathustra and the image of the overman remain remarkably pale. This is especially surprising because the speeches and parables of Zarathustra display a real depth and profundity. Nietzsche employs all the stylistic means of his seductive language, the entire force of his appeal in order to elevate Zarathustra above the human measure and to make this dream figure of his soul believable. Yet the figure of Zarathustra remains onedimensional, the ventriloquist's dummy of the philosopher. Therefore, this figure does not successfully capture the reality that is central to

Nietzsche's philosophy and life. This is not meant as a critical observation: the correspondence of man and the world is not an empirical given or a task to be completed, but a process of alteration and rearrangement that swirls the boundaries and limits of time and space and things through each other.

Indeed, there are certain aspects of our sojourn in the world that we all experience. We find ourselves in a natural world that surrounds and interpenetrates us. We discover that we are natural creatures who not only eat and drink but also speak and think, name and judge things, according to their "core" and attributes, according to their condition and motion, according to their countless structures. We thus discover that we employ a multifaceted and articulated understanding of being whenever we experience the world. We find ourselves not only in an allegedly natural world but also in a culture that is superimposed upon it, in a social world with institutions, laws, mores, and value systems.

The thesis with which Nietzsche launches his attack in order to break through man's self-alienation is that the superhuman and transcendent is, in fact, only man's externalization and self-forgetting. God and morality are thus taken back into man. Man's being is expanded beyond all previous limits, and the infinite is reinterpreted as an anthropological phenomenon. The collapse of values that occurs as a result of tracing them back to the value-establishing force in man transcends the narrowness of man's previous self-understanding. However, this new human being who has thus been unbound loses the contours of finitude. Is it not an inflation of the human essence to suppose man is everything, to claim he is the creator of the whole cultural world?

The intellectual impulse that comes to the fore in Nietzsche is another form of the impulse that led modern idealism to absolutize the subject, the central notion of "transcendental reflection." Nietzsche characterizes this thought in the first speech of Zarathustra in book 1, the "Three Metamorphoses of Spirit." Spirit is transformed first into the "camel," that is, into the reverential spirit that is capable of bearing a heavy load. Spirit is then suddenly transformed into the "lion," that is, into the radical negation of the apparent transcendence of God and morality. Finally, spirit becomes the "child at play," who symbolizes creative design.

The radical orientation toward creativity that Nietzsche traces out in his image of man understands creation above all else in terms of value setting. In this way, the moral interpretation of the will as practical reason plays a paradigmatic role, especially when the will arises out of fullness, strength, and superiority. One could show that Nietzsche's criteria of originality, developed earlier, already employ such moral concepts, although they are never explicitly developed. Similarly, he does not stop with *human* creativity, but alienates man's value-setting autonomy anew, driving it beyond itself, and relating it to the "overman." In an earlier age, the human world was ruled by God and filled with the blinding light of binding norms. In this world, men were lifted above themselves by the attraction of objective ideals. So today, in a world in which God has been done away with, the "principle of hope" is supposed to be sunken into the living depths of man's being: "What is great in man is that he is a bridge and not a purpose; what can be loved in man is that he is a transition and a perishing" (VI 1, 10–11).

Nietzsche attempts to establish a bridge from man to overman with his reference to the highest possibilities of humanity. With a view to his "passing over," he lists some of these possibilities: the great despisers who sacrifice the earth to themselves; those who know unconditionally; the workers and inventors; those who love virtue and perish of it; the spendthrifts of the spirit; those who are shameful of their happiness; the justifiers of the past and the future; those who cultivate their god; the deep souls; those who are overrich; the free spirits. Nietzsche takes his honey from many strange flowers in the human garden. In all these precursors, the overman collects and prepares himself. What is still scattered in these types is elevated and united in the overman: "I love all those who are dark drops, falling singly out of the dark clouds which hang over men: they herald the lightning and as heralds perish. Behold, I am a herald of the lightning and a heavy drop out of the cloud: the lightning, however, is the overman" (VI 1, 12). While it looked at first as if the entirety of our culture and all the works and deeds of men that make it up would be fully dissolved into man, man is suddenly transcended anew. What transcends man, however, is not already in heaven and on earth. Rather, it is supposed to come out of man and through him. Is Nietzsche's philosophy, one might ask, a new teaching about the creative power of man and his self-alienation, his self-overcoming that leads to a higher level of existence? In short, is it an anthropology of his own making? Culture precedes the "natural" world in which man finds himself as merely one natural creature among others. Man perceives nature, comprehends it according to facts and laws, defines it with concepts and judgments of the language with which he communicates, and gains insights and truths, if only of a preliminary sort.

■   II

In view of this perception of the dependence of nature upon culture, Nietzsche launches his second attack. He denounces the manifold things and regions of things around us as a delusive image and labels as a fiction the system of categories with which we determine substance, causality, the structure of things, the process of movement, and all forms of thought and objects. It is "being," according to Nietzsche, that is the delusion which conquers and enthralls the human imagination. It establishes a false network of concepts in which men commonly catch themselves and halts, binds, and lays to rest the supposedly actual. Concepts falsify and counterfeit the actual insofar as they arrest its movement in their static schema. As a result of this deep distrust of concepts, Nietzsche prefers "contemplation," not, however, simple seeing and hearing but rather the contemplation of strongly symbolic images, in which a deeper reality that cannot be held fast in concepts shines forth. Human cognition that relies upon concepts is a "lie in the extramoral sense," a lie that counterfeits the world, that distorts it into a fixed order of individual things connected through genera and species. The truly actual, Nietzsche postulates, is becoming, not being. Being is the lie of reason, the deception of concepts that conceals the surging play of becoming. Cognition in the ordinary sense is experimental, empirical. As the cognition of the essential principle of the categories by means of which we grasp being as a thing, as a substance with attributes, in other words as a single thing with a universal essence, cognition is also a priori. Nietzsche asserts then that there is emphatically no "being" but only the surging flood of life, only the stream of becoming. There is nothing persistent, nothing static, nothing that remains the same—everything flows. Our cognitive capacity falsifies the image of the actual, distorts the flowing stream into a pretended being of lasting things, a being that remains in the midst of change and persists through the change of conditions. "Thing" or "substance" is a fiction through which we forcibly "make" the flowing actuality "thinkable," with which we fix it and subordinate it to concepts, *forgetting* in the process, however, this act of force to such an extent that we fancy we understand the actual in concepts that are intrinsic to it. Man believes in "things," although there are none; he believes in "being," although this is his own creation, his net of concepts that he throws time and again into the stream of becoming.

Phenomenally, the environment is presented to us as dissociated single things, through which manifold processes of movement run

211

their course and in which we continually deploy a conceptually articulated preunderstanding of individuality and universality. However, this a priori structure, the understanding of being characteristic of things which we think with the categories, that is, the concepts of understanding, is not "objectively valid" at all but rather a mendacious presupposition of human reason. The authentically real is simply and solely *becoming*—not the becoming *of* an already existing being that only alters itself but a pure becoming, an incessant flowing and evolving, an unending movement. It is the "life" of the world that springs forth in everything that occurs, that brings everything forth and destroys everything. What we human beings ordinarily call "things" conceal from us the view of the unlimited, uncontained, unrestrained whole. The phenomena distort the world.

Obviously, we cannot live unprotected in the flowing world sea of pure becoming and must falsify actuality. "Falsification" is a biological necessity—but for whom? Necessity is the mother of invention, and this is equally true of the necessity that we live in a world where everything always glides about, dwindles away, flits past, and whirls around. *Whom* does it make inventive? Is it the man who says "I" to himself, who believes that he is a unique, irreplaceable "individual?" Or is he himself a fiction? Do the categories mean a humanization of the world, an anthropomorphic interpretation which "puts us in place" (*uns "in Stand setzt"*) in that it establishes a permanent place (*ein Ständiges*)? Categories are fictions, the "thing" is a delusive image, a rational instrument of life—nothing more. Strictly understood, is it man who projects himself into all forms and shapes the world in his image? Or is he in the end also only a falsification, also a fictive product? When he daily calls himself I, he believes he is something that persists and remains the same in the manifold flux of the subjective content of experience. This I that presupposes itself, however, *cannot* be the bearer of ontological illusions, because it is itself already a fiction, indeed the basic model for the fictional representation of being. According to Nietzsche, we transpose the presumed persistence of the I onto things and then believe that substance relates to its attributes as the I relates to its circumstances and actions. The concept of substance is thus the consequence of the concept of the I. Nietzsche formulates this as follows: "Man . . . has projected the will, the spirit, the I outside himself—he first took the concept of being out of the concept of I, he established 'things' as beings in his own image, according to the concept of the I as a cause" (VI 3, 85).

What is problematic about such a way of speaking becomes apparent when one asks how man can be a falsifier when he himself is a falsification and not the purveyor of falsehoods. The provocative abbreviation that Nietzsche gives his strident thesis makes it easy for his opponents to point out the circularity of his argument. He certainly does not achieve this interpretation of human cognition as fictional through a critique of reason or through a methodical investigation of the cognitive capacity. Rather, he calls upon the testimony of experience. To be sure, this is an unusual and strange experience, even an oracular intuition which breaks through the bars of concepts, and especially ontological concepts, to behold the life stream of worldwide becoming behind the stony mask of being. Nietzsche calls upon Heraclitus, the tragic philosopher, whom he sets up against the Eleatic Parmenides. What is decisive for him is a universal melting, a liquidation of the torpid thought of being. This melting means, then, the true destruction of the illusory human, all-too-human, of the human world that has been rationalized and secured conceptually. The "lie of being" must first be revealed and undermined before becoming, which foams forth, can surface in its unique maturity. The idea of permanence must be overthrown before the dance and the roundelay of the world-actuality can shine forth. Nietzsche here propounds a challenging thesis that is in fact a radical, self-completing skepticism. At first, the skeptical thesis traces everything back to man and then traces man himself back to a nameless shaping power. This power is conceptually indeterminable and no "*fundamentum inconcussum*"; it is world-becoming.

■ III

Man vanishes when he "thinks" himself "to the end" as a creative project in Nietzsche's sense. He penetrates to the ground of all things in the self-overcoming of his human being. Where does this way lead? Into a world in which man as a natural being belongs not only as a particular form but much more as a gateway and a part of the way. In this light, it is no longer possible on the one hand to assume that the world is a complex collection of things in which man is both a thing and also the subject that underlies all things including himself, and on the other to set man over against the universe as an eye that sees all things. Man's being and the universe are bound together in Nietzsche's optics. His anthropology is cosmomorphic, and his cosmology is anthropomorphic. This is no capricious fancy nor is it an extreme microcosmic-macrocosmic analogy. He needs a guiding thread in order to understand the world and man as an interpenetrating double motion. Man dissolves in universal becoming; the world concentrates itself into man. Nothing of all this, however, is noticed in the phenomena.

And yet several noteworthy features that point to it can be discerned in man's phenomenal being, above all in those aspects of his existence that otherwise concern and determine his coexistence with other men, his being-with-others. Man produces his life in that he produces the means of his life. This he accomplishes by working upon nature, subordinating it, and thus gaining power over things. Moreover, through the power of exchange that these things give him, he also gains power over other products and his fellow workers. This does not bespeak a definitive, unchanging condition but rather a *relative* level of power that suddenly grows, and suddenly declines, that rises and falls, and that thus continually finds itself in fluctuation. We also find a continual struggle among men who aim at imposing themselves upon others and overpowering them. This struggle appears at its harshest in war. In the world of men, the will to power is thus predominant in work and war. This will to power accentuates the singleness of each single person, separates a people into friends and enemies, raises up the one only at the cost of the other.

An exceptional and essential form of being-with-others is the love between the sexes, which is grounded in a natural interest. Man and woman are always single individuals who at the height of life procreate, grow old, and finally die. The same life passes through the chain of generations, lasts beyond death, is mortal and immortal alike. Love and death are a likeness of identity in difference, of an eternal return of the same. And finally, human life shows us that play is one of life's monstrous powers, that it scintillates through all the dimensions of life as the play of being and appearance and envelops them in the splendor of beauty. The will to power, the recurrence of the same, the clarifying image of play are central phenomena and indeed fundamental features of human being-with-others. Moreover, they are the anthropological models which Nietzsche's cosmology employs. He seeks to understand the world from the perspective of man. Human being becomes a cosmic key for him, the guiding thread in the labyrinth of the world.

The great and decisive difficulty of Nietzsche's model of the world is that it pulls the ground out from under its own feet. It shatters this ground and leaves it in ruins; it destroys the path of understanding that this model wants to establish. As the worker and the work of the will to power, man himself is not only the producer but the product of fictions. Nietzsche's anthropomorphic cosmology is extremely problematic as a philosophical assertion. As the art metaphysics that draws upon Schopenhauer, as the "dawning" liberation of the "free spirit," as the oracular world vision of Zarathustra, Nietzsche's thought always completes itself in a proud loneliness that pays no attention to replicability, proof, or the preservation of the "things themselves," and that shies away from the toil of verification and declares the method of verification itself to be a leading problem. He announces but does not reveal the way that leads him to his wisdom. It would certainly be a mistake to see a hidden incapacity in this attitude or to close off in advance the possibility that his theses are true. The "will to power," which is Nietzsche's one fundamental thesis about the world, is demonstrable in the circle of human phenomena. It is evident in the area of social life, in the struggle of peoples and races, in the conflict of classes and individuals; in short, it courses a thousandfold through the relations among men. While it is certainly not the only fundamental form of human existence, it is an evident and demonstrable phenomenon that makes man's relationship to the animals, that is, his own bestiality, clear.

From another perspective, Nietzsche believes that the phenomenon of organic life provides support for his theses and believes that he can demonstrate that the notion of organism is a key to understanding the cosmos. This thesis, however, contains several implicit presuppositions: First, it assumes that the world as a whole is "life." The cosmos is thus presented in the image of a monstrous living being. Such an image long ago was recognized by some philosophers as indispensable. In Plato's *Timaeus,* for example, the cosmos is characterized as a giant, spherical, living being, a *zōon* that has no extremities, that does not live in an environment, that takes nothing in and expels nothing, and that represents a temporal likeness of the highest idea. It is strange, however, that this analogy to the organic leaves out such essential features of the "phenomenal organism" as self-preservation, manifest in metabolism, as well as growth and aging. Second, the term "life" is vastly extended beyond the phenomenon of life when Nietzsche uses it to point to everything that is in motion. Third, the difference between the human organism and that of plants and animals, which is evident in the phenomena, is done away with insofar as the moment of freedom that characterizes human being is not expressly separated from plant and animal being. The "life" of the world that is manifested in the notion of organism is instinctual impulse, self-assertion, and human aggression all in one. Nietzsche "plantizes" and animalizes man and humanizes plants and animals by placing them under the general name "life," and then uses this term, so understood, as a likeness of the world. "Where I found the living, there I found the will to power; and even in the will of these who serve I found the will to be master. . . . That the weaker should serve the stronger, to that it is persuaded by its own will which would be master over what is weaker still: This is the one pleasure it does not want to renounce. And as the small yields to the greater that it may have pleasure and power over the smallest, thus even the greatest yields, and for the sake of power risks life" (VI 1, 143–44).

What does this speech about the great and small mean? There is a phenomenal basis for it in the way the world is articulated into regions of larger and smaller things and larger and smaller individuals. Can one still speak of individuals, however, when the world is a single sea stream, an unceasing, surging becoming? Nietzsche presents a peculiar theory according to which life splits itself up within itself, shatters its unity, and out of the ruin seeks to reestablish this unity in a bellicose fashion by overpowering and suppressing particularity. The primordial will turns to dust in the will's "punctuation," in the temporary and finite establishment of the "quanta of will." This remarkable and highly speculative "quantum theory" is overlooked in many Nietzsche interpretations. Does the individuation that seemed to be excluded by the concept of "life" return as a principle of the quasi-monadological self-determination? Certainly, Nietzsche does not mean by this monads that are closed and sealed to the outside world but only monads that last for a short time, not "substances," only waves in the sea.

For this conception as well, there are many precursors in the history of philosophy, from the *philia kai neikos* (love and strife) of Empedocles, through the conception of an absolute being, which contains the pain of finitude and the monstrous power of negation but that recreates itself as a whole out of all alienation and tornness, to Hegel's formula of the "speculative Good Friday." There are many world formulas in history that assert the conjunction of unity and plurality, of identity and difference, of the contradiction of phenomena and essence that speak in dialectical or mystical sentences that contradict all sense, but one cannot point to the phenomenon of the *one* world incessantly tearing itself to pieces. Nietzsche's "will to power" is a cosmological metaphor that contains many elements from the phenomenal realm, but that capriciously leaves many others out and thereby overleaps the phenomenal world altogether. This doctrine thus does not recognize the phenomenal world as an instance before which the philosopher has to justify himself. The "will to power," which is an irrepressible tendency toward an increase in the quantum of power, toward the greatest increase, always passes beyond itself: it is the flowing will of life to self-overcoming (see the chapter from *Zarathustra,* "On Self-Overcoming"). How high can it climb? Apparently, until one quantum of power has embodied every-thing else within itself, until the conflict comes to an end as the result of the defeat of all opponents. So one is supposed to believe. Then, in principle, the open sea of life would suddenly have to change into a limited and finite, even if monstrously large, form, into a giant quan-tum of power. One would have to borrow new principles from the phenomena of destruction that we are familiar with in order to make the breakdown and disintegration of this greatest quantum of power conceivable. Nietzsche does not do this; he asserts that the increase in power of the quanta of will and the destruction of the unity of life are equally primordial: to build and to destroy, to join and to set asunder are mutually necessary ways in which the cosmic will to power rules.

The question thus arises, Does the process of becoming, in which everything finite comes to be and passes away, form a final state? Does the world, in other words, have a goal? Nietzsche's answer to this question is his teaching of the eternal recurrence of the same. However, this teaching is not "teachable"; it cannot be presented in a communicative discourse. It is rather Nietzsche's "esoteric wisdom," which Zarathustra imparts to his animals and to himself. It is the at-tempt to knock down the sharpest walls of separation, to overcome the fundamental distinction that divides the unity of time itself, to take the past as the future that is coming to be and the future as what is always already past, to assert the unique now, this single unique-ness, as eternally repeated. Nietzsche's attempt to develop founda-tional arguments for the eternal recurrence are weak. They show no profound understanding of time and remain far below the height of the problem presented by all metaphysical interpretations of time. And yet this vision of time fascinated not only Nietzsche but also many serious intellects. It is counted as the heart of Nietzsche's philosophy.

In my opinion, this has two grounds. First, it can call upon the ex-perience that we all have of the interruption of the everyday monot-ony of the linear passage of time when we feel the "eternity of the world" and time disappears for us in moments of great joy or deep anguish, in the momentary nearness of nature, when moonlight "again quietly fills coppice and valley with misty splendor." Second, this teaching of the eternity of the world in the eternal return of the same offers a victory over the transience of all things and also a unification of freedom and necessity in *amor fati.* Nietzsche describes the teaching of the eternal recurrence as the greatest conceivable burden on earth. In each moment, the deeds and their consequences are again decided forever, for endless repetitions. Only the strongest individuals and the strongest peoples can bear this teaching, and so it is itself a principle of selection of the greatest hardness and efficacy. However, one could also draw the opposite conclusion: if everything recurs, then everything is already decided. The teaching of the eternal recurrence could thus also become a hobbling quietism of the human will, a fatalistic laying of its unrest to rest. How the "will to power" and the "eternal recurrence of the same" cohere in Nietzsche's thinking is made especially clear in aphorism 1067 of the so-called *Will to Power:*

> And do you know what "the world" is to me? Shall I show it to you in my mirror? This world: a monster of energy, without beginning, without end; a firm, iron magnitude of force that does not grow bigger or smaller, that does not expend itself but only transforms itself; as a whole, of unalterable size, a household without expenses or losses, but likewise without increase or income; enclosed by "nothingness" as by a boundary; not something blurry or wasted, not something endlessly extended, but set in a definite space as a definite force, and not a space that might be "empty" here or there, but rather as force throughout, as a play of forces and waves of forces, at the same time one and many, increasing here and at the same time decreasing there; a sea of forces flowing and rushing together, eternally changing, eternally flooding back, with tremendous years of recurrence, with an ebb and a flood of its forms; out of the simplest forms striving toward the most complex, out of the stillest, most rigid, coldest forms toward the hottest, most turbulent, most self-contradictory, and then again returning home to the simple out of this abundance, out of the play of contradictions back to the joy of concord, still affirming itself in this uniformity of its course and its years, blessing itself as that which must return eternally, as a becoming that knows no satiety, no disgust, no weariness: this, my Dionysian world of the eternally self-creating, the eternally self-destroying, this mystery world of the twofold voluptuous delight, my "beyond good and evil," without goal, unless the joy of the circle is itself a goal; without will, unless a ring feels good will toward itself—do you want a name for this world? A solution for all its riddles? A light for you, too, you best-concealed, strongest, most intrepid, most midnightly men. This world is the will to power and nothing

besides? And you yourselves are also this will to power—
and nothing beside!

Is this only a drunken speech, the world-visionary incantation of a
poet for whom the words break, or is it the thinking out of a new experience of the world? This new experience lies not in Nietzsche's
"great war" against Western metaphysics, Christianity, and traditional morality. Rather, it is hesitantly articulated in those phrases in
which the world is celebrated as a game, as a roundelay, a happening
that is driven by accident and chance, as the theater of the god of
masks, Dionysus, in such songs of Zarathustra as "Before Sunrise"
and "On the Great Longing." Perhaps the old and ever-repeated question of every Nietzsche interpretation, whether he is a thinker or a
poet, remains unanswered as long as we are unable to formulate a
sufficient concept of WORLD, beyond subject and object, beyond the
alternatives of being-in-itself and appearance, beyond all categories
of things altogether, beyond an understanding of being that is oriented on the basis of a broken, that is, individuated, Being of beings,
beyond Western metaphysics. What is ever again brought into question as the unresolved conflict of poetry and thinking in Nietzsche is
not the duality of two creative capacities but much more the difference between thinking the innerworldly and thinking the world itself.
Understood philosophically, what we need to do in order to understand Nietzsche today is not to inquire into that which is thought in
the world formulas, the "will to power" and the "eternal recurrence,"
but, before all else, to bring into words the relationship of human
existence to the world, the experience of the world.

■   NOTE

1. Friedrich Nietzsche, *Unschuld des Werdens,* ed. Alfred Baeumler (Leipzig: Kroner, 1931), aphorism 1217.

CHAPTER 9

■ The Drama of Zarathustra

Hans-Georg Gadamer
Translated by Thomas Heilke

Nietzsche belongs, with Goethe and Heinrich Heine, to the greatest stylists of the German language. Their use of the German language is distinguished by the absence of all gravity. Thus they are something like the fulfillment of the great message of Zarathustra and his struggle against the spirit of gravity. To be sure, *Thus Spoke Zarathustra* is an exception among Nietzsche's works, and as much as one has reason to admire individual lyrical sections in this book, it is not the forced style of this book that allows one to rank Nietzsche with the great stylists of the German language.

It is certainly not easy to extract a comprehensible context from this book. For it is a half-poetic book that belongs to the species of mimesis, of imitation. It is a literary work of art. Therefore, it is certainly incorrect simply to identify Zarathustra with Nietzsche and his speeches with Nietzsche's philosophy. Rather, it is a hermeneutical task of the first order to determine the "in between" of teaching and action that we find here and that is inherent in every poetic text. We must be fully conscious of the problem of conceptualizing the message of a thinker who is so divided between conceptual and poetic speech.

To begin with, there is the hermeneutical difference between the speeches and epigrams on the one hand and the narrative sections on the other. Both are elements of Nietzsche's book. The speeches of Zarathustra are not a mere collection of speeches like the speeches of

Previously published in German in *Nietzschestudien* 15 (1986):1–15. An earlier version of the essay was published in *The Great Year of Zarathustra (1881–1981)*, ed. David Goicoechea (Lanham, Md.: University Press of America, 1983). Professor Gadamer welcomed a new translation of this revised essay.

Gautama Buddha, rather they are set into a story. This immediately implies two different viewpoints of interpretation: a speaker who makes a speech has his audience before him. He speaks to someone, and that means he speaks differently to different listeners. Nietzsche has expressly let us understand this. Near the end of "On Redemption," he writes: "But why does Zarathustra speak to his pupils other than to himself?" The address of the speaker introduces a dialectical point of view. We must flesh out the auditor and always ask ourselves, Why one would speak in just such a manner to this particular audience?

The second viewpoint, in contrast, is that of narrative. A narrative lays claim to a superior authenticity compared with the intention of the speaker about whom the story is being told, even when the former only claims to be of poetic value, a fiction. This has enormous conceptual consequences. On a first reading, one will read the book as the announcement of new tables of values that are set up in opposition to the old, Christian values. This reading is certainly not false, but it is somewhat superficial in contrast to the drama whose events are recounted in this book.

This is the task I set for myself: to inquire about the meaning of these events, which constitute the tragedy of the teacher Zarathustra. No one can deny that Nietzsche was an oversensitive moralist. His critique of the ordinary moral values of the Christian tradition is the critique of a moralist, whose truest passion was shame and suffering through shame. He could not endure the presumptuousness, self-assurance, and authoritarian pretentiousness that he found accepted as valid in social and religious institutions and in public opinion. Thus, a peculiar dialectic of emancipation is operative in Nietzsche's sayings. He says, "Giving is much more difficult than accepting gifts." For there the task is to overcome one's own shame, which wants to spare another's shame. The example illustrates in an almost disheartening manner how difficult it is to overcome such sensitivity and to understand correctly the whole series of these aphorisms and the role that they play in the story.

To this purpose, I would especially like to bring to light those passages which serve as points of connection from which one can see the composition as a whole. I must repeat that the style of this book is not to everyone's taste, in any event not to mine nor that of my generation. We Germans of today have difficulty understanding that one can admire the rhetoric, the pathos of these discourses, without harboring strong inner reservations. It is less a successful poetic effort than the ingenious product of a thinker, and therefore the composition of the whole is its most important aspect. It is not a cloak or a framework for the didactic speeches. Rather, the narrative action is itself that about which we want to discover the truth.

Naturally, I can only attempt such a thing in selected places. I begin with the first speech. I leave the prologue aside, the first appearance of Zarathustra in the marketplace of the city, and the adventure with the tightrope walker. These are well known and oft-discussed matters. If I begin with the first speech, I do so because the entire paradox of conceptual speech comes to light in it. "The Three Metamorphoses" is the story of the spirit and its forms of appearance. It appears as a camel, as a lion, as a child. The camel personifies the patience to bear everything heavy and to take all duties upon oneself. The spirit as camel says to itself, "You ought." The spirit in the form of the lion retains the freedom to reject all duties. He can say the holy No because he says to himself, "I will." The third transformation is that into the spirit of the child; it is the spirit of innocence, of play, of a complete lack of awareness of time, of a life completely for the moment, of being quickly consoled for all missed opportunities. According to Zarathustra, this is the highest form of the spirit and is the true content of his message.

Thus, the problem becomes immediately clear: How can one proclaim the innocence of a child as a goal? How can the proclaimer of a new doctrine of the overman exhort us to something that we cannot want? This is the deepest tension in the proclamation of innocence and immediacy and the eternal recurrence of the same that runs through the entire book and that is familiar to us as the old tragic inheritance of German idealism: the paradox of restored immediacy, of mediated immediacy. Thus, all the speeches of Zarathustra are also in the same breath silences. Nietzsche himself says that one must learn to speak in order properly to remain silent. In that one says something, one is always at the same time concealing something. Whenever someone says something, he does not say something else that perhaps should be thought in the same moment. Thus, we must also look behind what is said. Then, the meaning of the action for the sense of the whole is revealed. In the action, a window is similarly opened time and again that allows us to view what lies at the bottom of the speeches, serving as an access to the reality that lies in the events themselves, that is, in the figure of Zarathustra and his tragedy, which he lives before us. We will attempt to take note of the signs that point to this tragedy.

In the first place, there is the end of book 1. I always especially pay attention to the end or the beginning of books, because it is certainly a hermeneutical requirement. Nietzsche wrote the work, which consists of four books, in such a manner that the first three books were produced relatively quickly, and the fourth considerably later. The fourth book was apparently not planned at the beginning. In contrast, the first three books arose from a well-considered composition. Therefore, the first window opens for us at the end of the first book, in the first parting of Zarathustra from his disciples. His speeches had won him a large audience and devoted followers. To them, he now gives the warning: you must free yourselves from your teacher. Each one must free himself from authority. But Zarathustra takes leave of his friends in such a way that one understands that he has not yet spoken his last word.

Then there are other foreshadowings, for instance, when in "On Redemption" he demands of the will to unlearn revenge, and hesitates: "'Who could teach him also to will backwards?'—At this point in his speech it happened that Zarathustra suddenly stopped and looked altogether like one who had received a severe shock." This is one of the most elegant forms of allusion. The subsequent conversation with the hunchback further underlines it. He accuses him of speaking to him and to the crowd differently than he speaks to his pupils, and, when Zarathustra defends himself, the hunchback responds, "All right, but why does Zarathustra speak otherwise to us than to his disciples?" This, too, means that something is still being held back. Finally, we have the highly dramatic and rousing scene in the chapter "The Stillest Hour." There, Nietzsche's Zarathustra reveals something of his inner struggle with himself and with the silent inner voice that exhorts him to speak. He continuously avoids this, so he is told, so he tells himself, "Oh, Zarathustra, your fruit is ripe, but you are not ripe for your fruit." So we arrive well prepared at the central section of the whole, and that, without doubt, is the third book. The burden that obviously presses on him is that he is the teacher of the eternal recurrence. He is to proclaim his teaching without being ashamed.

If one thus considers the book as a dramatic action into which Zarathustra's "speeches" are integrated, then something of its sequential nature, which gives this collection of biblical-antibiblical speeches the tone of a never-ending sermon, disappears. Further, one finds a point of entry that does not require one to accept and identify oneself with the largely "past" objectives of these discourses. The blustering, mendacious, neo-German imperial and hypocritical Christianity of the second half of the nineteenth century helped to determine the mode in which Nietzsche, the admirer and challenger of Richard Wagner, framed his anti-Christian reply. The form of speech in these discourses is far removed from us. Nietzsche himself saw one of his greatest achievements in his emancipation from the late classical and late Romantic enchantment of rhyme and his new orientation to the Old Testament and to Luther. Certainly, this has had consequences in our century, but of such severity that the effect of Nietzsche's poetic presentation—in contrast to the incomparably supple and forceful style of Nietzsche's prose—is "past" in the truest sense of the word. The extreme lucidity of his artistic means, the density of the assonances and alliterations as well as the frequent plays on words, allusions, metaphors, and variations chasing one another, are no longer comprehensible to us: one thinks of the false splendor of the historicism of the founding years of the *Reich,* even if the depth and luster of individual phrases shine forth again and again. In general, it is past.

If one considers the tragedy of the prophet who is approaching his end, and continually shrinking from it in terror, instead of these half-filled tablets which Zarathustra gives to himself, the whole work attains a new immediacy, intelligibility, unity, and tension. All this is intensified in the third book, which races toward the end, toward destruction, as if in a fury. That there was, finally, a fourth book, and that there were to have been others are other matters that do not concern us here. When *Thus Spoke Zarathustra,* this book for all and none, appeared, the end of the third book, especially "The Other Dancing Song" and the "Yes and Amen Song," was read as the fulfillment and resolution of the expectation permeating the entire work. Nietzsche himself perceived it as such, and called the third book a veritable finale. In fact, this third book does come to a particularly dramatic peak: it begins with the ascent into the last, lonely heights. There follows a story of the face of the loneliest, who does not truly free himself from the spirit of gravity which weighs him down and who only speaks in a dreamlike whisper with himself "of eternal things," of the "eternal recurrence of all things," "more and more softly; for I was afraid of my own thoughts and the thoughts behind my thoughts." He experiences his liberation only in another dream and a riddle in the image of a shepherd, who bites off the head of the snake choking him and breaks into the laughter of one who is freed, but in such a way that Zarathustra can only yearn for this laughter, and even the blessed hour, in which his abysmal thought seeks to appear, still cannot find its time. All these are only the first scenes of this ever more seductive expectation of the great noon. All speeches concerning the new tablets are dictated by such expectation and distress. It is hermeneutically naive to listen only to these speeches that Zarathustra delivers to his disciples or himself as things to be obeyed as if the deepest breakdown and the slowest convalescence did not follow immediately thereafter; and again it happens that it was the most abysmal thought that threw Zarathustra into revulsion and unconsciousness. When it threatened to speak, it is remarkable enough that this chapter of the greatest breakdown mentions nothing of it in the title but refers to it only indirectly. For the title is simply "The Convalescent" (as the rough preliminary drafts show, the title "The Exorcism" was dropped). The slow convalescence that Zarathustra undergoes in conversation with his animals is characterized in two ways. It is animals that through their own being tell him and sing him his teaching of the eternal recurrence of the same, and it is they who hinder him from speaking further and invite him to sing. They anticipate him, prespeak him, so to speak, and therein he finds his own convalescence, as the following piece, "The Great Longing," confirms.

Thus, the third section actually ends with song. Then, there is the other dancing song that in a metrically loose manner gives the unrefined rhymes in which it is delivered a nearly balladic accent. It is expressly characterized as "The Other Dancing Song," and thereby refers back to the first dancing song, the dancing song and burlesque on the spirit of gravity which Zarathustra sings to the girls. In the first dancing song, he confesses his love for life, which is so powerful that his wisdom still loses itself in it: "And into the unfathomable I then seemed to be sinking." Obviously, the same tension between Zarathustra's wisdom and "life" appeared there that now appears in "The Other Dancing Song" as a type of hunt and pursuit. A not completely unambiguous pursuit. It remains an open question whether "life" is a dog that loyally obeys the hunter, or a chamois, the pursued game. It is equally ambiguous whether life is to dance and cry to the time of his whip. Is this dancing song, in which his wisdom is to be sung out, not also full of the "great longing" of his soul for the great liberator *Lyaios, Bacchus, Dionysus,* "for whom future songs will first find names?

The song that the soul learns to sing is still not the "fulfillment," the great noon itself; once again the dialogue that life carries on with Zarathustra continues.

Again, we notice that the two following pieces, numbered two and three, appear under the main title "The Other Dancing Song, 1–3," as if the soul that acknowledges the eternal recurrence as its wisdom must first learn to sing its song. And has it really learned to sing and not to fall back on the teaching, on "Thus Spoke Zarathustra," when it finally sings forth in the "Yes and Amen Song"? Is that really the fulfillment? In truth, the dialogue between Zarathustra and life, which he himself recounts, much more nearly appears as the deepest point attained by his new wisdom. The dancing song was too loud: "Noise murders thought." But one asks oneself: "Can there be a song that is not too loud for this thought?" The philosophical problem that the Zarathustra book poses begins to develop its outlines.

In the end, does the dialogue of the soul with itself, the dialogue between wisdom and life that Zarathustra's soul carries on, conceal an insoluble diremption? If we follow the dialogue, we can hardly avoid this conclusion. That Zarathustra and "life" are good for one another—precisely because Zarathustra gives life its due, "beyond good and evil"—does not exclude the possibility that a tense relationship exists between his wisdom and life, a relationship of jealousy. The love of life for him is his love for life—life is inextricably bound to his wisdom, which consists in the prize of life, its incomprehensibility and readiness to dance: "If your wisdom ever ran away from you, then my love would quickly run away from you, too." "My love, too": so much are they nearly the same.

Yet not entirely, and this is the point at which the whole problem of Nietzsche and his Zarathustra comes together. It is something like a secret complaint that life harbors against him. Life looks around and says quickly (or does Zarathustra accuse life?), "You are not faithful enough to me. You do not love me nearly as much as you say; I know you are thinking of leaving me soon." And Zarathustra says, "Yes," even if hesitatingly. Hesitating perhaps because, like life itself, he knows nothing is ever completely over, and everything recurs. Life does know it, because it is the eternal recurrence. But no man knows it: "No one knows that." And then they weep together as they gaze into the evening: "But then life was dearer to me than all my wisdom ever was."

A scene of infinite grace and propriety. What does it mean that Zarathustra soon wants to leave life? What does it mean that he wants this? Is it despair about the meaning of life which overcomes him when the midnight bell reminds him of the passing time? But is he still not ripe? Does he still ask himself, as after that first dancing song, "Is it not folly still to be alive?" Then, where is the wisdom, which he has just whispered into her ear? Or is it indeed that he knows what no one knows and that he also does not know it? That he cannot stop wishing, "Woe implores: Go" and cannot stop, even in view of the whole of life, thinking about what is past. But that does not necessarily mean that he wishes to leave life, but rather that he lives all too much in the consciousness that he must leave it. It is death, the end, that stands before him, and, for life, which knows only itself and the eternal recurrence of the same, death is an infidelity.

Then, one would understand why they weep with one another, life and Zarathustra, and that "then" life was dearer to him than all his wisdom ever was—then, that is, in this moment of confession and final understanding with life. One would also understand why the midnight song ends at the stroke of twelve and is not followed by any more words. However, that the "Yes and Amen Song" follows is not so easy to understand. The "Yes and Amen Song" wants to be entirely in the present and is far removed from the "then." As present, it knows no "then." Indeed, one must ask oneself whether this hymn to eternity, with which the book closes, does not itself still stand in the ambiguity of having to sing its wisdom of the recurrence to itself. The singer calls himself "of a soothsaying (prophetic) spirit." This final piece of the whole "The Seven Seals," which are to seal the truth of his wisdom, is announced as a song by its refrain, but it is the song of a soothsayer, of one who is pregnant, of one who is "lusty" for the ring of rings, the ring of recurrence—the innocence of becoming, the innocence of the child, the "I am," saying Yes and Amen; this piece thus remains a message from elsewhere.

Is this last wisdom of Zarathustra, which he acknowledges in that he learns to say yes to everything, even to the recurrence of the least, a possible truth, a musical round, in which all "higher men" can unite?

The fourth part, added later, seeks an answer to this question. Perhaps in the 'Drunken Song," that wills the "once more" and thereby means "for all eternity"? In the end does Zarathustra not recognize that it is a delusion to unite the "higher men" in this musical round, and thus join company with the flock of doves and the lion?

Perhaps it is also meaningful that Nietzsche did not leave the ending of book 3 as the ending of *Thus Spoke Zarathustra.* He considered numerous plans for a continuation and carried out one of them, the fourth part, without sharing it outside the smallest circle. Nevertheless it is something like an authentic interpretation of the end of the third part—with all the ambiguities that are attached to this concept in Nietzsche (as in every poet). For, say what one will, this ending rings like a true ending, like an unambiguous curtain fall (*Untergang*). Zarathustra has finally expressed his most abysmal thought of the eternal recurrence, before which he always shrank back, and sealed it sevenfold in the "Yes and Amen Song." In fact, sketches also exist in which the death of Zarathustra was planned—in which thoughts of suicide, which otherwise lie close by, do not come into play. The existing fourth part, in contrast, sounds more like the overcoming of a final confusion—the confusion that arises from sympathy with the "higher men"—and like the departure of the teacher of "wisdom," who has become certain of his own victoriousness, to meet his "children."

It has become customary in recent Nietzsche scholarship to see a break between the semipoetic teaching style of *Zarathustra* and Nietzsche's later period, beginning with *Beyond Good and Evil*. Indeed, this scholarship recognizes a kind of self-confession that that way was a failure. This is understandable insofar as the great plan of a systematic presentation of his teaching under the title *The Will to Power* completely dominates Nietzsche's notebooks in the following period.

On the other hand, we have attained a certain consensus today that the posthumous *Will to Power,* which was composed and edited under the aegis of the Nietzsche Archive, gives a false impression, as if this major philosophical work were completed in its basic outlines. That this is not so has been established beyond all doubt by the new critical edition of Colli and Montinari. The "posthumous volumes," *The Will to Power* published by the Nietzsche Archive, are in fact a compilation, that in part even included older material. We have finally become aware that the entire work was set up according to completely inappropriate, conventional points of view. For example, when the oft-cited proverb, "not the victory of science, but the victory of method over science," is inserted under the heading "Epistemology," then this is characteristic of the nineteenth century. In truth, neither the title nor the exact content of the planned four books of the presentation of his teaching were fixed. Beside *The Will to Power, The Revaluation of All Values* appeared as a title. Above all, however, it is unclear how far the last publications of Nietzsche, in particular *The Antichrist* and *Twilight of the Idols,* are to count as a partial execution of the work, that is, are "extracts" of the planned work. It appears as if Nietzsche's new publisher, J. G. Naumann, contributed a good deal to Nietzsche's having produced a series of writings during his last creative years that sounded like announcing drumrolls, which faded away into emptiness with Nietzsche's mental breakdown.

The general difficulties that interpreters have had with the juxtaposition of the "will to power" and the "eternal recurrence" have recently been clarified, in particular through Heidegger's penetrating interpretation. Insofar as Heidegger assigns Nietzsche the extreme end position in the history of Western metaphysics, which he characterizes as the total "forgetfulness of Being," and therewith sees Nietzsche's thinking as tragically entangled in the empty essence of metaphysics, the general tendency to devalue the Zarathustra phase of Nietzsche's thinking becomes impossible. In fact, it turns into its opposite. In the tragic figure of Zarathustra, surrounded by storms and wrestling for the courage to bear his truth, the self-contradiction in which the magic circle of the modern reflexivity of consciousness is entangled finds its appropriate expression. Nietzsche did not hide from this: his great "new" inspiration, the theory of the eternal recurrence of the same, is itself entangled in this self-contradiction, and this is constantly present in the third part of *Zarathustra*. Already in that nocturnal whispering with the dwarf in the gateway, Zarathustra asks himself, "that this moment draws after it *all* that is to come. Therefore—itself too?" And the animals say it also, that Zarathustra should know it: "I come ever again to this same and self-same life, in its greatest and in its smallest things, that I again teach the eternal recurrence of all things." The working notes that were restlessly piled up and that were to serve as the basis for the great theoretical magnum opus, *The Will to Power,* or *The Revaluation of All Values,* contain an enormous quantity of material that allow the concept of subject, the concept of knowledge, and the concept of truth to appear as creations of the one true principle of being and becoming, the "will to power." The result of this reinterpretation is the self-dissolution of Nietzsche's own theoretical undertaking.

Before he sank into the night, Nietzsche planned to take up new natural-scientific studies in Leipzig for his theory of "the eternal recurrence of the same"—certainly not without being conscious of the paradox of this self-contradiction. He nevertheless took this into account; that is, he consciously placed "science" in the service of life. In a certain sense, he took physics, which he expected to provide him with the proofs of his theory, thoroughly seriously. But it is meaningful that *Breeding and Cultivation* figured beside the title *The Eternal Recurrence* in the plans for his theoretical work. This is very similar to the incident in *Zarathustra* when the struggle for the courage to face his teaching (which otherwise exceeds all bounds) is interrupted in the chapter "On Old and New Tablets." The moralist retains the upper hand. No path leads beyond the last seal that Zarathustra presses upon his "teaching," "Sing, speak no more."

This is neither retracted nor restricted by the added fourth part. Even if one does not enter into the particulars of the artistic invention of this part, the incorporation of the course of events portrayed here into the dramatic action is completely clear. Through his experiences with the "higher men," Zarathustra learns that he cannot let himself be distracted by them. This fishing from his high mountain, this invitation of the higher men to his cave gathers many sufferers together: the soothsayer, for whom nothing is worthwhile; the kings who seek for the highest man; the conscientious in spirit; the magician, whose mendacity Zarathustra sees through and who sees through his own mendacity; the old pope; the ugliest man; the voluntary beggar; the free spirit and wanderer who follows Zarathustra like a shadow— they all see in Zarathustra the great hope. As sufferers, they live on hope. But this means they are not capable of Zarathustra's wisdom: saying yes to everything.

This becomes Zarathustra's experience. It is not easy actually to free oneself, to accept suffering, evil, pain and limitations without any counterwilling. But that is precisely Zarathustra's message: to learn acceptance. *Amor fati.* In the end, Zarathustra realized that he must overcome pity for the sufferers who desire what is higher. They cannot follow him. The musical round of the Yes saying fails. It is like a sign to him that it is the animals, not only the doves, but also the lion, that nestle up to him and give him confidence in himself and in his talk, his work. One must also note the expectation with which Zarathustra strides into his great noon applies to his "children." "My children are near." It does not say "the right men" or even "the higher men," but his children. The innocence of the child, its "I am," is confirmed. That is something that one should not do and cannot will. Is this the end of tragedy? Or is it perhaps not much more truly: *Sic incipit tragoedia?*

The drama of Zarathustra is his becoming free to a Yes saying. Yet his drama is not so much about the suffering of the one who knows and says Yes to everything as it is about the one who now wants to teach his wisdom and cannot find the right men who are equal to this wisdom. There is no such division between knowing and communicating with others. The Zarathustra of the fourth part, who suffers because of the "higher men" and empathizes with them, is still the same person. He knows and yet is not what he knows. Nietzsche's theoretical attempt to justify Zarathustra's message conceptually on the basis of a general principle, the will to power, which culminates in the eternal recurrence of the same, was not completed. Could it ever have been completed? In the end, the inheritance of metaphysics is preserved in Nietzsche's radical critique of consciousness and self-consciousness from the perspective of life, and in his sketch of a universal theory of the will to power, and this metaphysics, as Heidegger has correctly seen, terminates in the mastery of all being, in the rule of technology. In contrast, the drama of Zarathustra imparts another teaching. The teacher and cultivator, the revaluater of all values, who wants to be Zarathustra, must in the end say to his soul, "Sing, speak no more!"

What does this aim at? Certainly to show that no doctrine that sees the will to power at work in everything and that tears the mask from truth, one after the other, can ever reach an end—rather, that all reaching and expecting remains suffering, the "I will" as well as the "thou shalt."

The free spirits too, the higher men, are such searchers and sufferers, who cannot cast off the spirit of gravity. It is the ease of the child, its easy forgetting, its timelessness, its arising in the there of the moment, its playing, that surpasses them all. It is like a song. Song is human existence (*Dasein*)—not something intentional, indeed, beyond all disclosing of intention, beyond all "unconcealing," something rather lying behind it, that fulfills itself entirely in itself. This is no desire to hold fast to what is past, no "spirit of revenge."

The scene in which at that time life was dearer to Zarathustra than all his wisdom ever was is unforgettable. It is the sorrow of the cool evening, but above all else the emotion of impending departure; "They wept with one another"—without complaint, gently.

◾ Contributors

KARSTEN HARRIES of Yale University is the author of *The Meaning of Modern Art: A Philosophical Interpretation.* He is a leading scholar of German existentialism and has written extensively on Heidegger, Wittgenstein, and language.

ROBERT B. PIPPIN of the University of California, San Diego, is the author of *Kant's Theory of Form* as well as numerous articles on Nietzsche, Hegel, and Wittgenstein.

JEAN-MICHEL REY of the University of Paris is the author of *Des mots à l'oeuvre; Parcours de Freud: Economie et discours;* and *L'Enjeu des signes: Lectures de Nietzsche.* He is prominent in the French new wave of thinking about Nietzsche and language.

CURT PAUL JANZ of Basel is the world's leading authority on Nietzsche's life and music. His *Friedrich Nietzsche: Biographie* is the definitive work on Nietzsche's life. He is also the editor of Nietzsche's musical works and has written extensively on Nietzsche and music.

MICHAEL ALLEN GILLESPIE of Duke University is the author of *Hegel, Heidegger, and the Ground of History* and other articles on Hegel, Heidegger, and Nietzsche.

TRACY B. STRONG of the University of California, San Diego, is the author of *Friedrich Nietzsche and the Politics of Transfiguration* and numerous articles on Nietzsche.

SARAH KOFMAN of the Sorbonne is one of the foremost French authorities on Nietzsche. She is the author of *Nietzsche et la scène philosophique;*

Nietzsche et la métaphore; Camera obscura de l'idéologie; and many other books and articles on Nietzsche, Freud, and feminism.

EUGEN FINK of the University of Freiburg was a leading German phenomenologist. He is the author of *Nietzsches Philosophie; Hegel: Phänomenologische Interpretation der "Phänomenologie des Geistes"*; and many other books and articles on topics in the history of Western philosophy.

HANS-GEORG GADAMER of the University of Heidelberg is the world's leading philosopher of hermeneutics. He is the author of *Truth and Method; Dialogue and Dialectic;* and *Hegel's Dialectic;* as well as numerous other books and articles that cover the whole range of Western philosophic thought.

◼ Index